T0383848

RADICAL ORGANISATION DEVELOPMENT

Contemporary organisation development (OD) in practice draws on sophisticated theory and tools to advance organisational change, using a range of concepts and techniques including positive psychology, appreciation, and active engagement with the workforce. OD is considered to be humanistic and, as a result, progressive. Mark Cole's original and thought-provoking treatise points at a hole at the heart of OD practice: it fails to consider the role of power in the workplace – and the result is disempowering.

Drawing from critical theory as a radical means to redefine practice, Mark Cole exposes this paradox and reveals the significant limitations and negative impacts of current OD practice. We need to replace the idea of the organisation with a focus on active human organising to enable individuals within systems to effect change from the grassroots up: this concept is Radical OD.

Essential reading for students, practitioners, and academics of OD; the wider HR community, and all with an interest in developing their understanding of organisational life, this ground-breaking manifesto offers unique and challenging insight into the corporate presence of OD – and challenges the willing reader to reimagine the focus and intent of this work.

Mark Cole is an OD practitioner with over 30 years' experience working with people and change management in organisations. A published author in both books and journals, he currently works at the NHS London Leadership Academy, where he focuses on organisation and leadership development; systems thinking in the workplace, and supporting meaningful and impactful workforce engagement.

RADICAL ORGANISATION DEVELOPMENT

Mark Cole

Routledge
Taylor & Francis Group

LONDON AND NEW YORK

First published 2020
by Routledge
2 Park Square, Milton Park, Abingdon, Oxon OX14 4RN

and by Routledge
52 Vanderbilt Avenue, New York, NY 10017

Routledge is an imprint of the Taylor & Francis Group, an informa business

British Library Cataloguing-in-Publication Data
A catalogue record for this book is available from the British Library

Library of Congress Cataloging-in-Publication Data
A catalog record has been requested for this book

ISBN: 978-1-138-59088-5 (hbk)
ISBN: 978-0-429-49079-8 (ebk)

Typeset in Joanna MT
by codeMantra

CONTENTS

Acknowledgements   vi

1   **Introduction**   1

2   **A Foucauldian preamble**   16

3   **A genealogy of the organisationally developed workplace**   40

4   **What does OD achieve?**   74

5   **Towards a truly Radical OD practice**   138

6   **And we land, where?**   198

Epilogue   213
Index   215

ACKNOWLEDGEMENTS

I have numerous people to thank for helping me to shape my ideas and to get them down on paper. First and foremost, I have benefited from boundless support from family and friends, in terms of their constant encouragement. In particular, thanks are due to my wife Sarah for helping me to maintain momentum over the 18 months that this took to write. And also to my five-year-old son Thomas, who – as he began school and started to learn to read – took an active interest in the fact that I was 'writing a book,' albeit one without illustrations by the wonderful Axel Scheffler!

In a professional context, there is a huge number of people that I need to mention. I would not have had the confidence to do this work were it not for Anne-Marie Archard, my director at the NHS London Leadership Academy, and everyone else in the team there who have been so interested in what I was doing and so tolerant of my enthusing about this title. It is a fabulous place to work, where thinking and ideas are respected and conversation encouraged, and I struggle to put into words just how beneficial that environment has been, in terms of developing both my thinking and my practice.

It is also a workplace that puts me in contact with countless interesting and fascinating people, all of whom have helped – to some degree or another – in terms of expanding my understanding and throwing down intellectual challenge. I need to make special mention here of my interlocutor

John Higgins, with whom I have spoken on so many occasions about this work and what I am trying to do, and Ben Fuchs, who is endlessly interesting and whose partner helped with the review of an early chapter. I have also benefitted hugely from conversations with Myron Rodgers, who has been generous with his thinking and his knowledge, and others in the wider OD community with whom I have been fortunate enough to work over the past few years.

Special thanks go to Amy Laurens, my editor at Routledge, who gave me the personal confidence and impetus to write this book by showing confidence in the fact that I could! Aside from some journal articles and a chapter in an edited collection, this is my first publication, so I greatly appreciate Amy's professional commitment to me as an untested author.

Whilst all these people have contributed to my thinking and writing through their conversations, comments, and advice, I have not necessarily heeded or incorporated what they have said, so I have to state clearly that any faults and errors in this book are entirely my responsibility.

1

INTRODUCTION

Back in 2017, I was leafing through an edition of *Fortune* magazine. There was article about a factory in the Mexican city of Nazareno, a supplier to Levi Strauss, the US jeans manufacturer. The report suggested the rewriting of the prevailing notion of the maquiladora as a sweatshop where poorly paid people cheaply create products which, on making the short journey over the border, acquire a substantial price tag. It was not so much the story itself as the illustration that accompanied it that piqued my interest and set me thinking.

It was a photo of a group of 25 or so people from the workforce from Linea 1 in the factory who were involved in a team-building exercise, which involved them standing in a circle and passing a ball of wool to one another. The article explained that,

> The players from Linea 1 are finishing a 10-week course designed to teach them about health, hygiene, and sanitation, as well as communication and critical thinking. The string game? That's intended to make everyone

feel personally invested in and accountable for acting on what they've learned. The cat's cradle is a web of commitments, representing their new connectedness—a physical reminder that their bonds are stronger, surer than before.

(Fry, 2017)

This was part of Levi's wider initiative that carried the title 'Improving Worker Well-Being.' And, in that regard, it was asserted that, 'The goal is to build a network of more productive, better-run factories—with happier, healthier employees and lower rates of costly absenteeism and turnover' (Fry, 2017). The report went on to suggest that the overall initiative was having a positive impact, in terms of engagement and hence productivity.

And yet, and yet. There was something about the photo which made me bridle somewhat. Certainly, it showed 25 or so people in what looked like a modern and clean manufacturing location engaged in something that most of us have been involved in at some point in our working lives. The article asserted that everyone looked happy – and drew attention to the number of people seen smiling. My take was a little different, though: some wore smiles but could not really be said to be smiling. And they could be read – and this, I am content to concede, was interpretative on my part – as smiles that might have derived from one or two possible circumstances: either they were the lightly worn smiles of a group of workmates watching each other do something that, by and large, looks foolish; or they were the smiles of those who were being paid at that time to pass around a ball of wool rather than sit on a production line and produce pair after pair of jeans for a global market.

The latter suggestion resonated with something shared with me by a colleague a while back. He tells the story of a Chief Executive who ran a number of 'town hall' meetings around his organisation and was consistently impressed by the fact that these gatherings regularly overran in terms of timing and that those from the shop floor seemed to have come armed with the most questions. My friend queried this with people in the workforce, who more or less confirmed that they preferred to sit on comfy chairs and ask pointless questions than spend that time at the hard edge of the work. I felt that something similar might apply in the picture from the Mexican factory; moreover, I was forced to wonder the extent to which, with a global mega-brand breathing down their necks, the employees in the photograph felt that they had any choice but to be absorbed into Levi's intrusive initiative to improve their well-being.

I was also moved to observe that there was an express connection being made between organisational effectiveness and the programme that was being offered to these employees. It was not an altruistic effort to improve the lot of the workers in and of itself: it was quite blatantly an exercise to incorporate the workforce in order to extract greater output from them. Now, one might argue that no one is being harmed in this: the employees are developing through the initiative and the employer is getting a bigger bang for their wage-buck. But I was intrigued at the transparency of this, as an approach, when oftentimes this sort of activity foregrounds the humanistic aspect and veils the payoff that is anticipated from a corporate perspective.

This coincided with a shift in my professional thinking as I found myself becoming more critical of what I was asked to do in the field of organisation development (OD) and the ways in which I might then approach to do it. Traditionally, I have worked in learning and development, by and large in (or around) the National Health Service. More recently, I have spent an increasing amount of my time engaged in OD activity, where I have worked under the personal suppositions that this work is humanistic and progressive. It is, after all, a field wherein practitioners focus positively on the way in which the workforce can be supported to gain more from their work – and thence enable the organisation to be more effective, in terms of its business performance.

This view was reinforced by what is broadly said about OD. There are myriad definitions of the work and how it is done, with every writer seemingly having their own. There are however themes that seem to either recur or speak strongly to the way in which the work is done in practice, which includes the efforts tend to be planned and long-term; it is underpinned by behavioural science (latterly, the blandishments of positive psychology) and demonstrates some obeisance to psychodynamics; it tends to pivot around the notion of change and its delivery, with a special emphasis on workforce participation in that; and it is ordinarily commissioned from the top of the organisation (Alban & Scherer, 2005, p. 103). Others have shaped a notion of what the work involves by articulating the circumstances where it might best be invoked: the overarching prerequisite in this respect is said to be that '...somebody in a *strategic position* really *feels the need* for change. In other words, somebody or something is really hurting' (Beckhard, 2006, p. 10).

It seems to me that this underscores just how flaky and imprecise the whole area of OD can be. There may be many people in work who are genuinely hurting: they are working at great intensity over long hours; they are poorly rewarded for their efforts; they are juggling myriad pressures outwith of work, whilst trying to stay focused in an environment where their performance is endlessly surveilled; there is a daily sense of insecurity, with the ongoing threat of upheaval and lay-offs, and flexible working practices such as zero-hours contracts. But I think that it is fair to say that senior leaders are not 'hurting' on the basis of wanting to commission some change in their firms. Underneath this notion of a senior leader 'jonesing' to transform the environment in which people work is an assumption that OD can usefully be deployed to engender change, a change envisioned and articulated solely from the top of the organisation. OD will manifest itself where there is a need to change culture, collaboration, and communication across an organisational setting. Moreover, it intervenes to work on people's motivations and their capacity for adaptation (Beckhard, 2006, pp. 10–12). But, behind these platitudes, there is for me a general sense of OD engendering compliance amongst the workforce in respect to new managerial imperatives.

If one looks for a point of origin for contemporary OD, it is possible to suggest that it emerged as a distinct field by invitation in 1939, when some of the key ideas of Kurt Lewin, one of the key figures in the history of this sort of work, were put into practice. In broad outline, the approach of Lewin, it is argued, '…meant, …, letting go of control and trusting the people themselves to figure out – with some support and guidance – what to do' (Alban & Scherer, 2005, p. 85). When asked in 1930 to enhance production levels at a pyjama company called The Harwood Manufacturing Company in the USA, a consultant and adherent of Lewin, John French, worked with a manager in the company called Lester Coch to suggest '…an experiment with the front-line people, to learn what might make a difference in their productivity' (Alban & Scherer, 2005, p. 86). All of which means that OD is generally seen as a way of working in the business setting where you seek to actively and meaningfully engage the workforce to resolve the problems faced by a business. This is, of course, a somewhat corporatist notion: it can be seen – and invariably is – as a humanising and engaging way of addressing these issues of effectiveness, although it is also possible to see it as compelling the workforce to be actively complicit in their ongoing exploitation.

It is also asserted that Lewin did not merely provide OD with its foundational ideas and practices; he also crafted the process through which practitioners would work in and through the organisations where they sought to consult. Turning his back on the standard tools of his trade as a social psychologist, Lewin instead took as his precept that '...you cannot know an institution until you try to change it. This meant studying companies with full immersion in their cultures, in partnership with managers who wanted to make changes' (Kleiner, 2008, p. 22). Hence, OD practitioners largely approach their work through a carefully crafted process of engagement, which often requires their immersion in the workplace. Obviously, this tends to carry a sense of something akin to scientific method itself, so neglects – in many ways – the very character of the workplace and, alongside that, the difficulty of using a method with an anthropological edge in a relatively superficial fashion.

Hence, the provenance of OD and the way in which most practitioners speak of it reassured me that I was doing work that was democratic and meaningful, in terms of giving people voice in the workplace. But something about that picture from the Mexican factory niggled at me, as did a more general and burgeoning sense of the significant limitations to what I could do and was doing as a practitioner. I was becoming increasingly critical of what I was being called to do – and the ways that were open to me by which to do it. Most significantly, there was sense for me that there was a disparity between what I assumed were my values (and those of OD at large) and what felt to me to be the reality of my practice.

Let me explain through the example of one element of my work. In one organisation in which I worked, I was responsible for overseeing the annual staff survey. This is a large-scale exercise that takes place across the whole NHS every autumn. Organisations become intensely focused on this work and on its apparent outcomes. At face value – and this was a view to which I very much subscribed – this seemed to be vital, from an OD perspective: it invites the workforce to give voice to the issues that they face day to day and thence prompts the whole organisation to take seriously and act upon the issues that flow from the responses that are received. Certainly, at the very beginning, I would throw myself into this work, trying to ensure maximum engagement, analysing the results in close detail when they appeared early each new year, and actively working to deliver an action plan that would be speedily crafted off the back of those results.

My first niggle came when there seemed to be a subtle shift in organisational attitude to the survey. From a *laissez-faire* approach, my organisation moved almost unnoticeably to a position of quite forcefully pressuring the workforce to complete the survey, even going so far as setting a key performance target for its HR function in terms of staff participation. This landed at around 55% and was a figure drawn from the ether on the basis of the participation rate in the previous year. Suddenly, the invitation to the workforce to complete the survey became a management imperative, with the learning and OD team as part of the wider HR function being charged with making this happen. Hence, we saw the situation where HR staff were sent out across the organisation to physically deliver the follow-up reminders to those who had not completed the survey.

Clearly, this caused not inconsiderable consternation amongst the workforce, who felt the dead hand of bureaucracy on their arm, forcing them to complete the questionnaires that are, as a key facet of the exercise, promoted to respondents as being completely anonymous. The negative reaction that I personally experienced whilst chasing down those who were yet to make a submission suggested a high level of both cynicism about the whole process (with people wondering aloud what the point of the initiative might be, when patently nothing ever really changed) and a significant degree of distrust of the leadership of the organisation, in respect to what their motivation might be in terms of enticing people to respond. As an OD practitioner, it was my job to assuage these concerns, despite the fact that – in my heart of hearts – I shared much of the scepticism that was apparent across large swathes of the workforce. I mentally embedded this exercise into my positive thinking about OD as an involving practice, setting aside any critical engagement with this notion.

My second concern came about as – over the course of a number of years, where I was charged to oversee this work – I came to feel that there was a ritual developing where the senior leadership actively invited the workforce to engage in the survey; the results were pondered (often with great concern over what the staff were saying about their experience of working in the organisation); and an action plan was designed, richly detailed in terms of timelines and anticipated outputs and outcomes. All this happened, of course, even as people came to realise that the results gave a superficial impression of what was happening but did not show us what was actually going on and, most importantly, why it was taking place. Even when one year we built some focus group meetings for staff off the back of the results and a carefully crafted follow up internal survey, the engagement was miniscule and the upshot utterly negligible. But OD, of course, had generated the illusion of concern and genuine response.

That said, it was interesting to see how this painfully and obviously limited engagement was parlayed by the leadership (and me, of course, as the OD practitioner, trying to pilot this to some sort of positive up-shot) into something meaningful. And this reinforced to me how the ritual worked and how – as a result – nothing actually happened, although the illusion of action was supposedly generated. A standard response to survey results began to take shape, broadly a defensive reaction where the leader-ship desperately wanted to broadcast the fact that they had heard the voice of the workforce and were doing something about what they had heard: it manifested itself in organisational communication of a 'You said, we did' message – although the extent to which the reactions outlined therein could actually be seen at the grassroots of the organisation, let alone felt by the workforce, was a moot issue.

This, then, led me to cast an extremely critical eye over my own practice – and to what now looked to be a chasm between the espoused values of OD as a practice (and my consonant values in this regard) and the practicality of the work on a day to day basis. This personal investigation was overlaid by my orientation in terms of engaging with the world from a critical perspec-tive. This derives largely from the work I undertook as part of my doctoral thesis, where I investigated the use of what is called reflective practice in the healthcare professions through an appreciation of the thought of the French philosopher Michel Foucault. This enticed me to look beyond the surface, to explore how OD nestled into organisational life and how it impacted and shaped that context. Similarly, this conceptual approach nudged me towards an exploration of this work with a foregrounding of novel ideas of power in the workplace.

For instance, in regard to the staff surveys that appeared each year, a reg-ular theme that appeared across the whole NHS, by and large, was a high reported incidence of bullying and harassment. In 2018, for instance, 28.3% of all respondents across the whole NHS reported experiencing bullying and harassment, a slight uptick on 2017 (Currie, 2019). Responses to this year on year did little to impact on that experience, not least – in my view – because the conversation that took place in the organisation in light of this included a great deal but omitted a number of key issues, which seemed to be wholly unacknowledged, let alone openly spoken about. Chief among these was the utter failure to allow the presence and nature of workplace power to be recognised and interrogated in this context. This was especially noteworthy in respect to the disconnect between a service committed to caring existing in a management context that seems at odds with that. Hence,

> For nurses in public sector agencies subjected to neoliberal management reforms, increasingly, the struggle has become how to perform caring work in a genuine and authentic manner while located in institutions that, despite claims to the contrary, have cultures that are antithetical to the value of caring.
>
> (Hutchinson & Jackson, 2015, p. 13)

With the key facet of power disregarded in this way, it meant that no one in my context could find the space to raise the deeper question of the extent to which the management and leadership culture of the NHS in general, with its continued reliance on command and control and the encouragement of an atmosphere of blame and penalisation, was, in itself, bullying and therefore gave permission for bullying to take place up, down and across the organisations. This led me into two linked positions: first, I began to shape up in my mind a deep critique of OD, particularly in respect to what seems to motivate many of us to do it, how it is experienced in practice, and what effect it might generate in light of how these two positions might run counter to one another. Second, I began to envisage a practice in respect to OD that genuinely embodied the values of humanism and engagement, one that abandoned the current approach to involvement and sought to embrace an authentic engagement with the workforce with the aim of meeting the espoused ambition of OD.

For the record, I am not of the opinion that OD as a practice merely needs to find its way back to its progressive points of origin, whereas some do take that position. So, in that regard, I do not take the view that 'By recovering and reaffirming a commitment to its original humanistic ideals, OD may avoid obsolescence and retain professional viability' (Harrison, 1984, p. 12). Indeed, as I will seek to demonstrate, I am unconvinced about this supposed provenance and take a considerable more nuanced view of how OD works, in terms of its outcomes and wider cultural impacts. Similarly, while I am largely sympathetic to the thinking that lies behind a project of defining a critical Human Resources Development (HRD) approach, I am unconvinced about the forging of a practice as '...a process of engaging human and organizational systems that relate, learn, change, and organize in ways that optimize human interest, organization advancement, and social impact' (Bierema & Callahan, 2014, p. 10). To my mind, this leaves the foundational issues largely undisturbed, unexplored and deeply challenged. This is why I prefer to speak of an authentically radical rethinking of current OD – and an OD for the future for those of us who are weary of the way in which OD is practised in most instances today.

In light of this, I recognise the following assertion and why it matters to the field of practice – but will seek to contest every single facet of this seemingly common sense declaration: 'OD was founded on humanistic values and ethical concerns like democracy and social justice, and most practitioners would agree that OD tends to emphasise human development, fairness, openness, choice, and balancing autonomy and constraint' (Worley & Feyerherm, 2003, p. 99). Interestingly, the modern practice of OD is often juxtaposed (or seen as a development from) the scientific management of F. W. Taylor. At least one chronology expressly announces this lineage, which is illustrative and implies a continuity between the earlier state – time and motion, workplace oversight – and those OD practices which are broadly seen as more positively focused (French & Bell, 1978, pp. 63–65). This runs counter to the generally accepted view that there is a general sense of an epistemological break between one and the other, which – to my mind – is self-justificatory for those who want for there to be distance between different modalities of management.

Hence, across a number of axes, OD is defined in contrast to the rendering of human beings as mere assets in a business; this conceit can be found in various histories of OD and authored by those with a significant presence in the field (Weisbord, 1987). As ever, though, the focus is on productivity; the debate is merely what means best suit this ambition. All of which calls into question what is truly foundational in OD – and my experience and my thinking has led me to doubt the presence of the values that people notionally ascribe to this area of work – and to wonder how OD is experienced in the field once you bracket off its supposed underpinnings and instead look at what it does and how it does it in a workplace context.

This has had a practical resonance for me as I have approached my work. I became over time extremely mindful of the fact that so much of what I am asked to do does not concur with the values that I hold dear – and which theoretically undergird OD in general. I have also been asked to facilitate countless 'away days' or events for people in the workplace to engage with a particular issue or to take time to explore where they are and where they want to be collectively. Like the Mexican workers in the photo, the people with whom I have interacted have acquiesced – to a greater or lesser extent – with what I have steered them to do at that time and in that space. But ultimately I have found it difficult to get a sense of something really positive coming out of those events. We all turn up, we all do as we are expected to do; oftentimes, the progress of the day is in some way captured – but those outputs and outcomes are often agreed during the commissioning process, so there is a sense in which the conversations that could take place do not happen – and those that we need to happen to meet those results are privileged.

This makes it easier in many ways for OD practitioners to demonstrate an impact of their work: if one defines the outcome in advance of the intervention, then that intervention ends up tailored – either openly or tacitly, on the basis of practice – to deliver on that expectation. As has been noted in respect to measuring OD effectiveness in healthcare settings, '…it can be difficult to attribute changes in performance to the intervention in the commonly adopted before-and-after analysis of outcomes' (McLeod, 2005, p. 249). Certainly, that is the case – and the limited amount of evidence available for OD effectiveness and the largely unsatisfactory nature of much of that evidence is noted in this context (McLeod, 2005, p. 249). Better then to define the 'after' in contrast to the 'before' – and thence build activity that steers towards that predetermined outcome.

I have lost track of the number of these types of events where some attempt at capture has been part of the work and where the artefact that supposedly codifies what was said and what was agreed is diligently written up from post-it notes and flip-chart paper, only to be circulated and instantly disregarded and promptly forgotten. There is no malice or overt intent in this: it is simply that the away day is a ritualised corporate carnival, and so is viewed as entirely separate to the actual day-to-day work that people seek to do. Indeed, much contemporary OD practice has the feel of Bakhtinian carnival about it, which is best encapsulated thus:

> in the Middle Ages, the carnival played a much more prominent role in
> the life of ordinary people, who inhabited a dual realm of existence: one

official, characterized by the authority of the church, the feudal system, work, and one unofficial, characterized by reversal, parody, song, and laughter.

(Vice, 2008, p. 150)

Participants fleetingly live in the carnival, which briefly dispenses with hierarchical structure and releases a wide range of ribaldry in contrast to the constraints that are ordinarily experienced in the quotidian (Vice, 2008, p. 152).

This, then, is the professional impasse in which I found myself. At root, I harbour a deep discontent about the workplace in a capitalist society, something which I happily recognise that others will not share, of course. It has always been a harsh, unequal and contentious domain – and much that we imagine as materially improving those circumstances is, to my mind, superficial and ultimately meaningless. As a result, there was a dissonance in values within OD and also between me as an individual in that field and the work that I was actually doing. I was finding it difficult to see the benefits of what I was doing, in terms of me as the interventionist, the people with (or, perhaps more accurately, on) whom I was working, and the organisation at large.

Given my critical orientation – particularly an open acknowledgement of the fundamental nature of the capitalist means of production and an adherence to key notions derived from Foucault, particularly in respect to our experiences of power – I sensed the possibility of unearthing fresh thinking about the work that gets done in the space called OD and an opportunity to craft an outline of a practice that I could engage in that would genuinely be true to its espoused values. The results of that relatively minor and very individual crisis is this book, which crystallises my thinking to date and offers a number of pointers – primarily to me, to be candid, but also to whomsoever might wish to join me on that road – that indicate how a new and more authentic OD practice might be developed through constant critical engagement of thought and experiments in how things might be done in practice.

So, the shape of this book follows in outline the way in which my thought in this has developed – and is built to enable the reader to trace how that thinking is supported and the direction that I feel that it is forced to take. Throughout, I have tried to speak candidly about my experience of the work whilst buttressing this with a level of scholarship which I hope the reader will find unobtrusive, reassuring – and, in terms of intellectual curiosity – enticing. This does not represent a definitive statement – no theoretical work can ever make such a claim – so I honestly hope that people will engage with this text as a starting point in a conversation. That said, I am adamant that – for me (at the very least) and for all those who think of their OD practice as democratic, engaging (and engaged), and humanistic – it is simply not possible to continue working in the old ways, considering the effects that I argue they have. For those who are content where they are in terms of current OD, I can simply hope that my observations encourage you to return to first principles to reassure yourselves in respect to the work that you do … and perhaps to adapt it in some fashion.

This can be seen to be a reformist position. More conservative practitioners might read my critique and not find anything negative there. At least we will then be clear whence they are coming and why it is that they do the work that they do. For me, I have cleaved to the title offered to me by my editor at Routledge, as it seems to go to the very heart of what I need to do in respect to my work and how I do it: go to the very root of the matter; deracinate my practice, and replant the patch with something fresh, new and nourishing. This, then, is the virtue of talking about Radical OD, as opposed to critical (or, indeed, reformed) OD.

The book is made up of two substantial chapters and a number of supporting essays, built around them in order to help the reader understand how they have been constructed, in terms of thinking. So, there follows a brief chapter that offers a hopefully accessible introduction to the Foucauldian framework that has supported the development of my work. This is followed by a brief section that applies some of those methods in terms of taking a fresh view of what we think of as the workplace and what happens in that space when human beings come together in an organised fashion in order to attain a common purpose.

This leads into the chapter that offers a detailed critique of OD. In light of the Foucauldian prism that is being used, it is fair to say that all that we accept as commonplace is herein open to close questioning. This goes as far as dismantling the very idea of the team, oftentimes seen as the key unit of analysis for the OD practitioner, and subjecting that to quite destructive scrutiny. If Radical OD is to be governed by any watchword, it would be that nothing is out of scope of our inquiries – and that inquiry is an intrinsic feature of working radically. I would not presume that the reader would subscribe to this detailed critique: it is presented not to persuade but to provoke, in the most positive sense of the word. Writing the book has, on many occasions, led me to an observation or an idea that was wholly unexpected. It is my earnest hope that the reader experiences – to some extent – something of the perturbation that I have endured (or, rather should I say, enjoyed) in taking my thinking for a walk, line after line down a blank page.

I have joked with people in the course of writing that – if this critique was to be viewed solely on its own – it could reasonably be seen as one of the longest resignation letters ever written. To that end, I became acutely aware that it would be important that this critical review of OD would need to be properly and subtly balanced with a vision of what OD could look like, if we chose to work differently. I should be quick to state here that I am not convinced that the reworked picture of OD that I offer is going to be immediately palatable in many organisational settings. It is, after all, a proposed orientation that holds closely to the idea of being radical in thought and practice. It does not shy away from articulating a vision of OD that would profoundly reshape our organisations – and not in a glib or fashionable way, with reference to flat structures or post-bureaucratic companies. But, without wishing to sound too grandiloquent, our organisations in the 21st century urgently need to be radically reshaped, as they are currently in no way suited to addressing the challenges we face now and in the future, economically, ecologically or personally.

Hence, the second large chapter offers a design for how a new OD might be explored and developed. It provides seven key precepts to support that reorientation. It is not a manifesto, as it hopefully avoids being too declarative and is written from a humble perspective. But, as suggested above, it offers me a way to think differently about my practice as I endeavour to sustain my position in the field and working where I do in health and social care. And it will be delightful to have company as I trace the route and pursue the bifurcations and new ways that will doubtless open up as that exploration unfolds. As with all radical projects, it is unclear as to whether it will carve out a new space in respect to OD – or whether it will be absorbed, in some fashion or another. It was, I think, Regis Debray who asserted that the revolution revolutionises the counter-revolution – and I have strangely often felt that this axiom has great currency within the field of organisational change management. It may be that the idea of Radical OD will prompt a negating response within the mainstream, although it is impossible to envisage what that might be at this stage. And, all that not-withstanding, the vision offered in the second large chapter may, of course, simply not have the vocabulary to offer a new possibility, in which case it will guide my work solely, for good or ill.

Some of the ideas utilised herein might seem somewhat incongruous in a book about business in its broadest sense. For instance, it takes it as read that we are working in a capitalist society, which was richly described from a technical perspective by Marx. It calls on some of those working in the Marxian tradition to reinforce some of the observations made herein. Similarly, it is the case that Foucault's thought is now recognised as '...a touchstone for debates about work, organization and identity, especially in the burgeoning field of 'critical management studies': Foucault has rapidly moved from the margins to the mainstream of organization studies' (McKinlay et al., 2012, p. 3). That said, many of those ideas are not familiar in the busy office or boardroom – and some will be seen to be decidedly outré in this sort of context. Perhaps most contentiously, my work respects the meaningful connection that scholars have made between poststructur-alist thinking such as that of Foucault and Gilles Deleuze and the politics of what is now called post-anarchism (May, 2011) and so invites anar-chism into the discussion, particularly in terms of what it has to say about organising and organisation, which is intriguingly productive.

All of which, I hope, will make for a provocative read – and one that peo-ple will find intellectually engaging and positively challenging of much-received wisdom. And, ultimately, I maintain a deep desire that we can rethink OD in order to make it an activity that is truly radical – and has the potential to make radical organisational change to the benefit of those labouring in the workplace and to society at large.

Bibliography

Alban, B. T. & Scherer, J. J., 2005. On the shoulders of giants: The origins of OD. In: W. J. Rothwell & R. Sullivan, eds. *Practicing organization development: A guide for consultants.* San Francisco, CA: Pfeiffer, pp. 81–105.

Beckhard, R., 2006. What is organization development?. In: J. V. Gallos, ed. *Organiza-tion development.* San Francisco, CA: Jossey-Bass, pp. 3–12.

Bierema, L. & Callahan, J. L., 2014. Transforming HRD: A framework for critical HRD practice. *Advances in Developing Human Resources,* 16, pp. 429–444.

Currie, A., 2019. NHS Staff Survey results 2018: Key findings. London: Bevan Brittan.

French, W. L. & Bell, C. H., 1978. Organization development: Behavioral science interventions for organization improvement. 6th ed. Upper Saddle River, NJ: Prentice Hall.

Fry, E., 2017. Can Levi's make life better for garment workers? Fortune, 8 September.

Harrison, R. G., 1984. Reasserting the radical potential of OD: Notes towards the establishment of a new basis for OD practice. Personnel Review, 13(2), pp. 12–18.

Hutchinson, M. & Jackson, D., 2015. The construction and legitimation of workplace bullying in the public sector: Insight into power dynamics and organisational failures in health and social care. Nursing Inquiry, 22(1), pp. 13–26.

Kleiner, A., 2008. The age of heretics: A history of the radical thinkers who invented corporate management. San Francisco, CA: Jossey-Bass.

May, T., 2011. Is post-structuralist political theory anarchist? In: D. Rousselle & S. Evren, eds. Post-anarchism: A reader. London: Pluto, pp. 41–45.

McKinlay, A., Carter, C. & Pezet, E., 2012. Governmentality, power and organization. Management & Organizational History, 7(1), pp. 3–15.

McLeod, H., 2005. A review of the evidence on organisational development in healthcare. In: E. Peck, ed. Organisational development in healthcare: Approaches, innovations, achievements. Abingdon: Radcliffe, pp. 247–271.

Vice, S., 2008. Introducing Bakhtin. Manchester: Manchester University Press.

Weisbord, M. R., 1987. Productive workplaces: Organizing and managing for dignity, meaning and community. San Francisco, CA: Jossey-Bass.

Worley, C. G. & Feyerherm, A. E., 2003. Reflections on the future of organization development. The Journal of Applied Behavioral Science, 39(1), pp. 97–115.

2

A FOUCAULDIAN PREAMBLE

My exploration of organisation development (OD) is heavily informed by the work of the French philosopher Michel Foucault. My interest in his approaches flowed from my doctoral work on reflective practice – and has come to play a key part in the way that I think about organisations and the way in which they intersect with wider society. Whilst Foucault himself would scoff at clumsy periodisations – indeed, his methods reject this type of linearity in favour of a more tessellated picture, as we shall hopefully see – there is a sense in which the author's corpus shows clear signs of intellectual development and reconciliation of theoretical tensions over time, as one would expect of a significant thinker of this sort.

There are some initial collisions over method, with two key concepts – archaeology and genealogy – in play. It might be reasonably argued that the former relates to work undertaken by Foucault, which, sharing a provenance with much continental philosophy of the time, privileges ideas of language as discourse, which derives from de Saussure's work on linguistics and the structuralism of Claude Levi-Strauss. The latter, however, comes to the fore as Foucault turns his attention to the general issue of power, a line of inquiry he develops to some extent in contradistinction to the field of Marxian thought that prevailed at the time. However, as is inevitable, partly due to the intellectual ferment of the time and also to do with shared milieu of many of these thinkers, there are resonances throughout: it is, for example, highly illustrative to read Althusser on ideology alongside Foucault on discourse, a term that I will seek to illuminate further on in this chapter.

A significant adjustment can be said to be visible between Foucault's early work on power, where some took it as a counsel of despair wherein the human subject enjoyed no agency in the face of it, and his later work on technologies of the self, which placed in the hands of that subject a far greater agency to engage in the web of power. Again, this can sometimes lead to a sense of inconsistency in the work, where initial conversations on what Foucault calls power/knowledge and the freedom that comes to human beings through the author's identification of technologies of the self. Again, both are explored more fully below.

This chapter offers a superficial introduction to these ideas, thereby surfacing the theoretical assumptions that I will mobilise throughout the rest of the book. This begins in the next chapter, where I offer an overview of the workplace as a location through a genealogical prism. Similarly, the chapter that offers an extensive critique of OD practice as it currently stands is obviously undergirded by Foucault's ideas, so this basic summary will hopefully help orient the reader. In this section, then, I will describe my understanding of the Foucauldian notions of surveillance, power/knowledge, technologies of the self, discourse and apparatus, governmentality, and genealogy. The latter will lead comfortably into the next chapter, which offers a genealogy of the workplace.

Surveillance

In his book entitled *Discipline and Punish*, Foucault lays the foundations for what has come to be called surveillance studies through his discussions therein on the Panopticon (Foucault, 1991a). He outlines the crucial role that he saw surveillance assume in regard to a shift at the end of the 18th and beginning of the 19th century in the way in which power exists in society, namely that from a sovereign power – where a ruler imbued oftentimes with a supposed 'divine right to rule' could exercise power on the bodies of their subjects – to disciplinary power, wherein more nuanced means of control were required for the new industrialising, massified and democratised population, that is to say, the key features of modernity.

Foucault seeks to establish a subtle connection between surveillance and the pervasiveness of this new disciplinary power. He borrows the idea of Panopticon from the work of the English Utilitarian philosopher Jeremy Bentham (1995). The Panopticon is an architectural design for a prison, which consists of a circular space in which the inmates reside in isolation from one another in open-fronted cells. The cells face into a central hub, wherein the inspector's tower sits. Crucially, while the inmates know that they might be being watched by the inspector, the design of the tower means that they cannot know whether or not, at any given point in time, the inspector's eyes are actually on them.

The visibility of the inmates is crucial in this model as it is this surveillance that allows for power to act upon them without having to rely on physical means. The gaze inherent in this model does not seek to adjust peoples' behaviours through mere action on their bodies, in terms of public acts of corporal punishment and execution that prevailed in pre-modernity; instead, it creates a situation in which behaviour is normalised so that, whether or not the individual is being watched, they will crucially assume that they are being watched and behave accordingly.

In an introductory essay to the collection of Bentham's writings on the topic of the Panopticon, it is explained that

> The inspector's partial visibility in the translucent lantern [the space at the core of the Panopticon – MC] does not allow the prisoner to determine whether the eye of the inspector is at that moment directed towards him any more than he can if the inspector is not at all visible. In this case, the inspector's partial visibility is equivalent to invisibility; his omnipresence is in no way affected, his gaze is still all-seeing, since the prisoner cannot see that he is not seen. *All that the prisoner can see inside the lantern is an opaque, dark spot which is always gazing back at him.* [My emphasis]
> (Bozovic, 1995, p. 13)

Whilst Bentham's prison was never built – although the Presidio Modelo prison in pre-revolutionary Cuba comes as close to the Panoptical model as any (Hernandez, 2005) – Foucault takes the idea as a metaphor for the new forms of power that came into existence in the 19th century. His use of the

Panopticon to describe the way in which surveillance was crucial to a new form of power anticipates the arrival of what has been called the 'surveillance society' (Ball et al., 2006), where notionally free citizens in a liberal democratic society such as that of the UK can be watched in a wide range of public and private places (Norris & Armstrong, 1999).

Foucault argues that such Panoptical surveillance engenders an 'automatic functioning of power' (Foucault, 1991a, p. 201). It is argued that 'to achieve this dream of total docility (and its corresponding increase of power), all dimensions of space, time, and motion must be codified and exercised incessantly' (Dreyfus & Rabinow, 1982, p. 154). However, others have indicated that, whilst the functioning of this power may be automatic, it is in no way irresistible: it is difficult, for instance, to identify 'docile subjects' in many places, not least '...prison riots, asylum sub-cultures, ego survival in the Gulag or concentration camp, retribalization in the Balkans' (Boyne, 2000, p. 302).

Foucault's use of the image of the Panopticon is a metaphor for the way in which surveillance is realised; this surveillance – as part of a wider assemblage of disciplinary techniques – has a tendency to render its subjects docile (Foucault, 1991a, pp. 135–169, 1991b). While there are contemporary writers on surveillance who see it in a more positive light – with at least one declaring that 'surveillance is sexy' (Bell, 2009) – a Panoptical surveillant regime, whether architectural, technological or personal, is a restraint on the individual subject and a key way in which disciplinary power is actualised. It is, then, the fact of being 'watched' by others – including the widest possible range of authorities, including governmental agencies, state proxies, and other organisations that are situated in the wider socio-economic fabric – that helps us to understand how Foucault understands power and his observations as to how we experience its action (and, through our actions, facilitate its presence and action).

Power/knowledge

As we have seen, Foucault links surveillance intimately with the functioning of a new form of power that emerged in the modern period. In contrast to the Marxian notion of power, the Foucauldian view is helpfully summarised thus:

> power is a relation between forces; or rather every relation between forces is a "power relation". In the first place we must understand that power is not a form, such as the State-form; and that the power relation does

not lie between two forms, as does knowledge. In the second place, force is never singular but essentially exists in relation with other forces, such that any force is already a relation, that is to say power: force has no other object or subject than force.

(Deleuze, 2006, p. 59)

In contrast to a Marxian 'zero-sum' view of power – a finite resource that, in being possessed by one person (or economic class) is thereby denied to another – Foucault argues

Power must, I think, be analyzed as something that circulates, or rather as something that functions only when it is part of a chain. It is never localized here or there, it is never in the hands of some, and it is never appropriated in the way that wealth or a commodity can be appropriated. Power functions. Power is exercised through networks, and individuals do not simply circulate in those networks; they are in a position to both sub-mit to and exercise this power. They are never inert or consenting targets of power; they are always its relays. In other words, power passes through individuals. It is not applied to them.

(Foucault, 2003a, p. 29)

Here, then, is the Foucauldian notion of power not as a commodity but as a phenomenon that inhabits the very capillaries of human society.

But this is just the opening gambit in Foucault's reconfiguration of the notion of power in society. It is – above all else – an anti-humanist conception of how power courses through the capillaries of society: in this view, power is not wielded by human beings; human beings become subjects by the action of power upon them. Foucault himself announced this when he declared that

I would like to say, first of all, what has been the goal of my work dur-ing the past twenty years. It has not been to analyze the phenomenon of power, nor to elaborate the foundations of such an analysis. My objective, instead, has been to create a history of the different modes by which, in our culture, human beings are made subjects.

(Foucault, 1982, p. 208)

In this sense, Foucault echoes a fundamental premise of Sartrean existen-tialism (Sartre, 2003), namely that there is no fundamental 'humanness' that philosophical inquiry needs to unearth. However, while Sartre pro-ceeds from this observation in a strongly humanistic fashion – arguing that we make ourselves (and the very nature of all humanity) by the decisions and acts that we pursue in life – Foucault sees discourse as constitutive of the human subject, although there is a different emphasis in terms of his earlier and later thought in this regard, with the latter arguably having a more existentialist orientation.

Foucault's notion of power, then, is two-fold: it does not see power as a commodity in society but as a characteristic of society; and, similarly, this power is a creative force, something that gives shape to the subject. In an important text in respect to his methods, Foucault helpfully spells this out:

> We must cease once and for all to describe the effects of power in negative terms: it "excludes", it "represses", it "censors", it "abstracts", it "masks", it "conceals". In fact, power produces; it produces reality; it produces domains of objects and rituals of truth. The individual and the knowledge that may be gained of him belong to this production.
>
> (Foucault, 1991b, p. 194)

But there is a third element that flows from the way in which Foucault marks a significant shift in the way in which power flows in society, one that is strongly hinged on the Panoptical notions of surveillance that he mobilises in his analyses. In *Discipline and Punish*, Foucault theorises a shift from sovereign power to one that Foucault calls disciplinary power, the latter being heavily dependent on two things: the development of a range of surveillant apparatuses and, linked to that, the growing recognition of the role played by the accumulation of knowledge in terms of its intimate (and, in Foucault's work, concatenated) relationship with power (Foucault, 1991a).

In practice, Foucault maps the transition not merely from a society ruled by a sovereign endowed with the right to exercise their power over their subjects, oftentimes in a brutal physical fashion, but to one where the question of maintaining social order was problematised by the emergence of notions associated with liberal democracy, such as liberty and human rights. This political shift was coterminous with wider social changes, such as industrialisation, urbanisation and (in consequence) greater concentrations of population, a population that needed to be managed but which was simultaneously being promised freedom and equality.

In addressing this problematic, Foucault (1991a) discusses in *Discipline and Punish* the arrival of disciplinary institutions – the factory, the prison, the hospital, the school, some of which *in extremis* find a place in Goffman's insightful analysis of total institutions (Goffman, 1961) – and makes the following crucial observation as to how disciplinary power works in this specific context – and thence in a wider social context: 'The perpetual penalty that traverses all points and supervises every instant in the disciplinary institutions compares, differentiates, hierarchizes, homogenizes, excludes. In short, it *normalizes*' (Foucault, 1991a). This idea of normalisation is crucial to an understanding of how power pulses through liberal democracy.

Importantly in this regard, the human sciences – and, in particular, psychology and psychiatry – have played a critical role in creating this dichotomous notion of normalcy/abnormality that occupies such a foundational basis for disciplinary power. Foucault makes a key observation about these human sciences and their emergence, which serves to underscore their intimate link to the development of this new power: he points out that a field was not mapped out, a space in human knowledge, into which these disciplines emerged in light of the expansion of scientific method; equally, they did not appear in response to a problem in which humankind was closely implicated and that demanded the application of such method, although he concedes that a certain element of wider problematisation of society, as discussed above, provides a circumstance in which they might unfurl. Instead, Foucault observes that human beings becoming an object of knowledge at that time is '…an event in the order of knowledge' (Foucault, 2002a, p. 376, 2002b).

These observations serve to ensure that Foucault's notion of surveillance does not become too strongly identified with particular types of technology in our society, such as CCTV. Here, however, is a richer sense of what Foucault is driving at when he mobilises the Benthamite notion of the Panopticon to discuss surveillance; human beings in society have become the object of a surveillant technology that is built around scientific method. It is not merely a question of watching someone to engender a sense for them of being surveilled; it is that this surveillance is likely to be oriented towards accumulating knowledge about the person and thereby make the key judgement of their relationship to the idea of 'normality.' In the classroom, for example, the marks and grades of school students are used to compare one to another in terms of who is 'good' at a subject and who is not. In the contemporary setting, there are those whose relationship to 'good' is so negative that their relationship to normality is reviewed and their 'special needs' in respect to education are identified through testing and examination.

As noted above, one of the key means by which normalisation is seen to take place for Foucault is through the development and actions of the human sciences, chief amongst which is psychology and its medicalised presence in terms of psychiatry. Of course, Foucault undertook substantial work on the emergence of madness and helps to illustrate the point explored above in the following observation: 'What we call psychiatric practice is a certain moral tactic contemporaneous with the late eighteenth century, which is preserved in the rituals of life in asylums, covered over by the myths of positivism' (Foucault, 2009, p. 509).

The following example allows for greater appreciation of the crucial relationship between human sciences and normalisation. The core text of psychiatry is the DSM, the *Diagnostic and Statistical Manual of Mental Disorders* (American Psychiatric Association, 2000). The provenance of this significant work is interesting: 'Not only did the DSM become the bible of psychiatry, but like the real Bible, it depended a lot on something akin to revelation. There are no citations of scientific studies to support its decisions' (Angell, 2011, p. 20). Instead, the inclusion of conditions is at the whim of a panel of psychiatrists, notionally experts in their field.

Noting that the list of included conditions looks set to expand considerably in DSM-V, it was suggested that

> ...diagnostic boundaries will be broadened to include precursors of disorders, such as "psychosis risk syndrome" and "mild cognitive impairment" (possibly early Alzheimer's disease). The term "spectrum" is used to widen categories, for example, "obsessive-compulsive disorder spectrum," "schizophrenia spectrum disorder," and "autism spectrum disorder." And there are proposals for entirely new entries, such as "hypersexual disorder," "restless legs syndrome," and "binge eating".
>
> (Angell, 2011, p. 22)

All of which underscores the processes of normalisation and pathologisation that the human sciences engender. Indeed, it might be argued that increasingly pathologisation actually precedes normalisation, rather than the other way around.

A final remark needs to be made about the way Foucault discusses one of the specific ways in which the surveillance creates the circumstances for the automatic functioning of (disciplinary) power, with an emphasis on the notion of docility. It draws very much on the centrality of ideas of normality and hence – by negative implication – of what might come to be considered to be abnormal. Relatively late in his career, Foucault began work on a history of sexuality that sought to locate this in the wider context of power and knowledge that he had theorised in his earlier work. To an extent, however, this endeavour conceptually eased a little way ahead of Foucault's material on disciplinary power by introducing a new notion, which he calls 'technologies of the self' (Foucault, 1988).

Technologies of the self

Foucault's starting point in his analysis of the history of sexuality is that the common-sense notion that sex was repressed with the advent of bourgeois society in the 19th century sits incongruously with what he sees as an increase in discussion about it that can be seen to occur at exactly the same time. Foucault argues: 'What is peculiar to modern societies, ..., is not that they consigned sex to a shadow existence, but that they dedicated themselves to speaking of it *ad infinitum*, while exploiting it as the secret' (Foucault, 1990, p. 35). Patently, Foucault's wide-ranging examination of sexuality leads him into detailed discussions of sin, the care of the self and the confessional act.

This latter is for Foucault crucial. I suggested earlier in this chapter that surveillance is central to disciplinary power and that, using the Panopticon as a metaphor, such surveillance facilitates the automatic functioning of power. I made mention of the 'opaque, dark spot' that sits within the Panopticon; eventually, that spot becomes incorporated into the human subject. The system is no longer merely surveillant; it now relies – to a large extent – on my own self-surveillance. I have argued elsewhere (Cole, 2004) that a surveillant infrastructure – cameras, leads, screens, control room, security guards keeping a watchful eye on all that is happening – is not needed to generate this effect: it can be achieved through the presence of a surveillant superstructure, in this case, the myriad signs in public and private spaces that alert us to the presence of surveillance.

In addition to these observations about the way in which surveillance acts, the role of the human sciences in defining normality – and, by implication, abnormality – was discussed earlier in this chapter. This also has a surveillant effect: the implications of being thought of as abnormal by a psychologist or psychiatrist are potentially profound, so the clichéd phrase 'Act normal' has particular resonance for most of us. In his discussion of the confessional, however, Foucault pulls together these elements to discuss the human subject's intimate relationship with the idea of normalcy. In a remark shown to be all the more prescient by the development of the reality TV genre, Foucault states:

> The confession has spread its effects far and wide. It plays a part in justice, medicine, education, family relationships, and love relations, in the most ordinary affairs of everyday life, and in the most solemn rites; one confesses one's crimes, one's sins, one's thoughts and desires, one's illnesses and troubles; one goes about telling, with the greatest precision, whatever is most difficult to tell. One confesses in public and in private, to one's parents, one's educators, one's doctor, to those one loves; one admits to oneself, in pleasure and in pain, things it would be impossible to tell to anyone else, the things people write books about. One confesses – or is forced to confess.... Western man has become a confessing animal.
>
> (Foucault, 1990, p. 59)

Traditionally, confession has been seen as an act of release, a purgative event that allows the confessant to release whatever it is that they have been harbouring and thereby to discharge the weight of carrying around their concern over whatever it is that they have done or thought. There is an implication that this release allows the subject to know themselves better, to be slightly closer to the 'truth' about themselves. Foucault struggles with such a humanist and essentialist view – and ascribes the confessional (and, in particular, its Christian variant) a role in terms of the automatic functioning of power. As I have explained elsewhere: '...the act of confession is not – as we might ordinarily be led to believe – something that brings us liberation; it is, instead, something that inscribes the confessant in power, by the subjection implicit in the process' (Cole, 2006, pp. 218–219). Moreover, the Christian confessional is not the sole preserve of the church; it can be equally be found in the consulting room of the psychoanalyst or in the office of one's manager at work during, for instance, the annual performance appraisal (Findlay & Newton, 1998).

All of the above serves to show very clearly how disciplinary power generates circumstances in which the notionally free are actually caught in a complex mesh of practices and popular conceptions that creates control without those controls being apparent. As I intend to show in the chapters that follow, the workplace is a location wherein surveillance and normalisation are incredibly significant – and hence where power is noticeably inscribed.

Discourse and apparatus

I mention above the notion of 'discourse', a somewhat slippery concept found extensively in the work of (and about) Foucault. I want to take a little time here to unpack this idea to avoid any confusion in my usage of it. I will begin with a pithy summary and work back from there to show how I understand the Foucauldian use of this analytic tool, which suggests that: 'Discourse must be understood as referring to an array of social practices, institutions and projects' (Joseph, 2004, p. 146). This is helpful as it draws discourse away from an exclusively linguistic concern. Indeed, some of Foucault's early methodological work places a very heavy emphasis on the constitutive character of language (Foucault, 2002b). However, his usage of the term gradually expands to encompass a wide range of elements, leading to the observation that Foucault seeks to move away from purely linguistic concerns and '...to centre the analysis of discourse within the field of political action' (Hook, 2001, pp. 522–523).

Elsewhere, a more fully rounded understanding of how discourse might best be understood from a Foucauldian perspective is provided, which is worthwhile citing in full here:

> Language plays a major part in constituting human subjects, the subjectivities and identities of persons, their relations and the field in which they exist, but only within a context of institutional practices. Thus to be a woman, or a man, or a parent, etc. is not just a biological label, but is encrusted with all the complex things that it means to be a woman, a man, or a parent in a particular culture at some particular point in time. This reading of the concept "discourse" encourages questions such as: how did it happen that some particular way of thinking, speaking and doing came to prominence at a particular time? Why this way of thinking, speaking and doing rather than another? Discourse emphasises the processes that produce the kinds of people, with characteristic ways of thinking and feeling and doing, that live lives in specific contexts.
>
> (Hunt & Wickham, 1998, p. 7)

A connection can usefully be made here between this developing concept of discourse and some of the points that were made earlier in this chapter in respect to the central importance of 'normalisation' in Foucault's work. Discourse is the way in which normalisation is realised, insofar as it shapes the subject through the action of (amongst other things) language, practices, policies, and institutions. To take this a further: discourse is the conveyance of all that is deemed to be commonsensical in society. And, in keeping with this observation, within Foucault's work, there is a sense in which discourse makes reference to the knowledges that are privileged at a given time and the truth-claims that contemporaneously secure pre-eminence, while thereby ensuring that competing notions are subjugated. To para-phrase this, there are knowledges and ideas that achieve superiority – that is, a status of 'normality' in terms of discussion and practice – and those that stand in contrast to this definition of normalcy.

But it is not enough to leave it there. To do so omits any attempt to describe the practical means by which such normalisation is achieved. In response to this, the work of Foucault throws up the concept of an apparatus (*dispositif*), which he describes as a grouping of '...discourses, institutions, architectural forms, regulatory decisions, laws, administrative measures, scientific statements, philosophical, moral and philanthropic propositions – in short, the said as much as the unsaid' (Foucault, 1980, pp. 194–195). Elsewhere, Foucault's notion of an apparatus is summarised by reference to three things:

> a. It is a heterogenous set that includes virtually anything, linguistic and non-linguistic, under the same heading: discourses, institutions, build-ings, laws, police measures, philosophical propositions, and so on. The apparatus itself is the network that is established between these elements; b. The apparatus always has a concrete strategic function and is always located in a power relation; c. As such, it appears at the intersection of power relations and relations of knowledge.
>
> (Agamben, 2009, pp. 2–3)

Governmentality

So far in this chapter, I have outlined a number of key Foucauldian concepts that will have relevance to the analysis that I am seeking to undertake in this book. The pivotal role occupied by surveillance has been stressed. Spe-cifically, an understanding of the way in which Foucault uses surveillance leads to a greater comprehension of his distinctive approach to the notion of power – and its intimate relationship with knowledge. An appreciation of the position occupied by power in his thought offers a gateway into what is meant by the move he describes from sovereign to disciplinary power and the implications around that, such as the move from power acting (often literally) upon people to the problematic of control in a society that is growing both more complex and – nominally, at least – more free.

Foucault, however, also speaks of the idea of governmentality. This concept to an extent gives practical shape and scope to the way in which disciplinary power is instantiated. Foucault describes governmentality as possessing three facets:

> First, by "governmentality", I understand the ensemble formed by institutions, procedures, analyses and reflections, calculations, and tactics that allow the exercise of this very specific, albeit very complex, power that has the population as its target, political economy as its major form of knowledge, and apparatuses of security as its essential technical instrument. Second, by "governmentality" I understand the tendency, the line of force, that for a long time, and throughout the West, has constantly led towards the pre-eminence over all other types of power – sovereignty, discipline, and so on – of the type of power that we can call "government" and which has led to the development of a series of specific governmental apparatuses (appareils) on the one hand, [and, on the other] to the development of a series of knowledges (savoirs). Finally, by "governmentality" I think we should understand the process, or rather, the result of the process by which the state of justice of the Middle Ages became the administrative state in the fifteenth and sixteenth centuries and was gradually "governmentalized".
>
> (Foucault, 2007, pp. 108–109)

Foucault is using the term to encompass the fact of the emergence of government as a practice at the time when the issue of the measurement and management of populations becomes significant. It refers to the apparatus – and, in particular, the governmental agencies that grow up – that develop as we follow social and political development from the turn of the 19th century onwards. With greater specificity, it is argued that

> Governmentality emerges in Western European societies in the "early modern period" when the art of government of the state becomes a distinct activity, and when the forms of knowledge and techniques of the human and social sciences become integral to it.
>
> (Dean, 1999, p. 19)

Importantly, this term is not used by Foucault to refer simply to the State. Governmentality is less about the actual institutions that arise at this time and more about the sensibility that sees the application of the human sciences – psychology and sociology pre-eminently – to the question of managing populations that exist in conditions of supposed freedom and social justice. To that extent, the scope of governmentality exists within but extends beyond the confines of formal government. This is succinctly expressed thus:

> The rapid crystallization of expertise and the establishment of professional associations in the nineteenth century was directly linked to the problems of governmentality – including the classification and surveillance of populations, the normalization of the subject-citizen and the discipline of the aberrant subject.... Far from emerging autonomously in a period of separation between state and society, the professions were part of the process of state formation.
>
> (Johnson, 1995, p. 11)

In large part, those professions were built on the burgeoning human sciences.

This observation extends even to the practice of medicine, which is seen to be crucial to the effectiveness of governmentality. Foucault's important work on the emergence of clinical medicine highlights the transposition of medical practice from the patient's personal bed to a specific clinical space in light of changing notions of medical practice and its wider role in society, relating to what Foucault calls '...an effective supervision of the nation's health' (Foucault, 1989, p. 45) Because Foucault foregrounds the professions – including, as we see, medicine (and especially psychiatry) – in respect to the human sciences that underpin them, the issue of governmentality is an extremely productive notion in considering how power/ knowledge coalesces and enjoys the widest possible currency.

Governmentality encapsulates a far more nuanced idea of how the liberal democratic state oversees and manages its populations. It refutes the Marxian idea of the state as merely an edifice through which power is exercised over subaltern classes; similarly, it avoids the fiction of the liberal democratic state being a neutral arbiter, lacking any type of agenda in terms of managing the population overall, the urban centres, the economy, and so on. In that sense, then, it reinforces the idea that one needs to think very differently about power, focusing on its productivity in respect to subjectivity and the ways in which it courses through relations rather than sits at one point to the exclusion of another.

Confession and parrhesia

Foucault's thinking develops, as one might expect, as he engages with a wider conversation about the question of power and his particular take on it. In particular, he responds to the idea that his perspective on power/knowledge as originally articulated as something that exclusively determines human subjectivity leaves no leeway for the idea of resistance (and, through that, to shaping one's own subjectivity in contrast to that which is being discursively determined). Hence, as the author begins his exploration of human sexuality, it is possible to discern a shift to a position where the subject can be seen to exercise a greater influence and is not merely subsumed into the discourse that operates around and through them. Partly, this originates in Foucault's exploration of the confessional, with the way in which this technology begins in classical times, with its emphasis on self-awareness and development, and is adapted through Christian practice, so that it is a more externalised practice, linked to a wider power discourse (Cole, 2006).

This supports Foucault to transition to a position where he begins to speak about the whole notion of technologies of the self, namely practices – many drawn from the classical period – wherein the individual assumes responsibility for their own development as a subject, enmeshed in discourse (and hence shaped very heavily by it) yet equally enabled to undertake some self-definition in contradistinction to that wider situation (Foucault, 1988). This, in turn, leads to the idea of parrhesia, the idea that, in the face of power, the individual – regardless of the implications of this act – engages in 'fearless speech' by speaking out (Foucault, 2001a).

This has great relevance, as the reader will see, as I start to articulate how a practitioner might think about engaging in truly radical OD work – and resonates very strongly with our wider social and organisational debates on speaking truth to power and whistleblowing. The very idea of parrhesia and its practical application equips us with a means of undermining the silence and denial, with the former lyrically observed thus: '[S]ilence is not just a product, but also a major source of, fear.... To overcome fear we therefore often need to discuss the undiscussables that help to produce it in the first place' (Zerubavel, 2006, p. 81).

Genealogy as a method

The final element of the jigsaw is an explanation of how the preceding concepts might be explored in practice. This requires the introduction of the Foucauldian concept of 'genealogy' as a method for undertaking critical analysis. Such an approach has the following virtues: first, it is rooted in history without being historiographical; second, it is exploratory without being linear; and, third, it does not rely on a traditional notion of cause and effect but instead surveys situations and circumstances, fields of force, push and pull in a social context, in order to develop a rich, detailed, and deep description of the circumstances that Foucault seeks to investigate.

A useful starting point here is Foucault's specific description of the method: 'Genealogy is gray, meticulous and patiently documentary. It operates on a field of entangled and confused parchments, on documents that have been scratched over and recopied many times' (Foucault, 2002a, p. 369). He pushes this definition further:

> Genealogy ... requires patience and a knowledge of details, and it depends on a vast accumulation of source material.... In short, genealogy demands relentless erudition. Genealogy does not oppose itself to history as the lofty and profound gaze of the philosopher might compare to the mole like perspective of the scholar; on the contrary, it reflects the metahistorical deployment of ideal significations and indefinite teleologies. It opposes itself to the search for "origins".
>
> (Foucault, 2002a, p. 370)

Notwithstanding these useful observations, a better understanding of this approach can be formed by engaging with the material that Foucault produced using it. Specifically, Discipline and Punish is the best practical example of the use of genealogy, insofar as the work explores the emergence of a new discourse of punishment without starting the analysis with the traditional historiographical question of 'What circumstances and events led to this?' Foucault's anti-humanist and anti-essentialist underpinnings are especially noticeable in this methodological approach (Foucault, 1991a). To expand on this, 'Foucault argues, drawing on Nietzsche, that history should instead be seen as a process of discontinuities and temporality, without essence' (Fejes, 2008, p. 12). The idea of linearity is absent in Foucault's writings – as, indeed, in the early work, is a sense of human agency.

It is said that Foucault

> ...offers historicist views of truth, knowledge, and rationality. He thinks that the most important philosophical projects have to do with understanding how and why we hold some things to be true, how and why we deem some things to be knowledge, and how and why we consider some

procedures rational and others not. Foucault also offers a historicist view
of the subject. Basic to his work is the idea that subjectivity is a complex
product rather than a pre-existent condition.'

(Prado, 2000, pp. 9–10)

Foucault's genealogical method acknowledges the emergence of things –
practices, ideas, behaviours, notions taken to be commonsensical – and
seeks to describe that emergence without necessarily scouring history for
relationships of cause and effect; it is, in effect, an historical analysis that
seeks to bracket off a linear notion of history. To take this a little further,
it is a method that does not seek to find a reality below the surface; instead, it takes the surface itself as the object of investigation (Ferguson,
1991, p. 327).

The way in which genealogy focuses on the surface rather than seeking explanation notionally hidden beneath that surface has another important implication in terms of method. Put simply, Foucault's genealogy does
not simply eschew a notion of chronology, events and instances occurring
as history inexorably rolls on; it also states openly that the rejection of
chronology is accompanied by a rejection of an idea of the unfurling of
history, particularly that this unfurling should be seen as one that has a
progressive direction. In *Discipline and Punish*, Foucault merely notes the shift
from regimes of punishment from sovereign to disciplinary power, without opining that the latter is necessarily better than the former (Foucault,
1991a). For Foucault, it is merely *different* – and the trick is to develop an
appreciation of that difference. As Kendall and Wickham (1999) observe,

> Foucault's approach to history is to select a *problem* rather than an histor-
> ical period for investigation. The problem might be "How did the prison
> emerge as the major form of punishment?", or "How did sex come to be
> seen as so important in terms of who we are?" But, whatever, it is crucial
> that we allow our investigations of a problem to surprise us.
>
> (Kendall & Wickham, 1999, p. 22)

Elsewhere, Foucault's detailed writings in respect to the development of a
modern idea of 'madness' is particularly illustrative of his methods. First,
Foucault's analysis notes a shift wherein those afflicted by madness move
from exclusion to confinement – and a confinement that, to all intents
and purposes, seems kindly and beneficent. In the modern asylum – such

as Samuel Tuke's Retreat in York – the mentally ill are free of shackles and treated with dignity (Foucault, 2001b, p. 233) – unless and until they misbehave, when it is explained that the shackles will be reapplied. But Foucault encourages his reader to question whether this is truly a progressive development, a 'better' way of treating the insane than before, despite first and superficial appearances.

But Foucault takes the analysis a step further, arguing that we should

> ...re-evaluate the meanings assigned to Tuke's work: liberation of the insane, abolition of constraint, constitution of a human milieu – these are only justifications. The real operations were different. In fact Tuke created an asylum where he substituted for the free terror of madness the stifling anguish of responsibility; fear no longer reigned on the other side of the prison gates, it now raged under the seals of conscience.
>
> (Foucault, 2001b, p. 234)

Moreover, he observes elsewhere that the asylum was where the burgeoning discipline of psychiatry – the crucial applied human science of the mind, so clearly yoked to the shift towards governmentality – met the mad – and importantly allowed them to remain (Foucault, 2009).

While Foucault avoids historical linearity and, in particular, any sense of progression, he does not thereby argue that the modern period has not been more humane and progressive. This is a significant distinction in respect to what we ordinarily expect from critical analyses. This is helpfully elucidated here:

> To deny the assumption of a progressive history does not require that one embrace the assumption of a regressive history. The inversion Foucault's studies perform seeks to show that what has been called a progressive history moment is accompanied by a movement that is also deleterious. This does not *reverse* the assumption of historical progress; it *complicates* it.
>
> (May, 2006, p. 68)

The second way in which his analysis of madness lays bare his method is the way in which Foucault thinks about madness in relation to the development of a wider sense of rationality. He demonstrates – in a very broad sense – that the mad can only be defined in respect to a prevailing notion of normalcy, namely those in possession of their reason. Foucault notes

that 'After defusing its violence, the Renaissance had liberated the voice
of Madness. The age of reason, in a strange takeover, was then to reduce
it to silence' (Foucault, 2009, p. 44). His analysis of this is complex and
detailed, exploring the way in which different notions of reason related
to the public experience of 'unreason' – and how those defined by their
'unreason' were viewed and practically managed. A remark by Foucault in
respect to this very idea of madness gives additional definition to his genealogical method: 'Let's suppose that madness does not exist. If we suppose
that it does not exist, then what can history make of these different events
and practices which are apparently organized around something that is supposed to be madness?' (Foucault, 2008, p. 3).

Foucault's genealogy was deeply influenced by the philosopher Nietzsche,
particularly in this regard through his work 'The Genealogy of Morals'
(Nietzsche, 2003). In terms of genealogy, Foucault states that two Nietzs-
chean concepts are crucial to his approach: these are the ideas of *descent* and
emergence (Foucault, 2002a, pp. 373–379). These are best explained in relation
to the example of madness cited above. In respect to the notion of emergence,
Foucault means the appearance of things at a given time and in a given place.
In methodological terms, emergence allows the genealogist to describe the
notions and practices that arise without reference to any sense of origin. In
respect to the notion of descent, Foucault views it as marked by an attempt to
explore backwards through myriad discontinuities and accidents without an
attempt to be comprehensive or to expose any sense of linearity.

The concept of *emergence* permits Foucault to describe the development of
the asylum, as discussed earlier, without feeling an obligation to talk as to
whence this development came. Meanwhile, *descent* gives Foucault licence to
mark a transition from sovereign to disciplinary power in terms of the practices about which he speaks (the juxtaposition of the regular use of torture
and a system of surveillance that serves to tap into notions of conscience)
with reference to the ideas that surround these practices (including those
ideas that surfaced but subsequently submerged and/or disappeared) rather
than a simple chronology of X leading to Y.

While Foucault is closely associated with genealogy, he is equally linked
to a method that can be said to be *archaeological*, which is oftentimes discussed as an approach that preceded genealogy. Indeed, there are authors in
the field who seek to periodise Foucault's work in a linear fashion in this
regard (May, 2006, p. 24) but even such periodisation tends to be tempered

with an acknowledgement that there is both overlap and, perhaps more importantly, the actual presence – as underpinning or overlay – of each method in the periods ascribed to others (Andersen, 2003, p. 7). From Foucault's perspective, the term archaeology is one that he chose to use strategically:

> Studying the history of ideas, as they evolve, is not my problem so much as trying to discern beneath them how one or another object could take shape as a possible object of knowledge. Why, for instance, did madness become, at a given moment, an object of knowledge corresponding to a certain type of knowledge? By using the word "archaeology" rather than "history", I tried to designate this desynchronization between ideas about madness and the constitution of madness as an object.
>
> (Foucault, 2000, p. 445)

Archaeology and genealogy are not two separate approaches that relate to different phases of Foucault's scholarship; they are complementary and overlap in many practical instances. Foucault explains:

> To put it in a nutshell: archaeology is the method specific to the analysis of local discursivities, and genealogy is the tactic which, once it has described these local discursivities, brings into play the desubjugated knowledges that have been released from them. That just about sums up the whole project.
>
> (Foucault, 2003, pp. 10–11)

In essence, then, archaeology examines discourses while genealogy looks at those discourses and their relationship to wider issues of power.

This underscores the way in which genealogy, in particular, is concerned with critique. The contrast between archaeology and genealogy is said to be Foucault's addition to the latter of '…a new concern with the analysis of power, a concern that manifests itself in the 'history of the present'' (Kendall & Wickham, 1999, p. 29). From a feminist perspective, it is pointed out that

> Genealogy is more of an activity rather than a theory in the interpretative sense in that it takes up a posture of subversion toward fixed meaning claims. Yet its emphasis on subversion positions it at odds with authority, inclining it to the side of the powerless and the marginal.
>
> (Ferguson, 1991, p. 324)

Foucault's analyses speak of the emergence of key practices and ideas, for sure, but they also use the genealogical method to question and contest them, with the suggestion that '[l]ike Nietzsche, [Foucault] also wanted to use genealogy as an argument against particular possibilities that had become realities' (Visker, 1995, p. 100).

In practice, then, a genealogy undertaken based on an appreciation of Foucauldian concepts involves an investigation of a wide range of material – policy documents and other material from recognised authorities; academic publication; 'grey' literature – that allows the investigator to discern the shape and style of a particular discourse. There is no sense in a genealogy of a simple historical progression and a seeking for straightforward causal linkages. Genealogy looks for the prefiguration of the present in the past – but also takes a critical perspective on the very nature of that present. Genealogy highlights those truth-claims that enjoy preeminence and explores why they enjoy that privilege, while – at the same time – acknowledging the presence amidst all of this of the bodies of knowledge that were placed in a subaltern position through the establishment of that privilege.

Application

My intention here has been to outline the thinking that derives from the work of Michel Foucault in light of the fact that I will be using this prism through which to judge OD and to outline how we might rethink that practice so that it has far greater radical impact in organisational (and hence wider social) settings. Hence, I will build my critique of OD as it is currently practised on the foundation of Foucault's thinking about power/knowledge and its associated concepts. I will also expound a vision of future practice off the back of Foucauldian notions such as *parrhesia*. Similarly, all of this work will be undergirded by the key methodological approach of genealogy, which offers both fresh insight into common-sense practices and gives greater scope for fresh thinking in regard to how things are done and why.

So, to pursue this, I will now carry forward the idea of genealogy into the context of thinking about the workplace as a social site. This offers a foundation on which to build the wider critique that I hope to offer – OD is a workplace practice, so its context needs scrutiny in itself and as the site in which it takes place – and it also gives insight into the way in which a Foucauldian approach can be actively applied in order to generate a more nuanced perspective on things which are ordinarily so common-place that they cannot be even perceived, let alone subjected to meaningful critical review. The next chapter, then, offers an outline for a genealogy of the workplace.

Bibliography

Agamben, G., 2009. *What is an apparatus? And other essays.* Stanford, CA: Stanford University Press.

American Psychiatric Association, 2000. *Diagnostic and Statistical Manual of Mental Disorders.* 4th ed. Arlington, TX: APA.

Andersen, N. A., 2003. *Discursive analytical strategies: Understanding Foucault, Koselleck, Laclau, Luhmann.* Bristol: Policy Press.

Angell, M., 2011. The illusions of psychiatry. *The New York Review of Books,* LVII(12), pp. 20–22.

Ball, K. et al., 2006. *A report on the surveillance society for the Information Commissioner by the Surveillance Studies Network.* s.l.: Surveillance Studies Network.

Bell, D., 2009. Surveillance is sexy. *Surveillance & Society,* 6(3), pp. 203–212.

Bentham, J., 1995. *The Panopticon writings.* London: Verso.

Boyne, R., 2000. Post-Panopticism. *Economy & Society,* 29(2), pp. 285–307.

Bozovic, M., 1995. Introduction – 'An utterly dark spot.' In: J. Bentham, ed. *The Panopticon writings.* London: Verso, pp. 1–27.

Cole, M., 2004. Signage and surveillance: Interrogating the textual context of CCTV in the UK. *Surveillance & Society,* 2(2/3), pp. 430–445.

Cole, M., 2006. The role of confession in reflective practice: Monitored continuing professional development (CPD) in health care and the paradox of professional autonomy. In: D. Lyon, ed. *Theorizing surveillance: The panopticon and beyond.* Cullompton: Willan Publishing, pp. 206–229.

Dean, M., 1999. *Governmentality: Power and rule in modern society.* London: Sage.

Deleuze, G., 2006. *Foucault.* London: Continuum.

Dreyfus, H. L. & Rabinow, P., 1982. *Michel Foucault: Beyond structuralism and hermeneutics.* Brighton: Harvester.

Fejes, A., 2008. What's the use of Foucault in research on lifelong learning and post-compulsory education? A review of four academic journals. *Studies in the Education of Adults,* 40(1), pp. 7–23.

Ferguson, K. E., 1991. Interpretation and genealogy in feminism. *Signs: Journal of Women in Culture and Society,* 16(2), pp. 322–339.

Findlay, P. & Newton, T., 1998. Re-framing Foucault: The case of performance appraisal. In: A. McKinlay & K. Starkey, eds. *Foucault, management and organization theory.* London: Sage, pp. 211–229.

Foucault, M., 1980. *Power/knowledge: Selected interviews and other writings, 1972–1977*. New York: Pantheon Books.

Foucault, M., 1982. The subject and power. In: H. L. Dreyfus & P. Rabinow, eds. *Michel Foucault: Beyond structuralism and hermeneutics*. Brighton: Harvester, pp. 208–226.

Foucault, M., 1988. Technologies of the self. In: L. H. Martin, H. Gutman & P. H. Hutton, eds. *Technologies of the self: A seminar with Michel Foucault*. Amherst: University of Massachusetts Press, pp. 16–49.

Foucault, M., 1989. *The birth of the clinic: An archaeology of medical perception*. London: Routledge.

Foucault, M., 1990. *The will to knowledge: The history of sexuality, Vol. 1*. London: Penguin.

Foucault, M., 1991a. *Discipline and punish: The birth of the prison*. London: Penguin.

Foucault, M., 1991b. Questions of method. In: G. Burchell, C. Gordon & P. Miller, eds. *The Foucault effect: Studies in governmentality*. Chicago: University of Chicago Press, pp. 73–86.

Foucault, M., 2000. Structuralism and post-structuralism. In: M. Foucault & J. Faubion, eds. *Aesthetics, method and epistemology: Essential works of Foucault 1954–1984, Vol. 2*. London: Penguin, pp. 433–458.

Foucault, M., 2001a. *Fearless speech*. Los Angeles, CA: Semiotext(e).

Foucault, M., 2001b. *Madness and Civilization: A history of insanity in the age of reason*. London: Routledge.

Foucault, M., 2002a. *The order of things: An archaeology of the human sciences*. Abingdon, Oxon: Routledge.

Foucault, M., 2002b. *The archaeology of knowledge*. Abingdon, Oxon: Routledge.

Foucault, M., 2003a. *'Society must be defended': Lectures at the College de France, 1975–76*. New York: Picador.

Foucault, M., 2003b. *Abnormal: Lectures at the College de France, 1974–75*. New York: Picador.

Foucault, M., 2007. *Security, territory, population: Lectures at the College de France, 1977–1978*. Basingstoke: Palgrave Macmillan.

Foucault, M., 2008. *The birth of biopolitics: Lectures at the College de France, 1978–79*. Basingstoke: Palgrave Macmillan.

Foucault, M., 2009. *History of madness*. Abingdon, Oxon: Routledge.

Goffman, E., 1961. *Asylums: Essays on the social situation of mental patients and other inmates*. New York: Anchor Books.

Hernandez, M., 2005. *Model prison on the island of Pines*. [Online]. Available at: http://modelprison.blogspot.com/ [Accessed 28 January 2012].

Hook, D., 2001. Discourse, knowledge, materiality, history: Foucault and discourse analysis. *Theory & Psychology*, 11(4), pp. 521–547.

Hunt, A. & Wickham, G., 1998. *Foucault and law: Towards a sociology of law as governance*. London: Verso.

Johnson, T., 1995. Governmentality and the institutionalization of expertise. In: T. Johnson, G. Larkin & M. Saks, eds. *Health professions and the state in Europe.* London: Routledge, pp. 7–24.

Joseph, J., 2004. Foucault and reality. *Capital & Class,* 82, pp. 143–165.

Kendall, G. & Wickham, G., 1999. *Using Foucault's methods.* London: Sage.

May, T., 2006. *The philosophy of Foucault.* Chesham: Acumen.

Nietzsche, F., 2003. *The genealogy of morals.* Mineola, NY: Dover Thrift Editions.

Norris, C. & Armstrong, G., 1999. *The maximum surveillance society: The rise of CCTV.* Oxford: Berg.

Prado, C. G., 2000. *Starting with Foucault: An introduction to genealogy.* Boulder, CO: Westview.

Sartre, J. P., 2003. *Being and nothingness.* London: Routledge.

Visker, R., 1995. *Michel Foucault: Genealogy as critique.* London: Verso.

Zerubavel, E., 2006. *The elephant in the room: Silence and denial in everyday life.* New York: Oxford University Press.

3

A GENEALOGY OF THE ORGANISATIONALLY DEVELOPED WORKPLACE

Theorists have devised myriad means by which to create understandings of the world. A good many of them rely on a sense of historicism and linearity. For instance, many of us learned in school that the First World War began with the assassination of someone called Archduke Ferdinand in Sarajevo. Such an isolated datum – divorced from context but placed in a notional sequence of events – creates a sense of progression. Yet, most of us now recognise that this sense of cause and effect, captured in my recollection by illustrations in my history textbooks of a man tossing a bomb into an open carriage occupied by someone in a plumed hat, is simplistic at best and illusory at worst. Quite simply, human affairs are significantly more complex than this type of notion allows and are best understood from a multifaceted perspective.

Even those perhaps more radical ways of making sense of things are fatally infected by this notion. The world view that underpins the work of Karl Marx, for instance, is inherently teleological. Underpinned by the notion of dialectical materialism, Marxian thought assumes the inevitability of the demise of capitalism at the hands of working people with a level of class consciousness. It assumes a progressive view, one that presupposes that

B follows A with a level of surety based solely on the internal logic of this mode of thinking. This internal logic prevails even when sense data intrudes to suggest that the certainty is questionable. The fact that capitalism has not collapsed under the weight of its own contradictions and that the proletariat has collectively eschewed the role of its gravedigger is not allowed to impact the unshakeable belief that these things will happen as surely as night follows day.

This way of thinking – derived in large part from the perspectives that constitute what is called the Enlightenment – does not simply assume a straight line of causality, as the Archduke Ferdinand example so ably illustrates. Underpinning it is also a key sense that this progress – the stepping from one point to another, with the route clearly mapped and patently discernible in retrospect – is leading us to betterment. Hence, in Marxism, it is unquestionably the case that the dictatorship of the proletariat will be better than capitalism for humanity. And human experience to date in terms of large-scale social experiments of a Marxian stamp – hallmarked with the horrors of the gulag or the grotesquery of Year Zero – is not allowed to confound the innate assurance of this supposed fact.

Trying to understand where we find ourselves in terms of such rationalistic notions as lineage and provenance creates the illusion of connections where none exist and assurances about directions of travel where none should exist. Into this space comes the idea of developing a perspective on things through the deployment of genealogy as a method, initially utilised by Nietzsche and latterly deployed in the work of Michel Foucault. This approach distinguishes itself by setting aside the notion of historical continuities in order to focus instead on discontinuities, anomalies, knowledges that run counter to the mainstream, and ideas and practices that run counter to the common sense notions that prevail at any given time. Genealogy does not deny history but neither does it privilege it: similarly, it does not disregard connectivity but, at the same time, it does not assume the idea of causality when looking at such constellations of ideas, structures, systems, and practices.

In Foucault's key analysis of the shift from sovereign to disciplinary power, he applies a genealogical approach to make sense of this change (Foucault, 1991). To posit the notion of such a change is to acknowledge events taking place in time and space. However, Foucault opts to explore the idea from beneath the notional historical timeline, investigating it in terms of wider transformations in society, such as industrialisation; the related development of large-scale urban populations; the growth of new professions and corpuses of scientific knowledge, particularly psychology; and the extension of the franchise. Foucault seeks not to write a history of power, wherein one event leads to another in a linear sequence because that generates a false surety of cause and effect.

Moreover, the whole notion of periodisation – the chunking of events and developments into discrete components that lead inexorably one to the other – misleads us into not noticing how threaded linkages and streams exist and are more apparent when one abandons a dateline. The way in which these streams constellate and inform one another gives a richer understanding of Foucault's concept of power/knowledge that might be possible by alighting on historical instances where one might assume a progressive linkage between the preceding event and the following one. This is an Enlightenment conceit which presupposes betterment and progress through the passage of history as humankind applies reason to the challenges that it faces. This is an ideological view, which serves to distort our appreciation of the way in which ideas, discourses, practices, and institutions – to use the Foucauldian term, the *dispositif* – are best understood rhizomatically rather than by using a tree-like model where trunk proceeds from root, bough from trunk, branch from bough.

Foucault's approach – in rejecting historicism – continuously highlights the perils of assuming that one thing follows another and (perhaps more significantly) that each successive state is better than the one that proceeded it, which can be described as the myth of progressivism. Hence, when Foucault explores disciplinary power, the premise that this work surfaces in respect to a new way of understanding power is that it is important not to assume that disciplinary power is in some way more progressive than traditional sovereign power, despite the liberal democratic discourse that surrounds and the ways in which its practical effect might be seen to be in some way more benign (Foucault, 1991). I shall return to this idea of power and its operation, specifically in the context of the workplace, a little later in this chapter.

From scientific management to staff engagement (1)

In terms of locating organisation development and making sense of it, then, a genealogical approach does not assume a sequential notion, despite the allure of periodisation as a means of tracking a supposed development in this area of practice. It would, for instance, be comforting to sketch out a history of organisation development as an assemblage of ideas and techniques over time, where we start with Taylorist notions of scientific management and progress through the human relations approach to arrive at today's notions of staff engagement, as so ably encapsulated by the Corporate Rebels and their work of trying to craft a picture of a genuinely modern 21st-century workplace (Corporate Rebels, 2018). But would this be accurate – or merely ideologically reassuring?

Moreover, to assume a genealogical approach is to get under the skin of things and to cast the most commonplace notions as enmeshed in a rich picture of interrelatedness. That which is not apparently connected may be viewed as enjoying the most intimate connection. So, at the start of a genealogy of the workplace and the activity that seeks to develop the organisation where it nestles, it is interesting to start with an examination of the significance of work. Hence, in an exploration of the way in which work and poverty intersect from a discursive perspective in terms of governmentality, it is suggested that poverty is economically necessary, particularly when one considers that the prevailing liberal democratic view is that poverty appears due to people not wishing to work (Lemke, 2019, p. 208). The intertwined quality of this observation leads the author to argue that 'Poverty simultaneously serves as the basis of, and motor for, moral and economic progress that pretends to aim at making it disappear' (Lemke, 2019, p. 207). So, this consideration of the workplace and the role that OD has played in fashioning it needs to assume a similar level of criticality – and to acknowledge this sort of underpinning to what we take to be the everyday and largely unquestionable.

When I began this book, I engaged with a number of my peers through LinkedIn. These were people who I respected, with whom I had a meaningful professional connection, and who all worked in the main in organisation development. Initially, I asked them to complete a quick online questionnaire, in advance of a conversation. I facilitated the latter by inviting people to connect on a specific date and time on the Zoom platform. In the end, 14 of my contacts made a response to the survey, so I am not claiming any scientific validity whatsoever for the observations that I am about to make off the back of that exercise. Nevertheless, for me, there is some insight to be gained from this slightly formalised professional exchange, which has helped me and my focus in terms of trying to undertake this work.

At the back end of the survey, respondents were asked to rate the extent to which they agreed or disagreed with a range of statements about the philosophy and practice of OD using a five-point Likert scale, with 1 the lowest and 5 the highest. At first glance, I was truly intrigued to spot the following apparent disjunction. In response to the statement that OD '…works to engender genuine engagement of everyone in the workplace,' there was a rated average across the group of 3.79; however, for the statement that OD '…is guided by truly democratic principles,' the response was just 2.79. As ever with the sort of 'data' that OD practitioners invariably seek to collate as part of the work that they do, this observation really cannot be seen to be telling us anything about the world in and of itself. However, it does provide idiographic insight, which might usefully be used to generate conversations. And so – for me – it raises this paradox: what does workplace engagement mean if it is not founded on democratic principles? Another response opened up an additional line of inquiry. The notion that OD '…seeks to make experience of the workplace more pleasant' attained a weighted average of 3.07, which could crudely be said to be suggesting that engagement in and of itself might not make your working life that much better.

A sidebar on data

As a sidebar here, I am eager to underscore my observation about the way in which OD seeks to give weight to its work by referencing data. The traditional model of OD practice is linear and sequential – oftentimes it connects to Peter Block's procedural approach to consulting (Block, 2011) – and ordinarily begins with a stage referred to as being diagnostic. Supposedly more enlightened practitioners relish offering up the mantra that even a diagnostic is an organisational intervention, a fact underscored by referencing the work of Elton Mayo and the identification of what has become to be known as the 'Hawthorne effect' (Mirvis, 2006, pp. 60–61). But, ultimately, this indicates an innate empiricism in much OD practice, where something akin to scientific method is applied: we cannot proceed without data, regardless of what that might look like.

Within organisations functioning in capitalist economy, this tends to be more about placating those for whom facts as described in numbers are privileged above all else when considering organisational life. I recall a few years back attending an OD event at which a noted guru delivered a keynote. He urged those assembled, when undertaking their diagnostic, to focus on the qualitative but also toss in one question where a Likert scale or similar is used. This offers a quantitative reassurance to those who need it. Such a distorted practice, of course, serves merely to reinforce that prevailing discourse, where key performance indicators, HR metrics, responses to staff surveys, and even psychometrics are seen to be truly reflective of reality, a reality into which one can intervene through activity to move those numbers in one or another direction. To an extent, though, such a practice substitutes a data reality for a human one, with numbers not merely superseding but effectively effacing the lived experience of those in the workplace.

Interestingly, as a reflection on my own practice, when crafting that short survey for my interlocutors on LinkedIn, I followed precisely this pattern. I wanted their observations about how they feel about day-to-day OD work – but ensured that one of my six questions was a quantitative item. These behaviours are ingrained – entrained, in fact, as Dave Snowden might observe (Snowden & Boone, 2007) – by the discursive formations in which OD practitioners work (the organisation itself, expectations around effectiveness and success, the imperatives of a capitalist society regarding profit and loss, and so on) and by the limitations that they place upon themselves in terms of their own thinking and their role in a capitalist marketplace. The radical response to circumstances faced will never be the easiest one, when we consider such constraints … and the fact that I have imported conservative rather than radical practices into the writing of this book underscores the challenges that exist in this regard.

From scientific management to staff engagement (2)

So, to come back to some genealogical observations in regard to the workplace, most historical accounts trace a simple lineage from specialist workshops through to increasing industrialisation. It is implied that these circumstances then create the condition for the appearance of scientific management, as defined in practice by F. W. Taylor (1919a). From a genealogical perspective, however, it is more important to survey panoramically and to and fro rather than from cause to effect. In that spirit, it seems relevant to attend to how new approaches to manufacture articulate with broader matters, such as population and its manageability. People moved towards – indeed, were drawn to – new and industrial workplaces that gave shape to the urban circumstances to which they migrated. Blake's 'dark, satanic mills' arose as a reflection of a present population but also as magnets to those who would seek to augment those populations. New methods of manufacture allowed production at scale – and perhaps for the first time encapsulated the notion of a 'workforce:' that living and breathing agglomeration of individuals who need to be inscribed into the method of production for it to be effective.

That act of inscription was indeed discursive – wage–labour forges an identity as a worker, the existence of the factory defines those therein as factory workers – but also entailed interventions. In many instances, this was about measurability: production is about inputs and outputs, as any economist (including Marx) will advise, and overseeing that requires the ability to quantify materials going in, products coming out, and (with particular reference to Marx) what happens in between to generate a measurable value (Mandel, 2002). In the summer of 1985, I spent six weeks where I seemed to be constantly sat at the top of a step ladder in the cavernous stockroom of a fax machine company, counting grommets – tiny sheaths of rubber that protect cabling as it runs through rough-edged metal holes – and reconciling that number (oftentimes in the thousands) with a figure that appeared on a large concertina of old-fashioned computer printer paper. I could never fathom what would count as a significant anomaly – or what would be done to address it, should it occur. But the experience taught me that capitalism loves to count things, and has done since we first began to monetise the exchange of goods and expand our manufacturing capability.

We still, of course, fetishize metrics, oftentimes at the cost of human wellbeing. I recall a busy team manager in an NHS trust telling me of her delight on receiving an email with the subject heading 'Outstanding.' Driven by a natural human desire for recognition and an excitement that this good news might be shared with those with whom she worked so diligently, she eagerly opened the missive, expecting to read praise for some noteworthy achievement of her team. Unfortunately, the senior manager sending the email was using the word in the subject line of the message differently: the text simply observed that the data required in respect to the measurement of the team's key performance indicators was 'outstanding' – that is to say, late – and needed to be submitted by no later than noon the following day. When the manager told me this story, I was instantly taken by the fact that she was reliving the disappointment and that the initial negative effect on her of this experience was profound. It reminded me of how unintentionally cruel the workplace can be when we allow day-to-day practices to go unchallenged.

The regimes of measurement that exist shape and determine the ways in which we exist as employees. A recent book (Gray et al., 2014) explored this idea of measurement in the workplace in a rich way, making observations that, first, we are often asked for data with no sense of why it's being requested and we do not see the use to which it is being put. It is a give and take, with us giving and someone else in the organisation taking with no connection or meaningful reciprocation. Second, the book noted that teams are invariably not engaged in any sort of prior or ongoing discussion about what should be measured and how: it is ordinarily a corporate given, an imposition or simple expectation.

The authors draw attention to the following example:

> Another famous story recounts how ... a carpet manufacturer in the North of England recorded "zero" on a daily basis against a measure labelled NART. Once again, nobody really knew what the measure was for, but any new person was told to record zero unless otherwise told. After 60 years somebody discovered that NART stood for Number of Air Raids Today.
>
> (Gray et al., 2014, p. 28)

This underscores our subjection in the workplace – we have no capacity to shape this regime and, importantly, we are, in a Foucauldian sense, made subjects by the practice of measurement, categorisation or taxonomy. Althusser – preceding Foucault in his explorations of this notion and retaining an unhelpful neo-Marxist orientation – suggests that one becomes a human subject when a police officer calls across the street 'Hey, you there!' (Althusser, 1984, pp. 44–51). Foucault sees the human subject emerging through a constellation of data points and categorisations: in his notion of disciplinary power, discourse determines normalcy (and hence, by exclusion, otherness) and scientific method – particularly the data that can be amassed from and about populations – supports that practice.

Between the input and the output sits activity that is delivered by people – or human resources, as the contemporary term so elegantly has it. (It's crude, but it's at least honest.) Here, then, once more, we see reason being interpolated into a social space and trying to render it sensible. In terms of the work of human beings, what was seen to be needed was the application of irrefutable scientific fact. Those facts were to be drawn from the day-to-day work of individuals – how quick, how often, how many, in terms of production – and then forced back into the productive process as standards; this is how you've done it to date, so at least maintain that level. But this is augmented by two things. First, there is a fundamental distrust of the workforce to apply themselves to the fullest extent. Taylor described this as 'soldiering,' which intimates that a worker is doing too little and taking too long to do it (Taylor, 1919b). Having driven the craft out of human endeavour by reducing production to a piecemeal process undertaken by deskilled individuals, small wonder that Taylor found 'soldiering' to be an issue.

Second, broadly in response to all of this, a new cadre of individuals arose whose role was to undertake the measurement and to identify ways in which production could be increased, either through changes to the ways in which things are produced (business process reengineering, anyone?) or through finding ways to make the workforce more productive. The latter ceaselessly fascinates a wide range of commentators, with seemingly endless debates about UK productivity or crude exhortations to 'sweat the assets.' This, then, is the managerial aspect of scientific management, which, in itself, marks a transition from crafts people overseeing – through their applied abilities and self-management – production on their own terms through to large-scale manufacturing where these people, with their talents scattered across a mechanical production line and their autonomy shackled to the rhythms of the factory and to the profit motive, are urged on to even higher levels of performance by people who oversee them.

It is perhaps worth noting in passing that a prime example of this type of focus can be found in Stakhanovism, which is how the Soviet Union chose to harness the capitalist ideology of scientific management (Bedeian & Phillips, 1990). Similarly, the popularity of lean methods in manufacturing, as first significantly exploited in the car producer Toyota, has led some to refer to this approach as 'Neo-Stakhanovism,' with the argument being posited that '... the logic of lean production is to reduce waste, to maximise the utilization of production factors notably labour so to reduce idle time and enhance the pace of work' (Askhenazy, 1998, p. 11). This author correlates engagement with lean techniques with an uptick in industrial injury, which makes lean look less like a progressive development in workplace organisation and more like a clumsy extension of scientific management.

Scientific management constitutes a discursive element of an overall workplace *dispositif*, in Foucauldian terms. The very presence of the practice intimates two things. First, that measurement and standardisation by a group that sits outwith the productive process – specifically a cadre of people with solely managerial concerns in this regard – is critical to ensuring that work is effective. The collection of data about that world serves not simply to reflect but more importantly to define that world in a subjective fashion – and to subjectify those who live in that world. For example, in respect to the ongoing debate about productivity in the UK economy, the figures used are argued to show – in an empirical fashion – that we fare worse than other countries; at the same time, it opens up a space for concern about why that might be, about what constitutes our otherness in respect to some intrinsic measure of normalcy for productivity in an advanced capitalist economy. That concern occasionally floods the system with anxiety about a crisis in this regard, and this, in turn, generates proposed responses to this discourse, in terms of remediation. All of this occurs within the discourse, with little reference to the reality of productive relationships in the workplace. To use the structuralist notion, this all exists amongst the signifiers, with limited practical connection to the signified; to take a further post-structuralist step, there is no true connection between the signifiers and the signified (Olssen, 2003).

Second, scientific management exists by displacing the capacity and willingness of the workforce to offer up new ways of doing things – and to experiment with those ideas in their day-to-day practice. Indeed, the internal logic of the measurability and notional efficiency that sits at the heart of scientific management supports the emergence of new ways of organising work, often referred to as Fordism (Doray, 1988). Here, the process of producing a good is seen to be amenable to being broken down to its smallest elements, so that the tiny tasks – none of which require a high level of understanding to execute – can be shared across an unskilled workforce. More importantly, it can be surveilled, closely watched via a superstructure of overseers, foremen and women, and managers. The outline of the modern workplace – striated into performers, managers of performers, and managers of managers – begins to appear.

Taylor's time and motion – a constrictive means of squeezing out the 'soldiering' he deemed a problem in manufacture – enjoys a remarkable segue with the efficiencies that were attainable through the application of

technology and the introduction of the production line. Within these practices, the subjectivity of certain individuals experienced a revision: their
role ceased to be about directly producing but instead homed in on managing production through oversight of processes through measurement and
direction of the people. At one point, a Managerial Revolution was declared
to have occurred, with cadres of managers acting to administer the economies of both the liberal democracies (viz, the USA, UK, and other countries
in Europe) and the Soviet Union (Burnham, 1960).

However, a society that promotes the notion of liberty, of the autono-
mous individual endowed with rights through a democratic system, while
at the same time tightly managing people in the workplace, is patently in
tension. It is not possible to be defined as a free subject in a sociopolitical
context whilst being surveilled, constrained and tightly managed in your
economic setting: if I am enfranchised to cast a ballot to choose the people
I think are best able to manage the country, surely I am entitled to more of
a say as to how the enterprise in which I work is run? The extent to which
casting that ballot is meaningful or truly impactful is moot, of course, but
is an act imbued with significance. I broadly subscribe to the view that, no
matter who you vote for, the government gets in, but it does not prevent me
from enjoying the carnivalesque qualities of polling day of the act of casting
my ballot. From a Foucauldian perspective, as well, I am less interested in
government and more interested in governmentality, in brief, how a state
formation manages its populations through measurement, applied science,
and categorisation (Rose et al., 2009). To go back to the key point, I cannot
exist in society as a free individual while in the workplace I am a serf.

There still persists, of course, the notion of betterment, as if the situation
of working people is in some way better as a result of the way in which
capitalism (and its sociopolitical corollary, liberal democracy) has developed.
But, to my thinking, that development is illusory, acting as a veil to disguise
the immutability of the relationships that underpin the workplace in this
context. Critics of this supposed refreshed or renewed capitalism made a
simple observation that underscores the argument that I am seeking to forge:

> [N]ew-style management does indeed offer various responses to the cri-
> tique of disenchantment by promoting the creation of products that are
> attuned to demand, personalized, and which satisfy "genuine needs", as
> well as more personal, more human forms of organization. Similarly, it

satisfies demands for liberation from the sway of bureaucracy associated with the critique of the second spirit of capitalism. These two dimensions help to give it salience and appeal, even if it proves to be somewhat lacking at the level of mechanisms of security and rests upon a form of justice which, while presenting characteristics that may be regarded as very specific, still remains largely implicit.

(Boltanski & Chiapello, 2007, p. 99)

Engagement as an illusion

The responses that we perceive in terms of the system working to reconcile this tension relate to the idea of staff involvement and engagement in the enterprises in which people work. In keeping with most other large corporations across the globe and as noted previously, the NHS undertakes an annual staff survey. Each year, the trusts and other NHS organisations jockey a little in terms of their league tabling off the back of this data: Are we better than our interlocutor trusts? Are we higher up the table than last year? Are we doing well amongst similar organisations in the sector in which we work, such as mental health? If the results make for miserable reading, the organisation will feel obliged to produce an action plan, not so much to do anything about it as to be seen as though something is being done. At this juncture, the workforce may be invited back in. I recall running focus groups of staff in response to staff survey results that suggested negative experiences in respect to bullying and harassment and discrimination. This involvement was honestly motivated but equally served the purpose of saying that the organisation had 'heard' the workforce and wanted to hear more. In this context, I fed back what staff had said in the survey – and asked the staff to speak about what they had said.

What's wrong with this, one might wonder? It seems a very positive organisational response to go back to the people and open up a discussion about the issues faced. Yes, it does ... at a superficial level. In reality, there are a number of issues with this type of reaction. First, the role of the workforce remains that of a stage army, brought into a specific space in order to speak with the organisation's senior leaders via the conduit of someone from the OD team. The material in the survey summary generates something akin to a legitimation crisis for the organisation (Habermas, 1976), so there becomes an imperative to work to assuage not the underlying causes but the character of that crisis. And, as a stage army, once those managed voices are heard in the space, they are invited to return whence they came – and the valued space, one that seemed to offer the prospect of meaningful organisational dialogue, is dismantled.

Second, the cyclical nature of this exercise is demotivating. The vast majority of senior leaders in organisations are not wicked villains, motivated by an intrinsically evil nature to do bad deeds. But they do have a tendency to be forgetful and reactive, due to the velocity of the workplace. Work can sometimes feel to be travelling faster than the speed of thought – and everyone in the workplace, especially the leaders, can be seen to be struggling to keep pace with it. This has the effect of erasing memory in many instances, so that they fail to acknowledge that the crisis they face at this point is largely the same as the one they faced at exactly the same time last year. They compensate for this impairment of memory through confabulation, the crafting of elaborate fictions about what actually happened in response to previous issues. This is oftentimes beautifully captured in a wantonly justifying communication from the corporate centre: at best, this is a defensive response to what is being heard from the workforce; at worst, it is an instrument that seeks to rework the organisational narrative.

Lastly, and by far the most significant in the context of the NHS, is the fact that the responses that can be seen in the staff survey, where the workforce is oftentimes complaining of negative experiences in respect to interpersonal relationships with those for whom they are endeavouring to offer care, those with whom they work, and those who manage them, are actually reflections of a working environment which in itself is harsh and lacking in compassion. Many argue that there is evidence to support this notion, noting in 2013 that a quarter of NHS staff had reported being bullied in the previous 12 months and highlighting a management culture described as both toxic and brutal (Klein, 2013). To give that assertion some richness of texture, in 2017, an erstwhile NHS CEO went on record to say that she had recognised that the ways in which she had managed in her trust were being described precisely in the bullying and harassment policy that she was at that time reviewing (Grimes, 2017). The fact that the NHS has been working to promote the notion of compassionate leadership (de Zulueta, 2016) seems strongly indicative of something of a deficit in this regard across the service.

There is a tendency to indicate that OD represents a humanising influence on workplace experience. I asked my LinkedIn colleagues to describe a piece of OD work in which they had recently been involved. One made the observation that those who had commissioned the work were looking for higher performance but the practitioner expressly said that they were hoping to encourage senior leaders to '…truly listen to the experience of employees.' Intriguingly, another of my correspondents, in responding to the question of what they were trying to achieve with the OD work they had undertaken as a practitioner, mentioned wanting to help a leadership group find a more '…grown up, functional way of working.' For me, this remark seemed double coded: on the one hand, it is referring – in a psychodynamic fashion – to the question of how best to ensure that human beings are authentically present in a workplace setting. And yet, it also seemed to me to offer insight into how OD activities can serve to reinforce our tacit experience of power in the workplace. For most of us, our first brush with power is through our relationships with our parents: the admonition to 'grow up' seems to carry with it a parental imperative.

A similar infantilism seemed to me to be at play in the remarks of another correspondent. Here, they were involved in delivering a programme to equip those working in HR and other parts of the business with skills traditionally ascribed to OD. Their individual practitioner ambition was that '…participants get they are agents of change, if they want to be, and internal agency has an edge to it.' Again, this is an entirely noble ambition, one that I have actively pursued in a wide range of settings – and one that I have openly espoused on public platforms. But my current focus allows me to cast a critical eye on all practice in my field – that of others as well as that of myself – and I return again to the notion that this carries two elements: an espoused commitment to putting the human being back into the centre of the workplace, alongside a supposed helplessness on the part of those subjects to be able to effect that manoeuvre without the explicit intervention of an OD expert.

Let me be quite explicit here: I am not using these observations to denigrate my colleagues (or, indeed, myself) in this regard, or to cast us as quislings, mindfully engaging in practices which are undergirded by an express commitment to engagement but which can be seen to disempower the people with whom we are working. Instead, I am using a Foucauldian idea of drawing attention to our immersion in the discourse and practices in which we find ourselves. The challenge is to denature that discourse, to render those practices strange to our own eyes, the better to engage critically with the common sense that supports it – and the better to be able to craft genuinely radical responses to the challenges faced in the workplace.

In recent years, this idea of 'engagement' has developed into an extreme manifestation where the workplace is seen to be 'demanagerialised,' through the adoption of flat organisational structures and enhanced individual autonomy. Interestingly, some of the precepts that define this liberated and seemingly radical vision of the workplace can be found undergirding the ideas of New Public Management (NPM), a political response to the fiscal crisis of the state (O'Connor, 2002) that saw administrations of a disparate variety of political hues flushing the public sector with business oriented practices in order to engender 'efficiency.' This looked towards flexibility, decentralisation and a new focus on leadership to reform these institutions, alongside less hierarchy and greater autonomy for those working there (Diefenbach, 2009).

In NPM, of course, managerialism remains, whereas more recent approaches assert that they have abandoned management altogether. In one such example of this type of thinking, human organisations are levered into a clumsily periodised analysis that sees us transition, through the pressure of a range of factors, from Red Organisations – excitingly referred to as a Wolf Pack – to Teal Organisations, which are seen as living organisms (Laloux, 2014). Such organisations – precious few but patently historically determined, insofar as they derive from what the sub-title of the book describes as 'the next stage of human consciousness' – are argued to have three key elements, namely self-management, evolutionary purpose, and wholeness. The latter intimates the arrival of a new *homo economicus*, one that is content to be their entire and authentic self in the workplace rather than merely a narrow professional simulacrum. By locating his arguments in broad brushstroke history and leavening them with an atheistic spirituality, he creates a simplistic expression of a wish that he desperately wants fulfilled. Laloux has already parlayed the work into an illustrated version of the original title (Laloux, 2016). Doubtless his audience eagerly await a colouring book edition of this scintillating volume.

Meanwhile, beyond Laloux's rarified palette, which does little more than apply a gloss to the foundational characteristics of the capitalist workplace, working people continue to struggle in colourless and hostile environments in face of numerous impositions. Never mind, though: a precious few people out in the global economy are having a rare old time, so those are the stories that fill the pages of the business press (Laloux, 2015). And cheerleaders for this reformist model cannot help but sound deterministic, certain that such observations portend an inescapable march to the beat of history across the whole economy:

> More progressive organizations are beginning to make move to greater openness; but, highly traditional organizations might find the ideas out-lined above too much to implement in the near future. Some top man-agers find they lack the privileges they have enjoyed in the past less than desirable, and many less progressive employees may feel uncomfortable with the uncertainty in their role within these structures – all of which could lead to organizational resistance. However, as we move forward it would seem clear that these more open, flexible, and agile structures are harbingers of even more open, flexible, and agile future set of organiza-tional structures to come – and this direction seem inevitable.
>
> (Coughlan, 2016, p. 16)

This seems akin to the old declarations that the socialist Valhalla was just around the corner.

Many of the new ideas about demanagerialised workplaces are closely enmeshed. Laloux offers a vision designed to inspire senior leaders who are seeking the next big thing or who are predisposed through a liberal world view to the idea that capitalism needs to be more effectively humanised. Meanwhile, Brian J. Robertson has popularised the concept of holacracy. According to the website promoting his book on the topic, 'Holacracy is a revolutionary management system that redefines management and turns everyone into a leader': meanwhile, we are advised that Robertson '…had previously launched a successful software company, where he first introduced the principles that would become Holacracy, making him not just a management theorist, but someone who has successfully imple-mented a holacracy-powered organization' (Robertson, n.d.).

In essence, the idea of holacracy is that there is a fundamental mismatch between, on the one hand, the current pace of business and the expecta-tions placed on firms to be responsive and agile, and, on the other, the tra-ditional structures of organisations, in terms of hierarchy and bureaucracy (HolacracyOne LLC, 2015). A white paper provided by Robertson's signif-icantly well-developed company that aims to promote holacracy intimates at one point that this notionally new and ground-breaking approach to 'distributing authority' in an organisational context traces its provenance back to Agile software development and Lean processes (HolacracyOne LLC, 2015, p. 3). That is significant, of course, insofar as the techniques that get bundled under the rubric of Lean are also notionally about harnessing the understanding of those in the workplace and encouraging them to assume responsibility for righting wrongs that they perceive around them. However, it is a practice that leaves the management cadre in an organisation largely untouched – and, in fact, can be argued to enhance their influence in the work context rather than actually diminish it (Beale, 1994).

I undertook a visit to an NHS organisation in the north-east some time back, where they had worked to introduce systematically the principles of Lean. These, of course, had been widely applied on the shop floor of Toyota – and they, in turn, had sought to popularise them and their uptake across a range of other organisations, including a healthcare facility in the USA called Virginia Mason, who had attempted to apply principles that had arisen out of manufacturing practice to the delivery of health services (Kenney, 2011). Virginia Mason had supported the adoption of these revised methods by the trust that I visited. The success stories that senior leaders were sharing on the day of my visit seemed at face value to be impressive and the processes that surrounded this work seemed to offer a high degree of staff involvement. They were particularly keen to showcase the charter that had been drafted in conjunction with staff, spelling out rights and responsibilities for the trust and for each individual member of staff.

My intuitive feel ran counter to the official message that was being offered and I longed for the opportunity to get among staff and have private conversations with them about their experiences. Sometimes, visiting an organisation that is pleased with itself in regard to work that it is doing on staff engagement feels something like being a tourist in a totalitarian state like the old East Germany: you know what you're being told, you can hear what people are saying publicly, but you sense very strongly that all of this is a very long way from the true picture, and if you could just give the tour guide the slip and speak to your taxi driver, you'd get an altogether different perspective. In other regimes, of course, staff are more than happy to share quite expressly their experience and their opinions: at one time, I escorted two consultants from Unipart Expert Practices around my organisation, exploring with them how they might work with us on Lean. Their division is, of course, a spin-off of the car parts manufacturer, which itself grew out of the old British Leyland to become successful using Lean as a way of trans-forming the business (alongside some quite hard-edged HR practices and a significant remaking of the firm). A social worker was in strained conversa-tion with them but eventually, she was unable to contain her true thoughts any longer: 'Our patients,' she explained, 'are not like exhaust pipes, you know!' My reflection on that experience now is that staff engagement is not about feeding that sort of heartfelt opinion into mollifying corporate channels but ensuring that everyone is offered time and space to express their opinions candidly as part of the day-to-day conversational exchanges in the organisation.

Research suggests that – in healthcare, at least – the application of Lean methods has a significant impact, with saving in terms of both time and costs; improvements in both quality and productivity; and improved staff experience, all being reported (Mazzocato et al., 2010). Certainly, it can be argued that the adoption of these types of techniques opens up a dialogue in the workplace between managers and staff that is oftentimes absent. But the voice of those on the shop floor is not free to express itself as it chooses: it is heard by invitation of the organisation's leaders and only through a formalised and externally defined process. In short, Lean allows everyone in the organisation to exercise their bureaucratic and corporate voice, but not necessarily their authentic one. Small wonder, then, that one senses – although might struggle to evidence – an uptick in staff experience, when people may be moving from organisational silence to an invitation – albeit a limited one – to exercise their voice in that space. It's good, as far as it goes. But there is an ominous sense that the conversation that you would wish to see as the lifeblood of organising for a purpose is mediated and constrained by the technocratic superstructure that surrounds the whole question of practices like Lean.

Holacracy, then, notionally takes up the challenge of following through on the promise of Lean. Even advocates of the latter concede that the tech-niques themselves cannot be successful without a defined management sys-tem that sees improvement as intrinsic to day-to-day operational oversight, a commitment to leadership, and a corporate culture that resonates with Lean practice (Kaplan et al., 2014). Therein is where OD is seen to be in play, picking up the human elements that sit alongside technical process changes. The latter would be felt as a management imposition without that smooth-ing off by OD, as later chapters herein will seek to show. Instead, process reengineering techniques can now be presented as staff engagement and empowerment (whereas, in reality, it is merely involvement of people in the workplace at the sole discretion of the managerial cadre, marched on at key points in a process and wheeled out when things get real).

I have had occasion to watch a senior leadership team wrestle with this very notion: some of the directors were extremely well disposed to the idea of undertaking a large-scale and unbounded exercise in staff engagement in order to address outstanding technical challenges in their business processes. But the anxiety arose as to whether that leadership would be able, with any legitimacy, to step in at some critical juncture to prevent the workforce from seeking to finish what they had been invited to begin. These observations from practice find conceptual insight thus:

> Every organization is an emotional place. It is an emotional place because it is a human invention, serving human purposes and dependent on human beings to function. And human beings are emotional animals; subject to anger, fear, surprise, disgust, happiness, or joy, ease, and unease. By the same token, organizations are interpersonal places and so necessarily arouse those more complex emotional constellations that shadow all interpersonal relations; love and hate, envy and gratitude, shame and guilt, contempt and pride.
>
> (Armstrong, 2004, pp. 11–12)

In this context, it is worth recognising two elements of the anxiety that might be experienced in a context such as this: signal anxiety, the small sense of discomfort that arises in a circumstance and which we can mentally manage; and actual anxiety, wherein this emotion moves from being a call to action to a burden, a '...force that becomes an increasingly regressed mental state where we may adopt an increasing use of fantasy, magic, and irrational methods' (Stapley, 2006, p. 46). This is important to note, lest anyone is expecting this radical approach to thinking about organisational life to seek to demonise those who end up in senior leadership positions. My sympathy extends to all in organisational life in the current context, whether on the frontline or in the boardroom – and my desire is to work to release the talents of everyone, regardless of their position or status, for organisational life as currently constructed constrains and stunts us all.

The observation that anxiety might manoeuvre us into behaviours that we would not necessarily want to indulge is another important one, particularly as it casts illumination on the idea that it is the organisational context and our emotional reaction to it that unwittingly leads to negative experiences for everyone. Some time ago, I was on board a commuter train into London King's Cross. Two men in suits boarded at Hatfield and opted to stand nearby where I was sitting and proceeded, for the duration of the journey, to speak endlessly about their organisation and the people with whom they worked, invariably in less than glowing terms: they gave so-and-so that project, but – by the judgement of one of the interlocutors – he was 'shit' and would not be able to deliver it. This irrational destructiveness towards the reputations of people best considered as colleagues or work-mates came from somewhere – and I was compelled to wonder two things: first, what sort of place was it that they worked in that rendered this normal; and, second, what might each say of the other in another conversational context.

To return to the idea of Holacracy, Robertson crafted his notion – and built his business around it – having managed a software company, and the precepts of the practice find great favour in such organisations. However, the firm that has embraced holacracy in a truly significant way is Zappos (Askin et al., 2016). Zappos is a shoe store, but actually began life simply as a plat-form company, akin to AirB&B and Uber. It used technology to connect con-sumers with products from a range of suppliers. Only later did it develop a model that included its own stock and storage facilities – and, unsurprisingly, given the avaricious nature of tech capitalism in the modern age, Zappos was acquired by Amazon in 2009. Throughout its existence, however, a central figure has been Tony Hsieh, who initially supported the concern through his venture capital company and latterly took the helm of Zappos as its CEO.

In an echo of the sort of paternalistic capitalism that attained its apoth-eosis in the UK with the development of company towns such as Port Sunlight, Bourneville, and Saltaire (Wray, 1996), Hsieh relocated Zappos from San Francisco to Las Vegas. Apparently, many of the staff made the move as well, which meant that they landed in that city that more or less defines postmodernism in terms of human geography (Venturi et al., 2001) without any social connections other than their Zappos workmates. But this suits the cult-like culture of the company, by all accounts: a 2015 article in The New Republic reports that 'Zapponians, as the employees call one an-other, like to talk about 'work-life integration' rather than work-life balance' (Hodge, 2015). But even with those at work already sipping at the Kool-Aid and self-defining in this way, this level of erasure of the boundary between public and professional life was not enough for Hsieh: using Laloux as his inspiration and holacracy as his model, he ensured that the firm moved to a notionally more fluid and flexible shape.

It is unclear the extent to which this decision was delivered as a managerial imperative (in this case, an edict from the CEO) or as part of a fully engaged discussion with staff across the organisation. Indeed, two years after the launch of the holacratic experiment, Hsieh was compelled to circulate an extraordinarily long email to Zapponians, urging them – through a fog of corporate speak and new age observations – to get with his programme (Groth, 2015). A quick look at the Zappos page on the Glassdoor employee feedback website shows positive numbers sitting alongside commentary that suggests that the Hsieh's boundless enthusiasm for driving Zappos to become a Teal Organisation, with holacracy as the first step on that process, may not be shared to the same level by the vast number of company employees (Glassdoor, 2018). Elsewhere, it was reported that between the release of the email in March 2015 and January 2016, the company had lost 260 staff members, representing 18% of its workforce (French, 2016).

Holacracy is sometimes clumsily denigrated as a model where managers have been stripped out of the system. Certainly, formal structuring of organisations does not feature in holacracy, but it stands to reason that simply rebadging management or affording it a different title does not do away with it in an organisational context. Instead, it is argued that

> Holacracy is just one example of a system that uses peer-to-peer self-organization and distributed control in lieu of more traditional approaches to achieving order. It reflects a broader societal trend toward a new way of structuring human systems and interactions, and it aspires to contribute to that shift by modelling the benefits of leaving behind outdated autocratic models.
>
> (HolacracyOne LLC, 2015, p. 7)

It is a self-organisation method that arranges around work itself rather than around position and command-and-control, so sets aside the standard organisational tree in favour of a corporate shape wherein teams (known as 'circles' in an holacracy) are the structure; those teams design and govern themselves, and leadership is situational rather than simply positional (Bernstein et al., 2016).

The crucial aspect of this analysis is not to produce a chronological analysis of better staff engagement over time. Such an approach would be unhelpful in this context for two reasons. First, it would indulge the historicist fiction that human life can be understood in a linear way in which one thing begets another. This disregards the complex way in which things interconnect across time, with prefiguration of contemporary concepts apparent in earlier historical periods. Second, such a linear approach, riven with the notion of causality, can oftentimes carry with it the presupposition of betterment, thereby indulging the questionable notion of progress occurring over time. In the narrative I have been exploring, it seems reasonable to observe that a self-organising workplace – where hierarchy is lightened and the focus is on the work and not the titles – is clearly a better place to work than an early Ford production line, overseen by Scientific Managers. The Foucauldian challenge is to say: is that actually so? And the reason that this question is posed relates to Foucault's refreshing ideas on power and how it operates.

The place of power

In work undertaken to support the wider issue of systems leadership in the health and social care context, I crafted a response along the lines of three streams of activity, namely being in a system, doing in a system, and developing a system. Whilst the latter two had a focus on leadership in practice within this new context, the first supported the exploration of the ontological challenges that accrue to individuals who need in the contemporary context to acknowledge the systems in which they reside at work rather than merely the structures or, indeed, their sovereign organisations. I had previously scoped out a theoretical position in respect to OD practice where I took the view that activity in this area could be considered to be anything that sought to facilitate conversation, connection, and the flow of knowledge between people in the workplace, the better to enable organisational effectiveness (Cole, 2017). However, in thinking about the reality of life in the workplace and the place of conversation therein, it seemed apparent that – with the exception of theoretical expositions within the broad academic area of critical management studies (CMS) – there was little discussion of power in respect to the organisation, or indeed of the basic acknowledgement of its presence.

A key response was to work with two expert faculty – my colleagues Ben Fuchs and John Higgins, the latter of whom had co-authored some impressive research in this regard (Reitz & Higgins, 2017) – to produce an introductory day to allow attenders to explore their comfort in respect both to speaking up in an organisational context (which is to say, speaking truth to power) and to listening up, by which was meant the climate that people create around themselves where their peers and those who work to them feel enabled to speak out. These events were deeply thought-provoking and very well attended. But the issue of power – whilst referenced in this context – was still not being critically interrogated: in a sense, it remained a given, something implicit to organisational context and inseparable from it. Hence, when we began to offer all participants the opportunity to invite the teams in which they worked and which they managed to complete an online survey on speaking up and listening up, the uptake was interestingly low. This despite – or perhaps because of the fact – that the survey generated a report that could be explored in a team session facilitated by John Higgins. It seemed as though three things were intersecting in people's minds: first, that power was indeed intrinsic to the workplace and something of concern; second, that the workshop represented somewhere to explore power once removed from its workplace context; and, third, that the exploration in itself did not then translate into a commitment to investigate directly the play of power in its workplace context.

Within Marxian theory, of course, particularly in its more classical and uninterrogated manifestations, power is a zero-sum commodity: if one class has it, then another does not (unless it is ceded to them or they organise to seize it). Marx, of course, saw class as a binary opposition – with bourgeoisie and proletariat facing each other across a class divide – and so his understanding of power was limited by that formal schema and by a view that saw it purely as a political resource. Later writers within this tradition who sought to develop this notion, such as Gramsci with his idea of hegemony (Gramsci, 1971), Althusser in terms of enriching an appreciation of ideology (Althusser, 1984), and Poulantzas who offers richer picture of how the capitalist state functions (Poulantzas, 2000), can often be seen to disappearing down rabbit holes as inconsistencies of internal logic fracture the ideas that they seek to posit in defence of Marx's original position. More recently, it has been suggested (somewhat simplistically, it must be said) that Foucault's thinking on power and discourse logically compliments the economic thinking of Marx (Bidet, 2016). There is much to be said for combining these apparently conflicting sets of ideas in order to forge a more comprehensive critique of contemporary society. However, in this instance, my focus is solely on the Foucauldian understanding of power.

Within organisational studies – and particularly from a critical perspective – a Foucauldian view of power as an intrinsic binding element in social relations rather than a commodity to be possessed by one party to the detriment of another brings a richness to our understanding of life in such a context. That said, there is a negative in respect to this view, which is that it might be said to offer limited space for resistance; if, in the workplace, we are enmeshed in relations of power rather than merely subject to its exercise by an authority figure, there is no exteriority where we might fight a battle against its imposition on us – and each constellation of power is no different from another (Knights & Vurdubakis, 1994, p. 175). Foucault himself was mindful of the counsel of despair that can be perceived in his more obviously structuralist early works. Latterly, he explored – particularly through his multi-part history of sexuality and his development of the notion of technologies of the self – how the individual subject might assert a presence in such a context (Foucault, 1988a).

The fact that power is intrinsic to the interconnectivity that we experience in the workplace makes it all the more remarkable that it is not expressly acknowledged in advance of trying to have conversations about organisational development. But therein is the key issue, which can be expressed as follows: there is a sense that we have progressed since the Industrial Revolution and that the workplace is significantly 'better' than it was. But, as Foucault seeks to underscore in his work around the move from sovereign to disciplinary power, in terms of analysis of how madness is understood (Foucault, 1988b), how medical practice developed (Foucault, 2003), and how punishment has been experienced (Foucault, 1991), the notion of progress is illusory insofar as power remains present but is merely better veiled. Foucault's contrast between the way in which sovereign power acts upon the body, through corporal and capital punishment, and how disciplinary power functions through definitions of normalcy and hence otherness stresses how the presence and effect of power are unaffected by changes in these modalities (Foucault, 1991).

Importantly, for Foucault, it is this concatenation of power and knowledge – the knowability of subjects being the currency of the power that inhabits social relations – that gives disciplinary power its distinctive and veiling quality (Foucault, 1980). It is the discursive formation – the dominant knowledges (contrasted with those held in a subaltern relationship), along with the institutions, practices, and procedures that accrue from that – that generates the power with the interrelationships of people, rather than an economic privilege or an assumed authority. And, in the workplace, it is suggested that such discourse both subjectifies the person therein – defining them as a valued employee or as a slacker, prone to Taylor's 'soldiering' – and objectifies them, insofar as the disciplinary elements of that power-knowledge formation acts upon them (Mumby & Stohl, 1991, pp. 316–317). I am no longer beaten or struck at work … but I undergo an appraisal that rates and ranks me, defining me in respect to my performance in the workplace. The lack of beating is patently a good thing but to dwell on the notion of progress ('Thank heavens we no longer do those things…') is to shroud – perhaps it is more appropriate to suggest that it sanitizes – the contemporary experience of power in the workplace.

Viva Rebellion!

When Mao unleashed the Cultural Revolution in China in August 1966, it appeared as though he was pushing back against the ossification of Communism in that country. In fact, as ever with such events, things were not altogether what they seemed. The Cultural Revolution called to the young people to act as a stage army in order to restore his particular faction to power. He unleashed the fervour of youth by closing schools and advocating a mass mobilisation on their part against what he chose to describe as reaction. This terror lasted just over ten years and, it is suggested,

> Some 1.5 million people were killed during the Cultural Revolution, and millions of others suffered imprisonment, seizure of property, torture or general humiliation. The Cultural Revolution's short-term effects may have been felt mainly in China's cities, but its long-term effects would impact the entire country for decades to come. Mao's large-scale attack on the party and system he had created would eventually produce a result opposite to what he intended, leading many Chinese to lose faith in their government altogether.
> (History.com Editors, 2018)

One of the early precepts – expressed in a letter to a group of Red Guards, as the young people who sought to drive forward the Cultural Revolution became known – was that 'it is right to rebel against the reactionaries' (Mao, 1966). This was granting permission to all of the Red Guards to pursue all those who might be seen as standing opposed to Mao's vision of the advancement of the somewhat faltering socialist experiment. As one commentator opines in relation to this apparently simple statement,

> Are we dealing with an observation, summarizing the Marxist analysis of objective contradictions, the ineluctable confrontation of revolution and counterrevolution? Is it a directive oriented toward the subjective mobilization of revolutionary forces? Is Marxist truth the following: one rebels, one is right? Or is it rather: one must rebel?
>
> (Badiou, 2005, p. 669)

This leads Badiou to argue that, in relation to the tension within this seemingly simple Marxist political phrase, 'Every knowledge is orientation, every description is prescription' (Badiou, 2005, p. 670).

I take issue with this at a number of levels: first, it seems – at face value – to be a simple call to action, an imperative for people to hold the old guard to account and to push the revolution forward. And, whilst it did achieve that essential aim, it did so not simply to return to an original principle, as this construction seems to suggest, but to advance the specific ambitions of a group within the senior leadership of the Chinese state. Certainly, it reinvigorated revolutionary sentiment, while at the same time subtly promoting the agenda and ambitions of a tiny group. And, secondly, linked to this, despite all the disruption that the Cultural Revolution unleashed, it did nothing to fundamentally alter or indeed meaningfully adjust the fundamentals of the situation: it simply maintained the old order by supposedly encouraging people to rebel against it. Each and every Red Guard, fervently waving a copy of Mao's Little Red Book, were rebelling in order to maintain the status quo, namely that China would aspire to become a successful socialist state. The acts of rebellion – the assumption of the role of rebel – all served to ensure that the fundamentals remained wholly untouched. Lastly, of course, unleashing this simulacrum of rebellion left the fundamentals unchanged – but adversely impacted millions of lives.

So, we turn our intention back to the workplace in the developed world in the 21st century, with this example of discursive practice firmly in our minds. And here, in outline, threaded through the discourse that dominates our thinking and practice in organisational settings, we find something curiously similar. First, we find that growing band of Corporate Rebels, as they have branded themselves, spinning out from their position as researchers and thought leaders into the role of consultant, as they announce the arrival of *Revolt by Corporate Rebels*, the provenance of which is described thus:

> In March 2017, fellow rebel and friend, Freek, joined the team. He's an idealist at heart, but also fiercely dedicated to turning ideas into reality. He pushes us from rebellious talk to tangible action—action that changes workplaces. Not long after Freek, Catelijne joined us. She is fiercely committed to the very same pursuit: helping organizations release the untapped potential of their employees.
>
> (Corporate Rebels, 2019)

Note the balance in this text, which I am taking at face value (although it may yet turn out to be a playful provocation to assess the reactions of the business world to these ideas); these rebels are dedicated to facilitating the further exploitation of the employees, which in this case is expressed as untapped potential which needs to be offered up to the organisation, rather than liberating the workforce in and of itself. Now, this is fine, of course: it's what so many consultancies offer as a service, including the big providers in the field. It offers us a simple point at which to direct our rejection of this type of activity. But dressing it up as rebellion partially disguises the fact that it is, in actual fact, no different, other than it might have greater currency amongst the workforce in light of the use of the ideas of rebellion and revolt. Hence, as with the Maoist example, it is an incitement to join a revolution to leave fundamentals completely intact and wholly untouched.

Now, I like the Corporate Rebels; I have had the pleasure of working alongside them on a number of occasions over recent years and I think I appreciate what motivates them. (Their back story – an intrinsic part of who and what they are in their roles as Corporate Rebels – is rich and interesting.) But this is a solemn reminder of how even those practices that seem most at odds with the dominant discourse can actually be a significant means by which they discourse sustains and reproduces itself, in the same way as the encouragement to rebel from Mao was about shoring up the status quo, albeit with a different group leading it. It is quite apparent, then, that the discourse is primed to absorb even the most leftfield practices in order to sustain itself.

Genealogically speaking, this idea of rebellion in the sterile world of corporate life echoes in a number of places alongside that of the Corporate

Rebels. In that pot-pourri approach to business writing that is increasingly used supposedly to engage the audience, the Professor of Business Administration at Harvard Business School, no less, proselytises thus:

> Rebel leadership means that you prefer working in a rebel organisation and that you support your organisation in that mission. Rebel leadership means fighting our natural human urges for the comfortable and familiar. We have an innate desire to be accepted by others and thus regularly conform to their views, preferences, and behaviour. We rarely question the status quo. We easily accept existing social roles and fall prey to unconscious biases like stereotypes. It's human nature to stay narrowly focused on our own perspective and on information that proves us right. By contrast, rebels know themselves and are aware of these limitations, but they don't believe there are limits on what they can accomplish. Like the pirates, rebels follow their own "articles".
>
> (Gino, 2019, p. 198)

One could be forgiven for thinking that a lot of that might quite easily have appeared on a large character poster penned by a Red Guard during the Maoist Cultural Revolution. But, no, it's a guide for business, which by its nature must pivot around the notion of improved efficiency. What follows, of course, is a series of precepts that indicate how the reader might connect with their own need to rebel (albeit within the tightly governed notion of corporate permission). And, as with the Corporate Rebels, the focus is not collective but solely on the individual: this is rebellion rendered merely as a technique for self-improvement and advancement in one's working life. It is not about coming together to engender significant change through a collective voice: it is – from a Foucauldian sense – a perversion of the idea of technologies of the self, all about inscribing that which might be defined as rebellion into me as a human subject.

And what on Earth was meant by the curious mention of pirates towards the end of the quotation from Gino's book? Well, the preamble to that chapter lingers on how enlightened life on a pirate ship would have been and sets up Blackbeard as a leadership exemplar. So, we rinse piracy of its negative connotations, the better to promote a sanitised version of rebellion, which can be usefully applied to the self in order to develop one's place in the workplace and which is denuded of its collective (and hence potent) implications. And pirates are busy in the corporate world, it has to be said. Their rehabilitation from a business perspective proceeds apace: it is asserted that their story has been distorted by the people who they threatened but that '...some of what they achieved could and should be an inspiration for our times' (Conniff Allende, 2018, p. 9). More importantly, the pirate trope can be effectively mobilised by cunning writers to create self-improvement books for downtrodden people in corporate life.

Hence, we are thereafter advised that,

> Becoming a rebel is the first decisive move you need to take to be more pirate, and all you have to do to begin is pick a rule to break.... Whether it's raising your voice, making a complaint, asking the difficult question or point blank refusal to follow even a small but stupid rule, the size of the first step has got to suit *you*.
>
> (Conniff Allende, 2018, p. 60)

All of which seems to indicate that we have moved away from the idea of the 'tempered radical' as a self-motivated agent of change in organisational life, someone who is committed to the values of the organisation but urgently seeks ways through which its purpose might be better realised (Meyerson & Scully, 1995). Instead, we have a solipsistic pirate figure, charting their own course for the purposes of self-actualisation without any real reference to the wider social context.

The workplace, then, is coated in a variety of varnishes, each over-layering merely adding to the thickness of lacquer that stops us seeing what truly lies underneath. These accretions, endlessly piled on top of one another, depending on context and circumstance, include scientific management, humanistic approaches, flattened post-bureaucracies and – as we have just seen – encouragement of 'rebellion' within a business context. They all serve to create the illusion of progression, when – genealogically – it is possible to assert quite simply that such practices co-exist (one does not precede the other, nor is there a logical trajectory of improvement opening up over the course of history) and that they are epiphenomenal in relation to the disciplinary power and its related discourse that prevails. Hence, for example, you are organisationally invited to 'rebel,' whilst anything akin to collective revolt would be very much frowned upon, not least by the busy 'rebels' around you. In fact, your rebellion is a means by which the firm might refresh itself and attend to the need to maintain profit margins.

Nothing, then, is quite as it seems ... and, while we busily carve out a pirate role for ourselves in corporate life, it is worth recalling that, once on the high seas, piracy persists and remains a genuinely cutthroat business. In 2010, researchers estimated that global piracy cost the globe US$28 million in trade destruction (Martínez-Zarzoso & Bensassi, 2010). And a richer and more comprehensive history of piracy from its earliest manifestations right up to the current day offers a more nuanced perspective on the practice – and introduces the important distinction between pirates and privateers. In this regard, it is suggested that,

> There were a number of reasons why a sovereign might commission pri-
> vateers. Most important, it offered a way to destroy a rival's shipping and
> create economic turmoil at virtually no cost to the issuing state. Large
> professional navies were expensive and often nonproductive; privateering
> represented a cheap form of naval warfare.
>
> (Elleman et al., 2010, p. 4)

In light of this, I am minded to suggest that we are not being invited to 'be more pirate;' we are being corporately commissioned to 'be more privateer' in service of the specific effectiveness needs of our organisations.

Engagement as 'Fallocracy'

A traditional view of historical workplace change would trace a developmental arc from the sharp edge of Taylorism through human relations and the growth of organisational development as a method for humanisation through to the modern ideas of teal organisations and holacracy. Our Foucauldian perspective, however, suggests to us that we set aside the progressive notion that underpins such a narrative; instead, we should focus on the way in which that shift from corporal supervision – Taylor's control of an employee's body in the course of production through segmentation of process and the application of time and motion measurement – up to a position where the employee's experience of disciplinary power acts upon their mind and their behaviour occurs. There exists a pretence that power can be evacuated in an organisational setting by the adoption of these modern methods: the experience of people at the sharp end suggests that this is a fallacy.

To this end, the next chapter will delve more deeply into how the practice forms part of an overall apparatus that sustains a dominant discourse of business and successful organisational life. In looking microscopically closely at that practice and the building of the outline review of the environment in which it takes place that has been the subject of this chapter, it will hopefully become apparent why I take the view that OD supports the generation of a progressive fiction, which obscures the real underpinnings of the workplace as we experience it. It will, of course, link to some of the broad brushstrokes observations sketched herein, in respect to the workplace as a location in which people are enmeshed and OD gives structure. But it will also look more deeply at the thinking that tends to undergird OD and the techniques that fall in – or alongside – its concerns.

Bibliography

Althusser, L., 1984. Ideology and ideological state apparatuses (Notes towards an Investigation). In: L. Althusser, ed. *Essays on ideology*. London: Verso, pp. 1–60.

Armstrong, D., 2004. Emotions in organizations: Disturbance or intelligence?. In: C. Huffington, et al. eds. *Working below the surface: The emotional life of contemporary organizations*. London: Karnac, pp. 11–27.

Askhenazy, P., 1998. *The neo-Stakhanovism*. Paris: Delta: Ecole Normale Superieure.

Askin, N., Petriglieri, G. & Lockard, J., 2016. *Tony Hsieh at Zappos: Structure, culture and change*. s.l.: Insead Business School.

Badiou, A., 2005. An essential philosophical thesis: 'It is right to rebel against the reactionaries.' *Positions – Asia Critique*, 13(3), pp. 669–677.

Beale, D., 1994. *Driven by Nissan: A critical guide to new management techniques*. London: Lawrence & Wishart.

Bedeian, A. G. & Phillips, C. R., 1990. Scientific management and Stakhanovism in the Soviet Union: A historical perspective. *International Journal of Social Economics*, 17(10), pp. 28–35.

Bernstein, E., Bunch, J., Canner, N. & Lee, M., 2016. Beyond the Holacracy hype. *Harvard Business Review*, July–August.

Bidet, J., 2016. *Foucault with Marx*. London: Zed Books.

Block, P., 2011. *Flawless consulting: A guide to getting your expertise used*. 3rd ed. s.l.: John Wiley & Sons.

Boltanski, L. & Chiapello, E., 2007. *The new spirit of capitalism*. London: Verso.

Burnham, J., 1960. *The managerial revolution*. Bloomington: Indiana University Press.

Carey, A., 1967. The Hawthorne studies: A radical criticism. *American Sociological Review*, 32(3), pp. 403–416.

Cole, M., 2017. Rethinking the practice of workplace learning and development: Utilizing 'knowledge, connections and conversation' in organizations. *International Journal of HRD Practice, Policy and Research*, 2(1), pp. 7–19.

Conniff Allende, S., 2018. *Be more pirate: Or how to take on the world and win*. London: Portfolio Penguin.

Corporate Rebels, 2018. *Bucket list*. [Online]. Available at: https://corporate-rebels.com/bucketlist/ [Accessed 14 February 2018].

Corporate Rebels, 2019. *Announcing revolt: A new weapon in the fight for better workplaces*. [Online]. Available at: https://corporate-rebels.com/revolt-announcement/ [Accessed 26 March 2019].

Coughlan, T., 2016. Structured for success: How the structure of today's professional organizations are changing. *Journal of Management and Innovation*, 2(Spring 1), pp. 1–18.

de Zulueta, P. C., 2016. Developing compassionate leadership in health care: An integrative review. *Journal of Healthcare Leadership*, 8, pp. 1–10.

Diefenbach, T., 2009. New public management in public sector organizations: The dark sides of managerialist 'enlightenment.' *Public Administration*, 87(4), pp. 892–909.

Doray, B., 1988. *From taylorism to fordism: A rational madness*. London: Free Association Books.

Elleman, B. A., Forbes, A. & Rosenberg, D., 2010. Introduction. In: B. A. Elleman, A. Forbes & D. Rosenberg, eds. *Piracy and maritime crime: Historical and modern case studies*. Newport, RI: Naval War College Press, pp. 1–18.

Foucault, M., 1980. *Power/knowledge: Selected interviews and other writings 1972–1977*. New York: Pantheon Books.

Foucault, M., 1988a. Technologies of the self. In: L. H. Martin, H. Gutman & P. H. Hutton, eds. *Technologies of the self: A seminar with Michel Foucault*. Amherst: University of Massachusetts Press, pp. 16–49.

Foucault, M., 1988b. *Madness and civilization: A history of insanity in the age of reason*. New York: Vintage Books.

Foucault, M., 1991. *Discipline and punish: The birth of the prison*. London: Penguin.

Foucault, M., 2003. *The birth of the clinic: An archaeology of medical perception*. Abingdon: Routledge.

French, L., 2016. *Zappos' weird management style is costing it more employees*. [Online]. Available at: http://time.com/4180791/zappos-holacracy-buyouts/ [Accessed 8 March 2018].

Gino, F., 2019. *Rebel talent: Why it pays to break the rules at work and in life*. London: Pan.

Glassdoor, 2018. *The Zappos Family*. [Online]. Available at: https://www.glassdoor.co.uk/Reviews/The-Zappos-Family-Reviews-E19906.htm?countryRedirect=true [Accessed 8 March 2018].

Gramsci, A., 1971. *Selections from the prison notebooks.* London: Lawrence and Wishart.

Gray, D., Micheli, P. & Pavlov, A., 2014. *Measurement madness: Recognizing and avoiding the pitfalls of performance measurement.* Chichester: John Wiley & Sons.

Grimes, K., 2017. *Bullying in the NHS – A bully's perspective.* [Online]. Available at: https://www.hsj.co.uk/workforce/bullying-in-the-nhs--a-bullys-perspective/7020654.article [Accessed 6 March 2018].

Groth, A., 2015. *Internal Memo: Zappos is offering severance to employees who aren't all in with Holacracy.* [Online]. Available at: https://qz.com/370616/internal-memo-zappos-is-offering-severance-to-employees-who-arent-all-in-with-holacracy/ [Accessed 8 March 2018].

Habermas, J., 1976. *Legitimation crisis.* London: Heinemann.

History.com Editors, 2018. *Cultural Revolution.* [Online]. Available at: https://www.history.com/topics/china/cultural-revolution [Accessed 26 March 2019].

Hodge, R. D., 2015. *First, let's get rid of all the bosses: A radical experiment at Zappos to end the office workplace as we know it.* [Online]. Available at: https://newrepublic.com/article/122965/can-billion-dollar-corporation-zappos-be-self-organized [Accessed 8 March 2018].

HolacracyOne LLC, 2015. *Holacracy: Discover a better way of working.* [Online]. Available at: https://www.holacracy.org/wp-content/uploads/2016/08/Holacracy-WhitePaper-v5.pdf [Accessed 7 March 2018].

Kaplan, G. S., Patterson, S. H., Ching, J. M. & Blackmore, C. C., 2014. Why Lean doesn't work for everyone. *Quality & Safety in Health Care,* 23, pp. 970–973.

Kenney, C., 2011. *Transforming health care: Virginia Mason Medical Center's pursuit of the perfect patient experience.* Boca Raton, FL: CRC Press.

Klein, R., 2013. *Bullying: The silent epidemic in the NHS.* [Online]. Available at: http://www.publicworld.org/blog/bullying_the_silent_epidemic_in_the_nhs [Accessed 6 March 2018].

Knights, D. & Vurdubakis, T., 1994. Foucault, power, resistance and all that. In: J. M. Jermier, D. Knights & W. R. Nord, eds. *Resistance and power in organizations.* London: Routledge, pp. 167–198.

Laloux, F., 2014. *Reinventing organizations: A guide to creating organizations inspired by the next stage of human consciousness.* s.l.: Nelson Parker.

Laloux, F., 2015. The future of management is teal. *Strategy+Business,* Autumn, Issue 80.

Laloux, F., 2016. *Reinventing organizations: An illustrated invitation to join the conversation on next stage organizations.* s.l.: Nelson Parker.

Lemke, T., 2019. *Foucault's analysis of modern governmentality: A critique of political reason.* London: Verso.

Mandel, E., 2002. *An introduction to Marxist economic theory.* Chippendale: Resistance Books.

Mao, T.-T., 1966. *A letter to the red guards of Tsinghua University Middle School*. [Online]. Available at: https://www.marxists.org/reference/archive/mao/selected-works/volume-9/mswv9_60.htm [Accessed 26 March 2019].

Martínez-Zarzoso, I. & Bensassi, S., 2010. *How costly is modern maritime piracy for the international community?* Discussion Paper No. 208. Goettingen: Ibero America Institute for Economic Research.

Mazzocato, P. et al., 2010. Lean thinking in healthcare: A realist review of the literature. *Quality & Safety in Health Care*, 19, pp. 376–382.

Meyerson, D. E. & Scully, M. A., 1995. Crossroads tempered radicalism and the politics of ambivalence and change. *Organization Science*, 6(5), pp. 585–600.

Mirvis, P. H., 2006. Revolutions in OD: The new and the new, new things. In: J. Gallos, ed. *Organization development*. San Francisco, CA: Jossey-Bass, pp. 39–88.

Mumby, D. K. & Stohl, C., 1991. Power and discourse in organization studies: Absence and the dialectic of control. *Discourse & Society*, 2(3), pp. 313–332.

O'Connor, J., 2002. *The fiscal crisis of the state*. New Brunswick: Transaction Books.

Olssen, M., 2003. Structuralism, post-structuralism, neo-liberalism: Assessing Foucault's legacy. *Journal of Education Policy*, 18(2), pp. 189–202.

Poulantzas, N., 2000. *State, power, socialism*. London: Verso.

Reitz, M. & Higgins, J., 2017. *Being silenced and silencing others: Developing the capacity to speak truth to power*. Berkhamsted: Hult Research.

Robertson, B. J., n.d. *Holacracy – Brian J. Robertson*. [Online]. Available at: http://holacracybook.com/ [Accessed 7 March 2018].

Rose, N., O'Malley, P. & Valverde, M., 2009. *Governmentality – Legal studies research paper 09/94*. Sydney: Sydney Law School.

Snowden, D. J. & Boone, M. E., 2007. A leader's framework for decision making. *Harvard Business Review*, November.

Stapley, L. F., 2006. *Individuals, groups, and organizations beneath the surface: An introduction*. London: Karnac.

Taylor, F. W., 1919a. *The principles of scientific management*. New York: Harper & Brothers.

Taylor, F. W., 1919b. *Shop management*. New York: Harper & Brothers.

Venturi, R., Scott Brown, D. & Izenour, S., 2001. *Learning from Las Vegas: The forgotten symbolism of architectural form*. Cambridge, MA: MIT Press.

Weick, K. E., 1969. *The social psychology of organizing*. Reading, MA: Addison-Wesley.

Wray, D., 1996. Paternalism and its discontents: A case study. *Work Employment Society*, 10(4), pp. 701–715.

4

WHAT DOES OD ACHIEVE?

I have argued that the workplace – and the people who work in it – maintains a regime of silence in respect to power, despite the fact that more or less all of us, notwithstanding how we think about power and the way in which it presents, are subtly aware on a daily basis of its constant presence. The previous chapter sought to demonstrate that, regardless of the shifts and changes that can be perceived in respect to workplace organisation, power remains a largely unchanged constant in this context. To that extent, the adjustments that we have notionally seen in the way in which work-places are organised are merely epiphenomenal, reflective of wider shifts and changes, but they leave power intact and unchanged.

Into this mix comes organisational development, which clearly sees the workplace as its playground. Importantly, the theory and practice of organ-isational development can be seen as double-coded: on the one hand, it has a functional purpose of supporting capitalist organisations to become more 'effective,' which invariably means more productive, efficient and (in many instances) profitable; on the other, however, it seeks to achieve this through supporting people in the workplace to work better, and it has a focus on things like engagement and culture. For many practitioners, this double-coding allows them to privilege the latter and to underplay the former. To an extent, this shifting of emphasis allows many OD (organisation development) practitioners who are notionally aligned to a progressive politics to justify what they do in terms making work life in some fashion better for people rather than to acknowledge the reason that many hard-edged corporations embrace the practice of OD, which is because it supports a liberal illusion of what it is to be an employee in capitalist society while guaranteeing their exploitation through ideas of engagement and autonomy.

There is a sense that OD has ended up being thought of as a radical and humanistic practice that contests capitalistic relations in order to reform the workplace into a more agreeable and satisfying location for those who reside therein for so many hours of their lives. This narrative is given voice in a number of settings, oftentimes drawing attention to the politics of OD practice – occasionally accompanied by a plea to return to a prelapsarian state (Harrison, 1984) – and those of the key thinkers and practitioners in the field. An example of this somewhat hagiographic approach can be found in a review of the life and work of Kurt Lewin, perhaps the central figure in the development of OD as a discipline, wherein he is described as a 'prophet' who 'passed away just before reaching the promised land' (Kleiner, 2008, p. 27).

This is not to denigrate Lewin's motivation or, indeed, the hinterland that compelled him to think in this way and to explore ways in which to democratise working relationships. He had left Germany in 1933 on a sabbatical but his mother perished at the hands of the Nazis. To an extent, he can be thought of, perhaps, as being as one with those in the Frankfurt School, whose experiences directly impacted their politics and the ways in which they sought to rethink Marxism (Anderson, 1979). However, his motivations notwithstanding, he was a psychologist – and, within that discipline, he looked at individuals and the group dynamics in the workplace. This presents a rich opportunity to work under the surface of an organisation, of course, but there is little suggestion that he was able to fashion a meaningful critique of the context in which he sought to explore these issues. Those with whom he worked were individuals in a capitalist economy; their group dynamics played out in that specific circumstance. But there was no apparent desire to tear away the shrouding and look into the mechanism that motors beneath these particular relations of production.

Others, with whom I am unsurprisingly sympathetic, take a profoundly critical perspective on the apparently commonplace notion that OD is a force for good in the workplace. It is suggested, for example, that OD compromises human freedom through engendering a tyranny of change. Indeed, planned organisational change – facilitated by OD practitioners – is seen to create uncertainty, adversely affect essential human relations in an organisational context, reassert the position of management, and serve to entrench the empowered position of management (McKendall, 1993). Elsewhere, it is argued that OD and its practitioners have failed to tackle power issues of the sort outlined above because OD puts a great stay in such espoused values as openness, transparency, and collaboration (McLean, 1981, p. 10). Those who practice OD work behind these screens and allow them to obscure entirely the issue of power.

These observations hold true, I would want to suggest, notwithstanding the schism that exists in the practice between those who hold to a somewhat traditional model of working – often described as Diagnostic OD – and those who cleave to the illusion that they have created a more positive approach, through a practice that is seen to be more humanistic because of its focus on dialogue (Bushe & Marshak, 2015). It is persuasively argued that this represents a false dichotomy, one where the dialogic approach is privileged in respect to things like its newness and in contrast with practices that existed prior to its articulation (Oswick, 2009). Even one of the foundational practices of dialogic OD, known as appreciative inquiry (Cooperrider & Srivastva, 1987) can be said to unwittingly mirror classic practices of OD, insofar as the four phases on that endeavour begins with one called 'Discover,' which is simply a diagnostic phase that orients towards the conversations amongst the people in the workplace.

Let me try and ground all of the thoughts expressed above in an experience from practice. In 2012, I worked for an organisation that – by design and by default – ended up tumbling into an extraordinarily wide-ranging organisational redesign. In human terms, this commitment was expressed primarily in the form of significant HR consultations: at one point, two-thirds of the workforce were formally 'at risk,' as work was redesigned and establishments reshaped. As ever in such significant circumstances, the discourse that formed around this work did a number of things: first and foremost, it justified what was being done, the speed at which it needed to be undertaken, and the fact that there was broadly only one course of action available. These discursive assertions flooded the system and served to define normalcy. I recall, in the midst of the hurly-burly of this significant exercise, embodying that discourse and actively pathologising those whose opinions ran counter to the accepted view.

Power/knowledge coursed through everyone's experience of this time, as measurement data – understandable only within its own terms, internal logic, and the dominant discourse that is produced and reproduced – became the reality, defining the subjects within this exercise. At its most brute level, it served to suppress ideas and opinions that ran counter to the dominant discourse – and the pathologising effect was expressed by conversationally referring to anyone who sought to express an attitude counter to that which was increasingly generally accepted as a 'change resister' (the most barbed weapon in the definitional armoury of the organisational change expert), someone who was not a 'corporate player,' or who lacked 'organisational awareness.'

Depressingly, I did this work on the assumption that I was in some way humanising the exercise, ensuring that people felt engaged (they didn't; they told us that they did not) and acting behind a pretence that my work – facilitating teams; encouraging new work groups of people to come together; adding an OD gloss to the hard-edged transactional activities of interviewing people for their own jobs, often at a band lower than that on which they had previously been employed – was in some way a more liberal and democratic means for reshaping the workplace in the face of business and economic imperatives.

As the dust settled (my choice of phrase here self-serving; for many people in the organisation, the dust never truly settled), I doubled down on my OD activity across the entire redesigned workforce. I recall facilitating an away day for a large team, where I revised my opinion of one of their leaders (who previously I had stowed away in my mind under the category of maverick) as he publicly and uncritically articulated the key elements of the justificatory discourse. Later, I exercised the duty of care that OD practitioners take so seriously, when – having been aware of one member of the group who had exhibited behaviours throughout the morning session that were out of step with the new reality (which most of her colleagues – no doubt performatively – had apparently already absorbed) – I engaged with her as she broke down and sobbed during the lunch break. Disingenuously, I spoke with her manager, intimating that she appeared not to have been able to make the necessary adjustment and enquiring as to her well-being. Her team had been broken up, her certainties fragmented, her job ripped from under her, colleagues had lost their jobs, and she had secured a role in a lower pay band: her reaction should have been the least remarkable – whilst those of all of her colleagues, locked into an away day and silently trying to make the most of a really bad circumstance, should have been worryingly noteworthy. But that is not how OD works in real organisational contexts, where the imperative is to apply a liberal veneer to an economic imperative.

Here, then, is an example of my OD activity that was notionally distinguished by a range of espoused values, all of which served to conceal a grimly hard-edged practice. The liberality and democracy of what I was publicly doing merely served to reinforce the unthinkability of any other way of thinking or being in that context. My datum, shared with the woman's manager, served to enmesh her in power/knowledge, subjectifying her as someone 'not coping' with change and perhaps as someone who would need other (possibly psychological) interventions to smooth off that negativity. (The increasingly cosy connection between OD practice and wider work from an HR perspective around issues of ensuring the 'health and well-being' of the workforce is worth noting in passing in light of this example.) My practice is directly implicated in power – from the Foucauldian perspective – but refused to allow the articulation of anything in respect to power in the workplace. Moreover, what I actually did in this context was to render human resistance something that merely needed to be resolved through the application of technique rather than a legitimate response to circumstance, one with which the organisation actually needed to engage.

This leads to a secondary observation about the way in which OD is experienced in context. Specifically, that organisations are places in which control and resistance can be argued to play out dialectically (Mumby, 2005). This observation reminds us of the need to wriggle past Foucault's early notion of power, where its pervasiveness and its exclusive role in subjectification simply left no space for human agency. Certainly, his later work opens up ways in which the human being can assume some individual responsibility for the subject that they become, rather than ascribing that mechanism solely to the exercise of power/knowledge. It is argued that workplace deviance occurs in reaction to obvious exercises of power and is expressed is a variety of ways, not all of which can be considered noble and may be inappropriately directed (Lawrence & Robinson, 2007), while elsewhere it has been suggested that cynicism is an identifiable and entirely legitimate means of resistance for many caught up in initiatives involving forced organisational change (Fleming & Spicer, 2003).

Back in the 1960s, John French wrote about his experience as a Personnel Manager in a US clothing factory (French, 1964). Specifically, he outlined an 'experiment' in staff engagement and organisational change. The company was seeking to introduce new technology to support production and French decided to break the affected staff into three groups, all of which were privy to the same information about the need for change and what was proposed. Now, the first group was communicated with about the change in this way but had no direct involvement in the change; the second was 'liberal democratic,' allowed to elect representatives to participate in the oversight of the transformation; and the third was an experiment in something akin to direct democracy, with staff encouraged to engage in group discussion to work through the change and decide how best to deliver it. His fundamental finding in this regard was simple: 'The greater the amount of participation, the greater the productivity' (French, 1964, p. 36).

This example – despite it having taken place over 50 years ago – strikes me as illustrative of OD both then and now. In this instance, formal authority in this institutional setting is commodified and bundled out by the management of the firm. Underlying this apparent act of generosity seems to be two things: first, a desire to veil the power that exists in the workplace through a liberal focus on involvement. That is to say, a Taylorist approach might simply seek to double down on the oversight of the workers, seeking greater corporeal control of their physical activity; however, this developmental approach seeks to achieve compliance through a practice of engagement that in truth leaves the relationships of power intact and yet pushed further into the shadowy organisational background.

Second, despite the process being overwritten by a notionally democratic commitment to involvement, it remains the case that the underlying purpose is to find a line of least resistance towards improved productivity. From the Foucauldian perspective, this reflects a shift in the modality of power, from sovereign to disciplinary, from a power that imposes itself on the individual to one that focuses on the definition of normalcy, management of populations, and the subtle integration of that power into the person so that it is intrinsic to their being rather than externally imposed. OD practice is implicated in this, as a key facet of the apparatus that supports the discourse of the modern workplace. It is, in fact, possible to persuasively argue from a Foucauldian position that the very nature of the workplace itself – and of the way in which work is organised in our societies – is a fundamental means by which disciplinary power acts on its subjects. Indeed, outwith the explicit operational and economic focus on production in this context, it is suggested that labour itself can be seen as 'dressage,' which involves processes of discipline, taming and performance (Jackson & Carter, 1998).

This idea of a different modality of power, one to which it is possible to argue that organisation development provides a significant underpinning, can be seen to erase the idea of human agency, particularly in respect to the leeway that a subject might have to oppose that power. At this juncture, it is worth underscoring the fact that, whilst trade union membership has declined and the number of strike days is on the slide, there are other ways in which human subjects might react to power in the workplace. Managerial control – however expressed, whether in Taylorist fashion or through the more subtle disciplinary modality – tends to obscure the significance of resistance in the workplace. And that resistance can perhaps be best appreciated, not so much as building barricades, picketing or literally throwing a spanner in the works, but as emerging from the dialectic that exists in organisations between control and the workforce (Mumby, 2005).

From a Foucauldian perspective, this is important, in that it underscores the fact that the presence of control is not merely a negative burden on the individual but is also a productive thing, one that shapes the human subject in terms of its selfhood and identity. For some, this is a challenging notion, where it is difficult to navigate the idea of control and subjectivity; some psychoanalytic thinking unsurprisingly takes a bleak view of resistance as a workplace activity – although one would assume that an individual might helpfully explore that subjectification through analytic work (Gabriel, 1999). Fortunately, there exists a more positive view of this idea of resistance: the idea of 'Švejkism' is advanced as a way of understanding new ways in which workers resist, which encompasses openly expressed attitudes of irony and cynicism (Fleming & Sewell, 2002). This less explicit and immediately observable manifestation of resistance, without doubt, reflects the increased precariousness of economic life. However, it is also, I would suggest, an immediate reaction to the shift from the stark realities of Taylorism to the subtle blandishments of modern managerial techniques, with OD practice at the core of this.

This offers up a false periodisation, of course, and one for which it is necessary to offer a corrective. Within Taylorism, one sees a prefiguration of the surveillance techniques that emerged strongly in the 1990s, whether through the presence of CCTV in the workplace or the capacity to track each click on a keyboard. This is oversight – but the overseer does not stand beside you with a clipboard; they sit in a control room once removed from the shop floor. Similarly, the paternalism that arose as Fordism became established finds echoes now in the soft HR practices, self-management approaches, and the focus on issues surrounding the health and well-being of the workforce (Thompson & van den Broek, 2010).

Indeed, Mir and Mir helpfully note in an insightful overview of the development of ideas of worker empowerment, that, 'While corporations were trying out scientific management (or its variants) in an attempt to address issues of organizational control, they were simultaneously experimenting with other forms of social regulation such as employee representation (company unions) and welfare capitalism' (Mir & Mir, 2005, p. 59). These authors draw out the contrast that exists in organisational life between the gaze and the embrace, between surveillant oversight and notions of worker involvement, although they are careful to locate this question within the context of capitalist relations of production. They begin by asking whether the embrace is ever truly possible in a capitalist context (Mir & Mir, 2005).

An early instance of this can be found in the Ford Motor Company, which established the somewhat euphemistically named Sociological Department to start to extend the reach of management and oversight of employees beyond the walls of the factory and into the very home lives of those workers. It arose in 1914 off the back of Ford's adoption of a new pay deal, called the Five Dollar Day, which was founded on the notion of profit sharing. The scheme worked in the following way:

> The Five Dollar Day was introduced. Shorter hours and twice the wages for those who qualified. Thirty investigators were employed by the Sociological Department. The foremen and the assembly line ensured that the men earned their money. It fell upon the investigators' shoulders to ensure that the new riches were spent right and that they only went to the deserving.
>
> (Benyon, 1975, p. 22)

So, a moral perspective intruded into an economic consideration. The move addressed two issues: the rise of worker collectivity and socialist thinking and a desire to enhance productivity. It allowed the company to introduce a classification of worker, namely, those who were deemed to be suitable to access the scheme and those who needed to adjust themselves in some defined fashion in order to be recognised as suitable to move into the scheme. As one author explains,

> Release from purgatory implied acceptance of company interference in one's private life, and conformity to criteria laid down by the company.... Workers were expected to improve their living conditions, to keep their houses clean and comfortable and to ensure that they lived in a healthy, well-ventilated and well-lit environment. In practice, about one hundred investigators were responsible for collecting information about the morality, respectability, habits and opinions of applicants over a period of several years.
>
> (Doray, 1988, p. 107)

This offers insight into the ways in which power acting through a notionally benign conduit retains its impactful quality. The illusion of active individual choice and autonomy is engendered – but the power involved is unchanged despite that. The worker has to accommodate to this and it will alter the way in which they are as a human subject, not just in the factory but in their kitchen and living room. And this causes me to make what I take to be a key observation in this regard: that power and the way in which it acts have found ways to become even more subtle in its action. Just over 100 years since this example, OD is busily supporting the crude categorisation of individual workers through practices such as 'talent management,' which manifests thus: Are you in the 'talent pool?' Where do you sit in the nine-box grid? How might you move from where you sit currently to become a 'hi-po,' a high potential worker?

Years back, in my faddish chase for new ideas to import into my organisation, I advocated the establishment of a localised talent management system for nurses. I promoted this crude notion in terms that explicitly referenced the way in which this intervention might lift nursing practice and enhance service delivery. Indeed, I ended up promoting this idea in light of an invitation on the part of the Chief Nurse to consider how we might raise the ambitions of the nursing workforce and develop their professionalism.

However, I recall her looking askance at me, as I enthusiastically outlined the idea of talent in this context. 'But what about the vast majority of the workforce who aren't in the talent pool?' she asked. 'They'll need to be encouraged to want to join the pool and to lift their performance in order to do so,' I replied. It seems to me now that I was unknowingly a beat away from suggesting establishing a 'Sociological Department' to help administer this.

Similarly, OD is oftentimes concatenated with work in organisations around employee well-being. Of course, the remarkable thing about this is the paradox that many organisations hold in terms of this practice. In the same way as Ford wanted a level of engagement in the lives of its employees outside of the confines of the workplace, so we see organisations attending to the interior mental and physical health of those who work in them. Weekly fruit drops, sports activities, staff choirs, yoga classes, lessons on resilience, flaky nonsense about encouraging people to engage in mindfulness, all of these interventions look to be altruistically attending to the health needs of the workers. And, of course, they are … and may, in fact, have a positive impact in a great many cases. Yet, the simple fact remains that a good many of those organisations sustain cultures of 'busyness,' where people feel obliged to be working for the business at all hours and where the performance expectations are overbearing. Quite simply, workplaces could attend in a truly meaningful way to the health and well-being of their employees by simply lifting the work pressures that most people find themselves enduring. But developing well-being and resilience initiatives shifts responsibility in this regard away from the firm and onto the individual, who needs to do additional work in order to find the personal resources necessary to do the intense amount of work that they are being compelled to do.

Let's return to the notion of the gaze and the embrace in the contemporary workplace about which we were speaking. If, for a moment, we assume that an authentic embrace is possible (and I am not at all persuaded that the constraints of capitalism in any of its variants – individualistic, corporatist or state – can genuinely be released to support authentic and meaningful staff empowerment, but be that as it may), then the practice of organisational development is crucial to its operability. Clearly, in such a situation, there are two possible perspectives: either OD is making a true and significant contribution to the reconfiguration of the workplace for the better, in keeping with a broad Enlightenment sense of 'things can only get better;' or it is – whether deliberately or inadvertently – serving to create an illusion of changed circumstances and veiling the fundamental nature of organisations in this context. Hence, OD practitioners may be working to create a genuinely better future or they may be sinister covert agents of the status quo, either as willing servants of managerialism (offering up OD practice as a means of working on the assets in order to improve effectiveness) or as useful idiots in unwitting service of that project.

Even within what might loosely be described as the field of OD, this delineation plays out in respect to how practitioners choose to approach their practice. There are those whose orientation tends towards an approach that mirrors traditional business thinking: they work on a consulting model where a diagnostic is undertaken using a range of data sources in order to define a problem that can be addressed through a prescribed intervention or set of activities (Block, 2011). Such a paradigm is premised on the sort of scientism through which organisations seek to reassure themselves. Key aspects of this discourse – outwith a fetishisation of scientific method – include an assumption of easily discerned and effective cause and effect, a linearity of thought that assumes that X leads to Y leads to Z with little acknowledgement of the tentative nature of those relationships, and the knowability of how a particular act will impact on the wider context. Abstract data are held in high regard – and there's a sense that more data are better, in that it will create a bigger and richer picture. (This is most obviously evidenced by Boards working to make sense of information provided for them and, instead of pausing to explore that which is in front of them, they opt unthinkingly to demand more data.) Similarly, it is worth noting in passing that the whole notion of data is far from as pure as scientism might wish us to believe. It is shaped by the narratives that precede it. This is not to assert that those that seek to collect and collate data are deliberately distorting the process; it is simply to note that the request for data does not sound in a pure void but is expressed from an inescapable context and takes shape in a place where suppositions are largely unspoken but are rife and hence impactful. Data, of course, reflect the world and, at the same time, shape the world. Hence, it is noted that men are more likely to be involved in car crashes than women but that the latter are more likely to be injured and to die in those collisions. This datum could be seen to lead us in a particular direction – until one adds an additional item of information, namely that it was not until 2011 that the USA started using a female crash-test dummy (Criado Perez, 2019, pp. 186–187). This author also finds that the datasets that underpin our internet usage, such as Google, linked female names and words such as woman and girl more to family than career, observing also that one analysis produced results wherein the top occupation attributed to women was 'homemaker,' whilst the top term for men in this context was 'maestro' (Criado Perez, 2019, p. 165). So, in a grim circularity, the data we use reflect the reality that the data we use produce.

All of which tends, as asserted earlier, to lead to a sense of OD being to some extent binary: it is largely seen (particularly by its practitioners but also by many organisations as well) as humanistic, egalitarian, and democratic, insofar as it seeks to engage with staff in order to enhance their lived experience of work and the workplace. However, equally, it is an approach that seeks to deliver on organisational effectiveness by working with (perhaps 'working on' would be more appropriate here) the human capital. That is to say, it is primarily a managerial technique that attains its economic end by generating the illusion of involvement and liberal democratic intent. This has in one instance been identified as a dichotomy between OD as a liberatory practice viewed in sharp contrast to the organisational context that actually relies on the brute exercise of power; the response to this analysis, however, was not to challenge the mesh of power in which OD finds itself operating but to colonise it, the better to exploit it as a resource in the service of ODs intentions (Greiner & Schein, 1989).

Credit to all of these authors for foregrounding power, although their decision to acquiesce to it rather than meaningfully support people to engage with it represents a theoretical cul-de-sac. It is an unsurprising position, though: in my work to date, I have managed a cognitive dissonance in this regard, forever managing an internal balance where I seek to generate outputs and outcomes from my work that benefit the organisation (occasionally to the detriment of the workforce) whilst persuading myself that I am offering those who work in that organisation the opportunity to genuinely express themselves and shape the purpose and direction of the enterprise. In reality, I have always suspected that the former overdetermines the latter; my view on this is all the more explicit now. And this is unaffected by more contemporary examples of writers broadly in the field who view power in an organisational setting as a clumsy binary opposition between 'old' and 'new,' the former articulated as an undoubtedly bad thing (Heimans &

Timms, 2014).The presumably unintended concatenation of 'old' and 'bad' in this schema unwittingly reinforces the cult of youth and our endless fixation on the idea of 'novelty' as a positive thing to be endlessly pursued. To what extent does this clumsy thinking lead to the following syllogism, with its dehumanising feel? 'Mark is nearly 59 years old; old is bad; Mark must be bad.'

In truth, this model – supposedly encapsulating fresh thinking about power in the workplace – is premised on the familiar notion of power as a resource. In the 'old' model, just a few people own it and use it in order to attain the ends that they – invariably as leaders – intend. The vision of 'new' power is actually not a reality but a filter overlaid on the world that generates the pretence of openness and engagement, things with which OD is all too intimately familiar. Drifting skyward in a celebration of their candy floss vision of the reality of the modern workplace, the authors wax poetic (in lieu of anything tangible to show) about 'new' power and how it

> ...operates differently, like a current. It is made by many. It is open, par-
> ticipatory, and peer-driven. It uploads, and it distributes. Like water or
> electricity, it's most forceful when it surges. The goal with new power is
> not to hoard it but to channel it.
>
> (Heimans & Timms, 2014, p. 50)

The most this hokum makes me want to do is go and check my water meter.

Interestingly, this work feels ridiculously overburdened by metaphor, which is an approach that enjoys great currency in the field of OD, alongside its companion of building narratives. Such ideas are proposed as means of making things accessible to the wider audience – but they are undertaken in lieu of serious thought and honest engagement. Moreover, they demonstrate an unhealthy disdain for workforce and customers: they won't understand the rarefied things with which senior leaders concern ourselves, so those leaders seek to infantilise their followers by offering them (tall) tales and meaningless metaphor in lieu of active dialogue. Storytelling, for instance, has colonised a wide range of social contexts, of which work is just one, and is seen to be a foundational practice around marketing, public relations, politics, and so on in the service of the capitalist economy (Salmon, 2017). This, of course, is just one way in which OD obfuscates the human relations in the workplace.The rest of this chapter seeks to apply a critical focus to other methods that often get used in this field of practice.

Some examples of the techniques of OD

In this regard, I want to critically explore ideas and techniques that relate to OD and its practice and which lend support to the idea of its espoused values. Practitioners will demonstrate a variety in terms of connection to the various activities that I am going to discuss, but all of the ideas henceforth discussed in this chapter figure in OD as a broad practice, to a greater and lesser extent, and thereby serve – to my mind – to expose the values in action of OD.

The imperative for all to speak

The techniques used in this type of endeavour are invariably couched in a language that suggests a humanistic and progressive underpinning. Take for example the method crafted by Nancy Kline, called Time To Think or, sometimes, the thinking environment (Kline, 1999). At face value, this is a generous approach to supporting diversity of voice, built upon a critique of the way in which most of us experience business meetings. Throughout my career, particularly as I moved up in terms of seniority, I have been expected to attend more and more meetings, particularly formal ones, such as governance committees and task and finish groups. For some senior leaders, of course, their working day is filled with these sorts of appointments, oftentimes sitting back to back between the hours of 8 am and 6 pm. As a result, they cannot help but have to work outside of their contracted hours, in the evenings and at weekends, in order simply to respond to emails and to actually get some work done. This is a serious matter, of course: it is asserted that executives are now spending 23 hours each week in meetings, not counting impromptu gatherings and conversations, as opposed to the 10 hours that was taken up with meetings in the 1960s – and unsurprisingly this effect is more pronounced in large as opposed to small organisations (Perlow et al., 2017).

My experience echoes what others have said to me about the way in which they engage in such gatherings: we attend but are not present; our energy and engagement is low, because in most instances we are there with marked reluctance; it is ritualistic – we wait to try to speak at an agreed point in the proceedings and allow our minds to wander until we are expected to play our part – and hence it squeezes out any vestige of creativity;

we arrive reflecting on the meeting we previously attended and spend time thinking about the meeting to which we are headed next; and the need to stay on top of things means we spend time when we are meant to be engaging with others about matters critical to our business distracted through the technology that is a constant appendage to human beings these days, namely the tablet, the laptop, and the smartphone.

Perhaps worst of all is the notion that most of us are merely pastiming in meetings, waiting for the HiPPO. This acronym – found buzzing across the internet and in the pages of the popular business press – stands for the 'highest paid person's opinion.' This observation is especially illustrative in the context of what I have been trying to argue thus far, namely that power is a defining element of organisational life but most of the time it is bracketed off and left unaddressed, at least in any open and conversational way. Indeed, it has been suggested that meetings – rather than offering genuine opportunities for useful exchange – can be either a vestige of past practice that acts as an organisational bottleneck or a terrain wherein organisational power is especially acutely experienced (Carucci, 2018). In the former instance, it is a meeting that once served a purpose but has been overtaken by events – and yet can still hinder progress in terms of business decisions. The latter, of course, is an arena where positional power (and proximity to it – oftentimes literally) is played out.

Of course, it is interesting that the notional move towards self-managing teams and holacratic organisations might indeed be contributing to the amount of time people spend in meetings (Rogelberg et al., 2007). Senior leaders might be managing countless invitations for a variety of gatherings – but it is surely also the case that the meeting is now a familiar element of everyone's working life, as the wider Human Resources agenda of 'engagement' (a key strut of OD practice) takes hold: at every level of an organisation, people are being forced to endure regular team meetings, town hall meetings, awaydays, and formalised appraisals, all of which management alone tends to see as a universal good. Using Foucault, it is possible to suggest that these are surveillant methods, an intrinsic part of disciplinary power, designed to engender compliance to the wider discourse and docility in the face of it (Foucault, 1991).

There are two issues with this wider agenda of 'engagement,' which – at face value, of course – seems a logical, humanistic, and liberal democratic development that appears largely to be a positive thing. But this presupposes that the nature of that involvement is not deeply inscribed with relation-ships of power, that it is to be taken to be a genuinely egalitarian gesture, unshaped by the wider discourse and the apparatus surrounding that. By way of illustration, consider the commonplace saw that suggests that a good manager always has an open door, so that workers have licence to approach them more or less at any time: this seems like an invitation uninhabited by anything other than generosity and attentiveness. However, by factoring in the mesh of power that surrounds such a statement, one can come to a different perspective. As two writers on speaking truth to power so pithily suggest,

> Consider the phrase "My door is always open." It contains a number of assumptions. First, people should meet you on your territory, rather than the other way around. Second, you have the luxury of a door. Third, you can choose when to close or open it.
>
> (Reitz & Higgins, 2017)

This is not to say that attentiveness is not an important facet for a manager to display. Off the back of a fascinating knowledge café event that I hosted with David Gurteen on this topic, I have written elsewhere that the contem-porary line manager faces a paradoxical challenge:

> Charged with wrangling their people to maximize delivery, as measured through abstract notions such as key performance indicators, arbitrary targets over which the individual has little or no influence (let alone con-trol), and behavioural expectations (realized through oftentimes explicit requirements for individuals to align themselves with organisational val-ues), the line manager is also – at the same time – expected to "contain" their team and attend to their essential human needs.
>
> (Cole, 2018)

For many managers, this tension in practice feels impossible to resolve successfully, which practically exemplifies what is being described when reference is made to the 'torn middle' in work on systemic working (Oshry, 2016).

One way of helping managers to consider how best to explore a possi-ble equilibrium in regard to these two effects is to try and articulate how an authentic attentiveness might be expressed in practice, which might be said to consist of three elements. The first relates to ensuring good quality conversation: in this context, the manager needs to be present and heedful, giving attention to those around them and being fully attuned to their being in the workplace. Second, there's a need to constantly reference back to our fundamental humanity, which in practice means that the manager avoids all aspects of objectification and categorisation, maintaining a perspective that sees people as people and not as human resources, human capital or indeed as assets. They concentrate on the individual and what it is that they uniquely bring to the workplace. Finally, it's vital to be alert to the ideas that people around us are regularly expressing. For this, the manager is constantly alert to fresh thinking and new ideas as and when these things appear, which means that they are finely attuned to the dialogic exchanges around them. This means that they are able to follow the thread of myriad conversations as they flow through and around them and support the surfacing of salient elements (Cole, 2018).

In the context of the modern workplace, of course, all of the above represents a significant challenge. How do you retain a focus on the people with whom you work when everything around you – including those staff – is expressed in terms of measurability, reducible very often to the expression of mere numbers? Subjectivity is crafted in the workplace through a cross-hatching of metrics: the pay band, the appraisal rating, the assessment as to whether one is calibrated as being in the high-potential pool of talent, the level of bonus, a dashboard of how well someone is progressing in terms of the performance targets that might exist for them.

This is what Foucault speaks of as biopolitics, the oversight of populations for the purposes of governmentality through techniques that quantify them in a variety of ways. This can be usefully summarised thus:

> Michel Foucault, through the concept of biopolitics, was already pointing out in the seventies what, nowadays, is well on its way to being obvious: "life" and "living beings" [*le vivant*] are at the heart of new political battles and new economic strategies. He also demonstrated that the "introduction of life into history" corresponds with the rise of capitalism. In effect, from the 18th Century, onwards the *dispositifs* of *power* and *knowledge* begin to take account the "processes of life" and the possibility of controlling or modifying them.
>
> (Lazzarato, 2002, p. 99)

This assemblage of numbers certainly creates human subjectivity – and enables managers (as a general term) to shape the workplace so that everyone is suitably enmeshed. To wriggle free of this discursive constraint might – within the terms of the debate – be argued to be impossible, although this notion is something to which I will return later in the book as I consider a radical OD practice.

Just to underscore briefly this notion of biopolitics as an ensemble of practices in service of wider governmentality, it is worth looking at the way in which one author has sought to develop this notion, which has particular resonance in respect to my investigations. It is argued here that,

> Disciplinary power discovered "population" as a productive and reproductive mass to be administered carefully. Biopolitics is devoted to this task. Reproductive cycles, birth and death rates, levels of general health, and life expectancy provide the objects of regulation. Biopolitics is the governmental technology of disciplinary power. However, this approach proves altogether unsuited to the neoliberal regime, which exploits the psyche above all.
>
> (Han, 2017, p. 21)

This attention to the interior and effort to externalise as part of a wider managerial effort indicates to me the presence of OD in this space as a key technology of power in terms of facilitating this.

To return to the *Time To Think* methodology, this seeks to reorient people when they are together so that they move beyond the formalistic sterility of traditional meetings towards a more authentic exchange. It does this through an acknowledgement of ten significant requirements for proper conversation to take place, the three most significant of which are attention, ease, and equality. In terms of attention, this is expressed clearly in the two key aspects of the method, namely working with a thinking partner and then giving voice in the wider group through the expression of one's freshest thinking on a defined question. In the former instance, people work in pairs, facing one another, and are accorded a defined and brief number of minutes to speak about the question without interruption by their partner. The only intervention that a partner can make is to query – if the person with whom they are working runs out of things to say before their allotted time is up: 'Is there anything more you'd like to say?'

When it comes to then moving back into the circle that has been created for the main group, a round will take place; one person will begin to speak in respect to what they are thinking – and the chance to speak will then move to either their left or right, until everyone in the circle has spoken. The person speaking may not be interrupted – and, perhaps more importantly, everyone in the circle has to be closely attentive to their remarks, so that the discussion moves around the group without interruption or the intrusion of those traditional discussions with which we are all well acquainted from meetings. Attention is offered to all, then, and everyone is granted a positive opportunity to speak, which engenders the notion of equality that is key to the practice. Similarly, the notion of ease in this context is taken to mean that the conversational process takes place outside of the tightly wound expectations that tend to overlay most workplace conversations, in terms of a general requirement to move quickly due to a generalised perception of urgency that haunts working life.

All of which sounds splendid to many, I am sure. And I have used this technique with a number of groups, from teams focusing on improvement in their work together through to steering groups of senior leaders who have become stuck in terms of the projects to which they were meant to be giving direction. In many of those circumstances, the technique – in releasing people from the ritual of their normal meeting practice – leaves them declaring that the conversation has been substantially better. But there are other considerations in regard to the use of a technique like this that need to be acknowledged that are fundamental to a more nuanced appreciation of OD and its supposed intent in a workplace setting.

First, there is a sense of compulsion about being expected to speak out in a group setting. Suddenly, the employee is denied the right to keep their peace, to say nothing on the matter, if that is what they choose. In a traditional meeting, there is ordinarily a place to hide, where there is no expectation of contribution and hence the opportunity for the worker to move into an interior space of comfort, where they might reside in safety and without intrusion by managers or peers. This is the place where people head for a reverie, a chance to bracket off the grim mechanical noise of organisational life – the ping of emails, the burr of phones, the clamour of myriad voices, the repetitive whirr of the photocopier, and so on – in order to get back in contact with their own humanity. This private space is closed off to them in Time To Think.

Second, at a more intimate level, this compulsion doubtless feels particularly oppressive to those who consider themselves to be introverts. Attention has turned recently to the importance of according introversion a parity of esteem in a range of contexts, which is a welcome intervention in a wider debate around how human subjects present in collective contexts (Cain, 2013). It also helpfully steers us to a Foucauldian perception in respect to normalcy and Otherness. While we are more attuned to the idea that the workplace has traditionally been dominated by extroverts – the blowhards who are constantly giving voice to things and filling communal space with the amplified noise of their own inchoate thoughts – it is my view that introversion is still somewhat pathologised in organisational life. I recall a senior leader commenting on what seemed to be a lack of confidence on my part in certain formalised organisational contexts. Certainly, in organisational meetings, which have always struck me as absurdly ritualised, I would keep my counsel until such time as I could sense the dynamics in the room ... and occasionally those dynamics would lead me to decide not to speak.

To remedy this shortcoming, it was suggested that I made sure that I made a contribution to every meeting within six minutes of it starting. For a while, I endeavoured to follow this advice: it did little more than to make me sound like an idiot, insofar as I was speaking in order to speak rather than speaking in order to say something. Naturally, it led me to wonder how many others at the grim tables around which we met were also following this arbitrary rule, which might go some way to explaining the unnatural character of the so-called conversations that I witnessed in such settings.

Third, it is the case that most meetings in organisational settings are stilted through ritual and unquestioned formality. While *organising meetings* – gatherings where people coalesce in order to authentically speak about issues at hand and responses that might make sense – tend to eschew rigidity of approach, due to their focus and the enthusiasm amongst those taking part, *organisational meetings* are often just tests of endurance on the part of participants and are structured via both explicit and implicit formality. (The former is expressed through the Terms of Reference over which people obsess, the crafting of agenda, the reams of minutes that are generated, the presence of a chair who holds a key positional power in this context, and so on. The latter is more cultural, a tacit understanding of the way things get done in this meeting space, with reference as to whose opinions carry added weight and who will make the final call in any discussion.)

Importantly, *Time To Think* does not abandon formality; instead, it merely replaces one form of structure with another. To take a Foucauldian perspective on this, it is neither a better nor worse way of encouraging organisational conversation, it is merely different from what we have ordinarily experienced. At first glance, it seems to address the issues that people feel inhibit rich conversation, with its emphasis on ease, attention, and equality. But it merely offers an alternative process – and one that might actually covertly leave those hindrances untouched.

For example, in respect to 'ease,' can it truly be said that the use of the *Time To Think* methodology removes the overall climate of urgency and pressure that people experience in organisational life? Only if an organisation abandoned traditional meetings in favour of encouraging the use of *Time To Think* in every circumstance, that is to say, only if a business fundamentally rewrote itself, would it be possible to say that urgency had been lifted – and, indeed, only then if all other aspects of organisational practice flushed out the pressure that people face in the workplace. It follows, therefore, that using the technique in isolation cannot meaningfully insulate those taking part from the urgency that defines their experience at work.

It is certainly the case that *Time To Think* allows everyone in a meeting to make a contribution, so there is an equality woven into the practice. In fact, as a method, it generates an expectation that everyone will contribute in the course of what is called a 'round,' when each person is given space and time to speak without interruption. And while those in the round have the option to say that they have nothing to say, the character of the method has the potential to leave people feeling remiss if they do not take time to say something. (There is a moot point as to whether the focus on each person making a contribution in a round is all that different to the advice that I received to speak within six minutes of each meeting starting.) Everyone takes a turn – and everyone is expected, in light of the ideology that underpins the method, to take that turn. And it is expected that this turn will be taken in a spirit of positivity.

Indeed, the method enforces this compliance into those involved in it by the way in which it privileges speech as opposed to silence, which may be mobilised by an individual in order to express a small gesture of resistance. But who would consider resisting when the workplace has been cleaned up and supposedly denuded of so many of the negative elements with which we feel acquainted with from the past? Who could possibly wish to resist that new workplace? Many, I would suggest, because its novelty is both superficial and, in fact, serves an ideological purpose. Similarly, resistance notwithstanding, it might simply be that a person seeks solace in silence in order to allow themselves the opportunity to reflect within themselves. To this extent, it could be seen to be a key facet of disciplinary power, from a Foucauldian position: it serves a wider discourse in respect to the value of each individual and encouraging what might be seen to be engagement of same, but – at the same time – engenders a docility in those who are subject to it, wherein reluctance to engage could be seen to be churlish in light of its notionally progressive appearance. It generates a psychopolitical imperative to externalise your thinking so that nothing can remain private. We have moved from where a senior leader might aggressively point to a subaltern and say, 'You. What do you think?' to one where those involved in *Time To Think* have internalised the expectation of having to say something.

This brings me to my final observation in this regard, which is that – as is so often the case with techniques such as this – the apparent flattening of the process in terms of hierarchy does not suck power out of the picture in any way. The imposition of a method that compels everyone in the team or work group to give voice to what they are thinking (or, crucially, what they feel that they should be thinking) does not impact on the positional power of each of the people sitting in the circle, waiting to speak in the course of the round. And, in that sense, it does not alter the personal calculations that each person will make in terms of what they will and will not say in such a context. This assessment might be said to operate at a number of levels, up to and including whether a person is content to speak truth to power when they spot unethical practice or things going wrong in a work context. Foucault's later work alighted on the classical notion of *parrhesia* as a way of conceptualising someone giving voice to 'fearless speech,' articulating a view that might lead to lethal conclusions in literal terms (Foucault, 1983).

Interestingly, some have suggested that *parrhesia* has the potential to be an intrinsic part of a truly authentic OD practice (Sementelli, 2016), a view to which I fully subscribe, as will be apparent later when I outline what I consider to be the defining characteristics of a radical approach to doing OD in a capitalist context. Certainly, the work that I have done over recent years around finding ways of developing a richer understanding of speaking out in an organisational context has steered me to the idea of power and speech as core aspects of life in the workplace – and has drawn me towards an understanding of this that: encompasses the idea of discursive 'regimes of silence' that exist amongst people at work; acknowledges the Butlerian notion of performativity and 'impossible speech' that help us to understand such regimes (Kenny, 2017), and the hope that parrhesia might offer a means for people to envisage a different sort of ontology in the face of the challenges and politics of the workplace.

As a slight sidebar here, it is worth considering the way in which the notions of empowerment in the workplace impact on this idea of giving voice to concerns. For example, it is argued that neoliberalism in terms of society and economy combines deregulation and active staff involvement, which decentres responsibility to ensure an ethical course from the state, the organisation and its senior leadership cadre to a localised individual responsibility of all who work in the enterprise (Bjorkelo & Madsen, 2013). This neoliberalism is said to have eroded any form of collectivism, whether expressed through state intervention or worker unionisation, in favour of an utterly individualised context wherein the employee experiences 'over-involvement' in work through the battery of engagement techniques that exist in corporate life – at the very time that the relationship between worker and organisation is made practically fragile (Bourdieu, 1998).

Notwithstanding the notion of positional power, the character of a process like Time To Think is riven with power, as it inhabits the very fabric of the interrelationships between people in the workplace. The expectation that each person will give voice to their freshest thoughts is coercive yet the underpinning idea is articulated as creating freedom for people to speak in order that engagement might be seen to be meaningful. But having to speak means intervening in that field of power, which, in turn, defines the individual subject. Parrhesia could be argued to be self-defining and truly empowering for the parrhesiaste; however, forced speech in an organisational context passes the definition to the organisational context itself and diminishes the capacity for power of the individual.

The ubiquitous 'awayday' and the myth of the 'team'

If one were to take OD at face value and within its own terms, it would appear that what people at work most crave is the opportunity to spend hours on end with their colleagues gathered at circular tables full of sweets and mineral water in garishly carpeted subterranean hotel spaces. These environments are ordinarily lacking in natural light and use climate control systems that produce either arctic chilliness or tropical warmth but nothing in between. Working in practice, I have regularly been asked to facilitate events of this sort, although very often it's difficult to determine, despite one's best diagnostic efforts, why such an intervention is being requested and what the commissioner of the work hopes might come out of the work.

A large-scale research study in the USA indicates that a majority of the workforce – 63% of the respondents – wanted more influence particularly in regard to workplace decisions, while another data point suggested that a third of the survey felt dissatisfied at work and a great deal of that dissatisfaction related to their perceived lack of influence (Freeman & Rogers, 2006, pp. 68–75). When exploring the question of what it was exactly that workers wanted to have more influence over, it was noteworthy that, at the top of the list, were decisions on pay and reward; at the very bottom sat decisions about organising their work, where they felt they enjoyed considerable autonomy (Freeman & Rogers, 2006, pp. 75–76).

Despite the corporatist dalliances of the advanced capitalist economies in the long boom that followed the Second World War, there is a structural incapacity to deliver on what the workers want in this instance. Collective bargaining made inroads into this issue but ultimately ran up against the imperative of profitability, which the incorporated trade unions were simply unable to contest. As noted above, neoliberalism, in response to the faltering of that boom post-1974 and thereafter up to the present day, dismantled that collectivist orientation, in favour of an individualised view of the economy. So, in light of the survey, workers can 'want' all they like, but our current society – and specifically the economy that both undergirds and overwrites it – cannot meet that need. The pressure felt in this context cannot be permitted to continue to act unattended in the economic sphere, for fear that it might find release politically. Instead, I argue that we see a refocusing away from the harsh realities of wages and salaries to practices that indulge the wider expectation of influence, of which the awayday is the most basic example, for the very purpose of absorbing the discontent that could end up creating wider social ramifications.

Underpinning, this, of course, is the widely accepted notion that teams and teamwork are crucial to organisational effectiveness. Guild workers and tradespeople were valued for their individual skills until such time as means were discovered to speed up production through technology and new technologies of human organisation. Taylorism and Fordism effaced the skilled worker, subsumed that person into a process, one that fractured the work into myriad unskilled pieces. Latterly, we have seen the virtue of working together with shared purpose and the 'team' has moved to the centre of organisational thinking (Sundstrom et al., 1990). Within the NHS, a huge amount of research effort and developmental activity has been invested, with the main concern being to ensure that teams are defined clearly so that they might work effectively (West & Markiewicz, 2016) and that they are authentic rather than what is referred to as 'pseudo-teams' (Lyubovnikova et al., 2015).

The emergence of the 'team' as the key unit of organisational prac-tice and business effectiveness can be argued to be one of the central and profoundly misleading achievements of OD. Indeed, the two elements – a search for efficiency alongside a commitment to engage people via the application of human sciences – are intertwined richly and through their action in concert have shaped the modern workplace. In the context of the team, there is an intimate connection with the work undertaken by Elton Mayo and the Hawthorne studies that he and his team undertook between 1924 and 1932 at a firm called Western Electric (Hassard, 2012). This work gave birth to the human relations approach to organisation, a perspective that stood in sharp contrast to the ideas of scientific management and its practical manifestation in the form of Fordism. As Mayo himself explains, 'The first inquiry we undertook ran headlong into illustration of the insuf-ficiency of the assumption that individual self-interest actually operates as adequate incentive' (Mayo, 1949, p. 51). These observations suggest a break between one approach and another, the latter being seen as an improve-ment on the former. In this instance, as well, there was an Enlightenment feel to the development, where our approach to people in the workplace was progressing over time. Mayo was arguing for a revision of our under-standing of human motivation, which laid the ground for a supposedly entirely different way of seeking to engage people in the workplace.

For others, of course, this was a position susceptible to critique. Purser (2000) is very clear that the human relations approach that grew out of Mayo's work has a mythical character in that it erroneously asserts that '... management could compensate for the loss of dignity, meaning and pride in work by showing interest in the worker' (Purser, 2000, p. 60). The mate-rial generated by the studies undertaken at the plant in Illinois, where a variety of electrical and telephonic products were built, could be argued to have been discursively integrated without much attention to the veracity of the claims that it made. As a seminal article wherein the author interrogated the research undertaken in order to undertake just such as assessment concludes,

> The results of these studies, far from supporting the various components of the "human relations approach", are surprisingly consistent with a rather old-world view about the value of monetary incentives, driving leadership, and discipline. It is only by massive and relentless reinterpretation that the evidence is made to yield contrary conclusions. To make these points is not to claim that the Hawthorne studies can provide serious support for any such old-world view. The limitations of the Hawthorne studies clearly render them incapable of yielding serious support for any sort of generalisation whatsoever.
>
> (Carey, 1967, p. 416)

Mayo's work is seen – within OD – to be a pivotal moment, where management as a practice was prompted, through the use of diagnostic research and applied science, to move to a more humanistic orientation towards the workforce. Carey's analysis throws into question how this transition was affected, although – as ever in such academic circles – there are counterpoints to his assertions that seek to reemphasise the virtue of the conclusions drawn from the studies and specifically to argue that the work did not underplay the dull compulsion of the economic in a workplace context but merely placed it in a wider social context (Shepard, 1971). All this notwithstanding, there was clearly a receptiveness abroad for the ideas that Mayo advanced and context doubtless played a part, as the world was reeling out of its first major global war wherein conscripted armies had fought bloody battles for the sake of patriotism and little more. The Bolshevik revolution in Russia in 1917 and a failed revolution in Germany a year later seemed to speak of a different way of being socially and politically.

Power made response to these wider developments. It appeared refreshed in response to this fast-changing set of circumstances but it was not transformed in any meaningful sense; instead, it was simply repositioning, experiencing a reconfiguration in light of the changed relationships across the terrain. Power in the workplace needed to be experienced differently in light of wider liberal democratic developments: supervision of work needed to shift from physical oversight – the manager with their stopwatch and clipboard – to an insidious regime of panoptic surveillance and the population needed to be moved from being an object of the action of power to subjects created out of the generative capacity of that power. The view of workers subtly elided from seeing them as interchangeable machine parts to valued assets whose contribution and engagement were essential to the success of the enterprise. The Hawthorne studies provided a foundation on which to base this shift, regardless of whether this work actually could be said to offer an evidential base for such a change. The change was immanent in the wider system. The Hawthorne studies were timely in terms of apparently connecting with this shift.

While the notional value of the individual's contribution is foregrounded in light of all of this, it is also the case that the vehicle for their respective efforts becomes – at around this time – the work group. There is something of a lacuna before these arrangements starting to be spoken about as teams or team working, but there is a point – somewhere in the 1980s, I think – where the idea of the centrality of teams to industrial practice starts to be actively asserted. However, there was little evidence for this supposed ubiquity, which might lead one to ponder whether people working in 'teams' is something of a fiction (Devine et al., 1999) – and that, far from being an outlier, the 'pseudo-team' about which I spoke earlier is actually what prevails in most situations. We are working teams because we – and others, especially those who oversee our work – assert that we work in teams. And the team has always been – and largely remains – the key unit of analysis and for action in the workplace for the practice of OD.

One working definition of the work team suggests that they are '...interdependent collections of individuals who share responsibility for specific outcomes in their organisations' (Sundstrom et al., 1990, p. 120). In respect to teamwork, there are said to be five key aspects that support its success: the team is adequately led towards a collective outcome; members have an acute awareness of the contribution of those around them to the overall goal; the team covers for one another to get the job done; the team shows an innate ability to adjust its approach in order to meet that goal; and individual members intrinsically see the value of working as part of a team (Salas et al., 2005). This is a wearisome process-oriented view of the work, unfortunately, which obscures the critical element to all human organising, which is communication and connectivity. These elements are effaced from the perspective expressed here, which regrettably enjoys extensive currency in the wider business world. As ever with business writing, the schema offered by Salas et al lends itself well to conversion into a helpful and instantly accessible checklist for the busy manager or executive (or, indeed, OD practitioner).

There are richly crafted insights into being in groups, borne of the experience of the author and their immersion in that context (Bion, 2001). Bion states that 'Every group, however casual, meets to 'do' something; in this activity, according to the capacities of the individuals, they co-operate' (Bion, 2001, p. 143). I am unconvinced that the business-oriented five-point definition of team working cited above gives any credence to the vital element of cooperation. Schrage (1995) takes this further: his argument is that the very notion of 'teams' and 'teamwork' are constructs that obscure the key practice of human organising, which – to his mind – is collaboration (Schrage, 1995). He suggests that the fiction of the 'team' arises to an extent from the work of Mayo and the 'human relations' school, as they sought a counterpoint to the atomised production undergirded by Taylorism and realised in Fordism: create a climate of respect and concern between managers and the workforce and cooperation will spontaneously arise (Schrage, 1995, pp. 49–51).

Yet, in my view, the constraints of 'organisation,' the ossified and hence inflexible remnants of previous efforts by humans to organise actively, actually work against any notion of spontaneity in this context. It does not matter how respectful, concerned, and engaging the management in a formalised structure might notionally be; ultimately, the dead weight of the fossilised organisation limits and constrains what people can do in the workplace, regardless of the values espoused therein and the policies drafted and put in place. Indeed, such policies are the documentary codification of the fossilisation about which I speak. At least one organisation that I came across some while back in the NHS was able to state that it had 40-odd policies governing HR practice; if one visualises this repository of strictures and requirements, the myriad threads from each policy caught in the organisation's current and becoming intertwined with one another, it rapidly assumes the quality of a net, within which both manager (in terms of discretion to act as a genuine manager) and staff member (as someone who is oftentimes being nominally invited to offer their creative views and to explore new ways of being in the workplace) find themselves entangled.

The idea of team and team working is best seen as an organisational imposition, one that is the modern-day notion of the production line: it is management's way of getting people to get things done but carries with it an illusion of discretion to act and creativity. This is why there are management textbooks that seek to help managers to 'create' teams. They are not natural, in the way that a human group has an organic feel to it: they are instead built by the organisation, which is why manuals exist that describe how this might be done (West, 2012). The fact that collaboration does not appear spontaneously, largely because the organisational environment is inhospitable to such developments and specifically because the forced presence of 'teams' occupies the space where authentic cooperation would take place in this context, necessitates the presence of OD practitioners to constantly steer teams towards some semblance of connectivity and effectiveness. The ubiquitous away day is not as positive as it seems: it is, in fact, borne of the need constantly to remediate 'teams,' a structure imposed discursively within organisations, because those teams actually inhibit collaboration and human organising.

Two contrasts between teams and meaningful collaboration need exploring here, in light of this blithe assertion about the complicity of OD practitioners in serving a wider organisational discourse at the expense of genuinely emancipatory practice where true human talent could flourish. The first is to draw attention to the fact that many managers work on the assumption that to create a team that works requires them to place human pieces together like a jigsaw (Schrage, 1995, p. 32). All manner of tools are offered to support them in this endeavour, such as the Belbin team tool (Belbin, 2010) and the Myers-Briggs Type Indicator (MBTI), which will be explored in more detail in the section that follows. In respect to the former, it is asserted by the promoters of this model that,

> Great teams start with Belbin! Belbin Team Roles is the language of teams, enabling individuals to be able to project and talk about their behavioural strengths in a productive, safe and non-confrontational way. By using Belbin, individuals have a greater self-understanding of their strengths, which leads to more effective communication between colleagues and managers. *Great teams can be put together*, existing teams can be understood and improved, and everyone can feel that they are making a difference in the workplace [My emphasis].
>
> (Belbin, n.d.)

Belbin's approach offers the manager nine possible jigsaw pieces. It's simply a technical exercise to use the roles that Belbin describes in order to categorise people – by which I mean, squeeze an individual into one of nine boxes – in order to craft the ideal and high-performing team. While Belbin's ideas derived from years of collaborative research, it is observed that little material has been published since these ideas gained purchase and have seen wide application in business settings that actually investigates the assertions being made by the model (Pritchard & Stanton, 1999). Meanwhile, the very idea of human collaboration is being overwritten by all of this epiphenomenal activity with a very limited evidence base – and it underscores for me the simple fact that organisations chase after the idea of teams and team working, while human beings simply seek to connect and work together in order to achieve their aims.

This is richly evidenced when one turns one's attention to those instances where people do come together in collaborative union. For example, when we look to people organising together for a wider political aim, we gain insight into the effectiveness of this – and, of course, to an extent, into the limitations that exist in that respect. The Occupy London initiative, for example, sprang up relatively spontaneously, with a collective of people coming together to protest about the iniquities of modern capitalist society in the UK and in the wider world. An encampment arose outside St Paul's Cathedral, where people sought to organise to promote an alternative view of the world – and to engage in exemplary practice that could be seen to prefigure that envisioned future. Research on that experience allows us to recognise the power of organising – but also to acknowledge the tendency towards 'organisation' (Reinecke, 2018). The collaboration that took place shows the power that derives when people authentically and openly work together, without overbearing constraint; it equally illustrates the way in which that collaboration can dissolve as intractable issues of praxis come to light – and the lapse into formality drains the positivity from the experience.

Similarly, there is the case of the Xerox engineers, who – while subsumed in formality and organisational expectation – nevertheless engaged with one another collaboratively, on an informal basis, so as to learn from one another in order to better understand their workplace practice (Orr, 1996). From this type of enactment of collaboration in and through practice came the wider understanding of situated learning (Lave & Wenger, 1991) and the associated development of Communities of Practice (Wenger, 1998).

Work undertaken by the RAND Corporation in terms of exploring the efficacy and benefits of a number of healthcare-based Communities of Practice came to the conclusion that,

> [T]he enthusiasm for CoPs observed at events and indicated through surveys is real. They appear to meet a hunger for working with others in non-hierarchical ways to deliver benefit for patients. The evidence provided here suggests that CoPs directly speak to the altruistic and professional motivations of staff and consequently mobilise energy and commitment. It is clear that CoPs come with their own limitations relating to managing sustained learning and delivering improvement, but it is equally clear that they generate commitment and loyalty that could, if well harnessed, greatly support healthcare improvement.
>
> (Garrod & Ling, 2018, p. 40)

This counterpoint is vital in relation to the discourse that exists in business about teams and teamwork. There is another way for people to be in the workplace, an ontology that derives from the quotidian experience of socially constructing a meaningful and collective understanding of that space and context. The idea of team – something pursued in the abstract by managers and the corporations in which they work – is an imposition; it is a mere overlay on the lived experience of people in work, something that effaces that experience and renders subaltern the range of alternative knowledges and practices, lest they grow and become overwhelming persuasive. And OD facilitates this, not least by promoting the 'human relations myth' alluded to earlier, wherein there is a read off from managers fostering an atmosphere of cooperative team working to organisational effectiveness (Purser, 2000, p. 69). This generates a fascinating paradox, wherein supportive management without meaningful autonomy is actually even more manipulative than direct and more austere oversight of the workforce. The latter allows room for resistance; the former seeks to smother resistance with a cloying kindness that serves to suffocate the human soul (Purser, 2000).

There is a persuasive argument that Elton Mayo and the Harvard Group's work at Western Electric at Hawthorne did not engender the paradigm shift from scientific management to a human relations approach, as popular management history might suggest. Instead, their activities amplified a context wherein 'welfare capitalism' was already apparent in the US corporate life – and that this flow of the tide might be seen to ebb at a point after the Hawthorne work, as the hard economic realities of the 1930s began to assert themselves (Hassard, 2012, p. 1453). A possible conclusion is that OD can be brought into the work context by management in organisations when its blandishments best suit the wider sociopolitical context – and hence can just as easily be shunted out of the workplace when those circumstances change and require a different approach. The growth of OD as a practice – and its increased focus on itself in terms of codification of its applied knowledge and efforts around professionalisation – would seem to coincide with the post-1974 economic paroxysm and the remedies in response – such as neoliberalism, in terms of politics and economics, and latterly the politics of austerity – that flourished from the 1980s until now. Such a view places OD in a purely supporting role, deployed manipulatively at those points when involvement, engagement, and empowerment are notionally the order of the day – and providing the semblance of that through its range of activities and practices. But, to assume that role, OD is working to formalise itself for no other purpose than to justify itself in that position: witness, for example, the curious spider-like spinning of a provider of OD services seeking to assume for itself the role of a professional body for OD (Institute for Organisational Development, 2019).

The idea of the 'team' offers the perfect vehicle for such intervention – and so OD finds itself heavily invested in working with teams and providing events that pivot around team working, the elusive idea of teams working well together. This orientation for OD practitioners has been noted along with a sense that, despite this concentration on team building to improve effectiveness amongst practitioners, the evidence for its effectiveness is inconclusive (Buller, 1986). Such OD work – intervening in teams via team training or the provision of time away from work for the team to consider its work – can be argued to work, however, if your aim is to make the team be team-like (which is a dramatically recursive notion – and one that is patently ideologised) and to enhance its performance (McEwan et al., 2017). So, we intervene in teams in order to encourage their 'teamness' – a notion that leaves no space for the interrogation of the supposition that teams are the best possible way for human beings to come together to cooperate – or for critique of the way in which this idea of the team is so seamlessly woven into the discourse that surrounds business. And we do so because of the correlation that is suggested to exist between team training and performance in the workplace (Salas et al., 2008).

In order to defamiliarise this concept of the team as a natural state that is best suited to meet organisational expectations, one that is so woven into our day-to-day experience that it seems impervious to critical scrutiny, it is worth viewing it through the prism of gender. Specifically, it has been suggested the very notion of the feminine and of women's experience of the workplace is not present in our notions of team working, wherein the individual's efforts are amplified by those working in concert around them, simply because the business writing in this area is founded on masculinist notions. In one case study, it was observed that the performance orientation of so much team thinking can be seen to render the feminine invisible, even when women are part of the team (Metcalfe & Linstead, 2003). Importantly, we tend to work with the idea of the 'team' as if it were an entirely neutral and natural phenomenon, when the reality is that they tend to be 'forced' work groups. The focus on delivery that is seen to be key to this arrangement is meant to smooth off the differences that might exist in such as context.

The supposed naturalness of the team and the expectation that everyone in the workplace should be a good team player (meaning, I suspect, that they are content to subsume their own individuality in order to assume a drone-like quality of merely meeting the imperative of the hive) means that it opens up as a space wherein the workplace discourse can assert itself through a range of ideas and practices. The centrality of the team facilitates the blurring of the worlds of work and non-work: teams do not just exist in the workplace, they are expected to bond outside. This porousness is seen to be virtuous – and reinforces the notion that managers should be seeking to engender a 'culture of fun' in order – and here it is again – to get the most out of the human capital that they are charged with overseeing (Fleming, 2005).

This resonates with the idea that everyday life is in the process of being 'managerialised;' we live in times when we quantify ourselves through fitness apps, attend endlessly to whether we are being personally effective, and oftentimes assume the role of entrepreneur for our own selves, assuming a managerial responsibility to develop ourselves and endlessly challenge ourselves (Hancock, 2009). In this regard, I have two friends, a married couple, who each year set themselves a set of joint objectives; these are then loaded into a spreadsheet, which is kept under monthly review in order to assess achievement and progress. If this indicates a managerialism of everyday life, the reverse is also said to be detectable: in this respect, it is suggested that 'Consumption, lifestyle factors, sexuality, and humour are neither externalized in favour of a collective normative alignment nor barred from the organization in the bureaucratic tradition, but 'celebrated' as a useful organizational resource' (Fleming & Study, 2009, p. 214).

Taking this as a part of the wider reconfiguration of the changing relations that serve to support the extant mode of production, it seems as though,

> Flexible hours, job enrichment, self-managed work teams, continued retraining (*formation permanente*): none of these innovations can be regarded as serious attempts to modify the capitalist regime. And in fact their ambition is not to transform the organization of production, but to change the relations of individuals to their productive work.
>
> (Donzelot, 1991, p. 251)

This is perceivable in a wide range of effects that can be isolated in the modern workplace. A study of Motorola factories, particularly those that were established in Scotland from 1969 onwards, offers fascinating insight into the way in which 'team working' plays a role in terms of the oversight of these facilities by viewing it through a Foucauldian prism (McKinlay & Taylor, 2018). For example, they identified the fact that – given the rhythm and pace of the plant – break times were invariably taken with immediate workmates, meaning that individuals were constantly in their teams. Newspapers were banned in the cafeteria so that teams sat together during breaks and talked about work issues rather than more general (and human) topics of conversation. These are not mere assertions and theorising by the authors of the study: it is explicitly stated in terms of text from company documents and observations by managerial staff (including an OD practitioner, of course). Interestingly, they note that 'For senior managers, a prime virtue of team working was that surveillance was both more intense and continuous than in hierarchical structures' (McKinlay & Taylor, 2018, p. 84). The authors then quote one of the Motorola managers who elaborates on this: 'The team can manage all the time, whereas a supervisor can only do so some of the time. Teams are fierce self-managers' (McKinlay & Taylor, 2018, p. 84).

Through this analysis, a shift in workplace practice is revealed in richer detail than might ordinarily appear, wherein some of the motivations and the implications become more apparent. Teams collectively supervise their own members – who could tolerate being referred to as not being a team player in the current discourse – and that regime inscribes power in the workplace very differently. The overseer or manager is an external authority, carrying positional power within a given hierarchy; they not only wield that power but act as a focal point for resentment and resistance. The internalised discipline of the team disperses power and gives no single node against which disgruntled workers might push. And OD works diligently to develop and sustain this state of affairs, thereby making the workplace so much more manageable – literally, of course, in the case of senior managers. What we think we are doing, in terms of creating a new kind of workforce, runs counter to what it is possible to define as the impact that we are having. We are creating the illusion of a new workplace in which the old workplace secretly nestles and operates unhindered.

Surveillance feels less like being watched by Big Brother when it's being undertaken unknowingly by all of your colleagues around you. Following Foucault's notion about the Panopticon, such a circumstance will see people incorporate the idea of constant observation into their very existence, which means that their compliance is attained without coercion and occasional oversight. During my college years, I had a vacation job in the office of a local authority which managed the stationery requests for the whole council offices. The work was dull and utterly unengaging and seemed – by my recollection – to pivot around the receipt and discharge of 'pinkies,' requisition chits that would land on my desk and which I was expected to meet. The tedium was amplified by the fact that the workflow was glacially slow. Oversight of my work was sporadic and hardly thorough, so I spent a huge amount of my time perched on a step ladder in the large stationery cupboard, avidly reading books. To be candid, I am to this day wholly unconvinced that inculcating the notion of being part of a 'team' in this context would have had any impact whatsoever. But this tale, hardly designed to show me in a good light, underscores that management cannot genuinely oversee everyone in a complex organisation, although teams create situations of permanent surveillance and strive to foster 'team spirit.'

Ultimately, the Foucauldian idea of a transformation of power from a resource held by a sovereign to an aspect of the interrelationships of human beings in certain circumstances and its capacity then to constrain behaviour through discipline seems to be in play as we consider these matters. In respect to power in this context, it is argued that

> The focus shifts from questions like "Who uses the power?" and "Through what formal channels?" to examining the ways in which power operates

WHAT DOES OD ACHIEVE?   109

in everyday organizational routines, is spoken about in everyday discourses, and is reproduced and exercised by the subjects over others and themselves.

(Valikangas & Seeck, 2011, p. 14)

This seems a pithy way to summarise the impact that teams in the workplace might have in terms of people's presence in that space.

The modern workplace tends to double down on surveillance, however, through both these cultural adjustments and the application of a wide range of technological methods for keeping track of us. A TUC report highlighted how organisations are now more than able, should they so choose, to monitor the computer and phone use of their employees and also to track their movements through CCTV and the company phone (Trades Union Congress, 2018, pp. 8–9). More than half of those sampled thought it was likely that they were being monitored at work – and 70% were of the opinion that this surveillance would become more common in the future (Trades Union Congress, 2018, p. 4). In an age of staff involvement, there will be few instances where employers have expressly engaged with their workforce to advise them of the overall regime of surveillance to which they are subjected; nearly 80% in the survey suggested that employers should be legally compelled to consult their workforces and reach agreement with them over the use of surveillance in this way (Trades Union Congress, 2018, p. 30).

Team working is reaching new heights, of course, in the context of so-called holacratic organisations, about which I spoke earlier. Here, the collective nature of the team is celebrated as a truly empowering way of working, one where the organisation is flattened and overseers are removed. But, as we have seen, this simply sees oversight inscribed into the team – and thence into the subjects that make up those teams. Each team ends up locked into a situation where each member watches – and is watched by – the other team members. As Foucault notes in mobilising Bentham's notion of the Panopticon (Foucault, 1991) to explain the surveillant and enveloping nature of disciplinary power, one does not need to be watched for watching to impact on a subject. Indeed, knowing that one is surveilled but not knowing when that is happening means that this idea of being viewed at all times becomes inscribed in our day-to-day lives. It encourages us towards normalcy at all times and engenders docility in us (Foucault, 1991).

Pathologising resistance

One of the issues that some have with Foucault's work in this regard is the apparently all-pervasive nature of that disciplinary power, which seems to leave little or no room for the notion of a subject engaging in resistance. However, it is clear that the latter exists and is significant particularly to our discussions. Back in the late '50s, of course, the argument was proposed that, as traditional ties unravelled, people were seeking to anchor themselves instead in their organisations, particularly as those extended in scale and scope. It linked this suggestion very tightly with the development of Mayo's human relations movement, which – as we have seen – is viewed as foundational to OD practice even now (Whyte, 1957). Importantly, drawing directly from Mayo (1949), it suggested that the organisation seems to offer the opportunity for belongingness and togetherness; the former is about membership, seen as a key human need, while the latter satisfies what is thought to be a requirement to connect with others in pursuit of action, via work groups, 'teams,' after hours drinks, social awaydays, and so on.

A key means by which this need for togetherness is met within organisations is via the formation of teams, not necessarily for a specific work purpose but because they meet this particular expectation. For some, this seems an innocuous development, but Whyte went so far as to observe that 'Just as [the team] has obscured the role of the individual in creation and discovery in such activities as research and communication, so in the regular work of running an organisation it is obscuring the function of leadership' (Whyte, 1957, p. 53). We can now also note that the team – that fundamental unit of analysis and practice for OD consultants – subtly subsumes the individual and operates a regime of power where each subject manages themselves as part of their commitment to an artificially confected collective.

And yet, and yet... We can still perceive resistance in the workplace, as individuals either openly – through perhaps a grand act of speaking truth to power – or more seditiously, through myriad micro-responses to the prevailing expectations that confront them in organisational life and with which they disagree, push back against the prevailing view of expected behaviours. This can be undertaken individually, of course, or in concert with others: in some cases, an entire team might resist an organisational direction of travel. For an individual, liberal thought – albeit from initial conversation as to how customers relate to firms but broadened to encompass other contexts – suggests three options when confronted with something with which they disagree in an organisational context: exit, voice, or loyalty (Hirschman, 1970). In a commercial context, a customer 'exiting' a firm in order to seek a good or service elsewhere is seen to be likely to have a positive impact on the company that they are leaving, through the supposedly pure market system.

Giving voice – even in a market context – is a more complex activity. It aims to change things directly and is purposeful in that regard. It seeks to change rather than escape from the circumstances (Hirschman, 1970, p. 30). Acting to change things in a circumstance where the contract of employment holds sway is problematic: it is not, in truth, an agreement between equals other than just before the employee signs it. Thereafter, it seems clear that they are beholden to the organisation they have joined for their sustenance and well-being, as the contract defines work to be delivered in return for an agreed payment. Broadly, the organisation can part ways with a worker without too much adverse impact; the same cannot be said for the worker sloughed off by the firm for whatever reason. Similarly, the workplace is a place constituted by individuals enmeshed in myriad intricacies of power. The role of the 'team' in managing the individuals that make it up renders giving voice even more contentious.

All of which means that for organisations – and their practitioners of OD – the notion of resistance is seen to run counter to organisational normalcy. It is an aberrant behaviour that needs to be managed out of the system. I have been approached professionally on countless occasions by a manager soliciting my services in terms of working with what is often referred to as a 'difficult team.' Early in my career, I would take these instructions at face value, and craft an intervention designed to explore the 'difficultness' and aiming to normalise that group. Latterly, I am more likely to respond with one simple question: 'Difficult in what way and for whom?' Oftentimes, the difficulty identified and pathologised in this context was simply a meaningful reaction to change, especially change designed, driven, and delivered by senior leaders with the rest in the organisation seen to be an object to be moved and manipulated. For some authors in the OD field, such resistance is a logical systemic response to new circumstances (Senge, 2006).

From the psychoanalytic perspective, this response – decried as negative in our modern business discourse and targeted for remediation – is merely a symptom of the release of anxiety ordinarily contained by the dynamics of the workplace, something revealed in work undertaken in respect to the provision of healthcare. In a further exploration of this mechanism, particularly in respect to the challenge of interagency or professional collaboration, it is asserted, very helpfully, that,

> Change is inevitably feared if it is perceived as threatening an identity evolved in large measure as a means of coping with unconscious conflict and anxiety... If in the course of human development anxiety, conscious and unconscious, is inescapable, it cannot in itself be said to be pathological.
>
> (Woodhouse & Pengelly, 1991, p. 11)

As organisations and people therein wrestle with the notions of closer strategic working and active partnership, this critical notion desperately needs revisiting – and this applies particularly in respect to health and social care, wherein integration is such an imperative at this time.

Resistance, then, in OD terms, is seen in one of two ways: either as evidence that change efforts are being effective or a challenge in terms of finding ways to encourage people to abandon their contrary positions in favour of aligning with the wider efforts of the organisation. This reminds me of a conversation that took place as part of a discussion on complexity and leadership that was facilitated by Professor Chris Mowles from the University of Hertfordshire. We opted – with Chris's help – to get under the common-sense notion of organisational values. The discussants were quick to suggest that it was important to encourage the workforce to *align* with the values of the firm. (I italicise that word to draw attention to its ideological impact: it suggests an exercise of free will on the part of the employee to achieve a soft positioning in the overall intention of the organisation. The reality is oftentimes extensive programmes of OD interventions to drive the workforce into the prescribed position in this regard.) Values, of course, are an essential part of the work of an OD practitioner, located very clearly in their responsibilities in relation to organisational culture. On some occasions, I have watched organisations assume that these values can be designed from scratch or actively revised without any meaningful reference to the cultural context within or without the organisation, which is a fascinating refusal to connect a number of very obvious dots.

Back at the workshop, the challenge came back: why do they need to align with these values? And, of course, once this type of thing is subject to genuine scrutiny and critical thought, it is possible to attain a very different perspective on it all. The group came to a conclusion that the values represented the front facing aspect of a large infrastructure of behavioural expectations in an organisation. It is, then, a means of defining how people should 'be' in the workplace. As with the team as a fierce manager, so the incorporation by individuals of a set of apparently innocuous values leads to a docile acceptance of two things: first, a set of behaviours to which all must subscribe in order to be recognised as truly corporate (and therefore a model citizen); and, second, a division between what can be said and – crucially – all that cannot be said in an organisation.

Hence, herein another contemporary organisational paradox: many companies now pursue the notion of diversity as extending beyond merely monitoring the composition of their workforce in order to ensure that it reflects the wider society, focusing alongside this on the importance of creating conditions for a diversity of voice within the organisation. Simultaneously, they are advocating the embodiment of a set of company values, ordinarily designed at the centre with little practical involvement by the workforce, which aims to homogenise the workforce and the opinions, ideas, and resistances to which they might be tempted to give voice.

Resistance, though, in a contemporary setting assumes a wide variety of forms, all of which are worthy of celebration when they seek to undermine any monolithic project that aims to impose itself on the individuals who find themselves subject to it. Even the workplace surveillance methods and the corrective of working in a team do not eliminate resistance altogether. Indeed, it is argued that the shift in workplace practices and managerial approaches may have generated the potential for a new and subtle repertoire of acts of resistance, where human agents supposedly inscribed in the organisation assert themselves in reaction to that pervasiveness and supposed incorporation (Thompson & Ackroyd, 1995). In fact, Thompson and Ackroyd (1995) are correctly highlighting how Foucauldian work in the field has become something of a counsel of despair, because of Foucault's fresh take on power as inescapably subjectifying and present in the interactivity of everyone regardless of context. However, as intimated earlier and as we will see later, Foucault found ways of reconciling this tension, particularly through his advocacy of technologies of the self (Foucault, 1988a).

One way in which this new modality of resistance is articulated is 'Švejkism,' mentioned earlier in another chapter, which draws on the main character of a novel by Jaroslav Hašek's, 'The Good Soldier, Švejk,' where the chief weapons are seen to be irony and cynicism (Fleming & Sewell, 2002). Interestingly, both individuals and their teams have the potential to engage in this type of behaviour, hence the way in which managers – as noted above – can end up describing groups of people that they oversee as 'difficult.' The team can certainly act as a fierce manager – but it also has the potential to resist, albeit in ways that take cognisance of the shift away from Taylorism and Fordism through the Human Relations approach to the way in which we experience the modern workplace. And the discourse that runs through business, of course, establishes normalcy – what is seen to be collectively acceptable thoughts and activity in that context – and otherness, by which is meant a category of people who stand outside of that normalcy and therefore need to be reincorporated. OD practitioners are on hand to use their techniques to support this, which is to say, to contribute to the discourse that crudely calibrates a population into the normal and the aberrant. The latter might be lacking in team spirit or change-resistant or not sharing sufficient allegiance to the cultural expectations of the organisation. OD helps to define these individuals and thereby supports them being ostracised, so that – of course – these 'outliers' might better be enticed and welcomed back into the organisational fold.

The technologies used to affect this do not appear constrictive, for that is how disciplinary power (in its concatenation with knowledge and the subjectification associated with that) inhabits the spaces where human beings interact. Far from it, in fact; they instead appear inclusive and authentically engaging, although it is possible, of course, to view them from a different perspective. Take, for example, the widespread use of the MBTI, the Myers-Briggs Type Indicator. Many will be acquainted with the back story of this instrument: built upon Carl Jung's notions of archetypes, this methodology and practice were created by people without specific expertise in this regard. So far, so flakey, not least because the very foundation upon which this curious edifice is built is questionable: 'There was no proof for Jung's type theory; as a matter of method Jung did not believe his conjectures ought to be validated by modern empirical methods' (Emre, 2018, p. 35). To an extent, the same might be said by Jung's partner and antagonist in psycho-fiction and confabulation, Sigmund Freud.

Despite being clothed in a notion of modernist practice, wherein – despite its provenance in an avowedly theoretical corpus of thought – it constantly seeks to reassure itself by reference to scientific method, a genealogical analysis underscores the idea that pre-modern notions such as astrology and alchemy lie at the heart of Jung's conceptualisation – and so must, by implication, sit underneath MBTI (Case & Phillipson, 2004). This is amplified by research work that confounds the claims of the instrument in regard to its scientific grounding (Boyle, 1995). In critiquing the foundation, the instrument and its claims, at least one serious researcher has argued that,

> The popularity of the MBTI as a consulting tool most likely reflects the success of the publisher's marketing campaign and the intuitive and simple sounding nature of the instrument's scoring scheme. Compared to a conventional measure of the Big Five [in terms of wider psychological thinking in respect to personality – MC], it is probably comforting to learn that one tends to be intuitive and feeling, rather than learning that one has scored high on the neuroticism and low on the consciousness scales. Consequently, the MBTI can serve as a nonthreatening vehicle to introduce the concept of individual differences in personality and the relation between personality constructs and behavior to a general audience. The instrument might even serve as a catalyst for exercises that lead to improved esprit de corps among employees.
>
> (Pittenger, 2005, p. 219)

Perhaps more worryingly in these benighted times, the willingness of the corporate world and a huge number of people therein (particularly practitioners of OD) to swallow this idea hook, line and sinker – despite a recognised lack of evidence and internal contradiction – is said to reflect on our poorly developed relationship with scientific theory and practice, with those making this observation also acknowledging that enthusiasts of the approach would be 'unphased' by the contrary evidence offered (Stein & Swan, 2019). That is certainly my experience amongst practitioners: some drink the Kool-Aid during the training that equips people to facilitate feedback on the instrument; some can be prompted to recognise the methodological problems and evidential shortcomings of this approach but cleave to it due to its 'usefulness' in the work that they do. It is unclear, then, within OD practice as to where this crude utility argument might reach its limits, which is a great concern to those who want to work seriously in the workplace.

Those completing MBTI see their responses translated into supposed preferences across four type pairs: extraversion–introversion, sensing–intuition, thinking–feeling, and judging–perceiving. The categorisation is expressed in a cluster of letters: when I indulged this particular fiction most recently, the instrument declared me an INTP, meaning I exhibited preferences through my responses for introversion, intuition, thinking, and perceiving. There are 16 possible clusters of such letters, given the way in which this is constructed … as, indeed, there are 12 signs of the zodiac, which is as robust a way as MBTI to make a judgement about an individual and their orientation to the world. And it is not, to my mind, an improved esprit de corps that the instrument fosters, although I am constantly amazed about how much credence teams of people compelled to run through this exercise ascribe to it. Instead, it is the very act of categorisation that is significant in terms of sustaining a particular discourse of power and docility in the workplace.

As noted above, practitioners are often moved to acknowledge, somewhat *sotto voce*, that the instrument assumes a pseudo-scientific mantle and has a problematic underpinning. There's also the defence that – just like signs of zodiac – it's merely an innocuous and amusing piece of fun to use with individuals and groups. I have heard myself offer a somewhat mealy-mouthed rationalisation for its use, one that separates the instrument from the 16 sets of type and favours using the theoretical grounding of it to work conversationally with groups. Such a hybridised application, of course, does not actually challenge the sense or applicability of the package. And it reinforces the way in which its usage merely underscores normalcy – don't worry, you'll be one of these 16 clusters and you'll be able to interrelate meaningfully then with others in clusters different, perhaps even 'opposite,' to your own – and, in so doing, generates an Other, namely those who will not accept the endless categorisation of human beings for the purposes of management of populations in the service of disciplinary power.

The MBTI – alongside other psychometrics and categorising technologies, such as Belbin with its nine team roles – serves also to undergird the notion of the workplace team, a concept critiqued earlier in this chapter. For example, I undertook training in the Wave Instrument – owned by a company called Saville Assessment, part now of a global concern called Willis Towers Watson – which encourages respondents to undertake an assessment that is meant to be a highly effective predictor of workplace performance. Specifically, they explain that,

> The Wave Questionnaire is the most valid indicator of competency potential and cultural fit. It identifies talents, motives and preferred culture in one dynamic questionnaire and uses dual response format to help control distortion. On completion, high-quality graphic reports are produced, which are available in over 30 languages.
>
> (Saville Assessment, n.d.)

In other words, it takes a human being and converts them into a static representation of enticing and colourful pictures.

Off the back of this, the company claims that use of Wave with people in your organisation will 'Illustrate team dynamics to cultivate better understanding and enhanced performance, improving the effectiveness of working relationships that employees have with each other.' So, it is promoting the mythology that one can categorise human beings – indeed, they can be prompted to categorise themselves through the completion of this questionnaire – in order that you can manage them into teams that work more effectively, given the capacity it provides you to build a balanced team. Interestingly, of course, such a view simply neglects the role of emotion that exists within the very individuals that one seeks to mould into a collective that can truly deliver for your endeavour. Completion of a psychometric – whatever it might be – notionally gives others insight into the human subject – but actually all that it does is facilitate the individual surrendering themselves to scrutiny and categorisation. It tells you nothing about the person other than that they have become enmeshed in the regime of power – and thence allow others to take a view of them that is mediated by a dehumanising mechanism. When OD practitioners use these sorts of instruments, they are abandoning their commitment to humanistic practice and person-centred thinking.

The report tells all – and the promoters of these instruments control very carefully who is licensed to work with a respondent to review and understand the report that is generated from their completion of an instrument. In reality, the report tells something, of course; it speaks of the way in which disciplinary power – and in particular the practices of governmentality that arise out of that regime of power – is effective through the subjectification that it achieves. I do not become a human subject, understandable (and incorporated) in the wider context until I know that I am an INTP, or a Plant in teams, or I have a sense of myself through the completion of a questionnaire. And that vast reserve of human experience – our happiness, our anxiety, our dread, our desire, our pleasure, our distress – is rationalised away by the condensation of a human existence into a series of questions and a glossy report.

Intriguingly, knowing one's MBTI type is simultaneously both an incorporation into a regime of power – but can also be seen as a technology of the self, a prompt to the individual not merely to be defined by this curious jumble of letters but to use it as a means to gain greater personal understanding, to work on oneself to become an even better – and more docile – subject (Emre, 2018, pp. xvii–xviii). It allows the individual to state, 'I'm normal … but in my own special and unique way.' And so two conditions of disciplinary power are met: it generates a means by which populations can be more seamlessly managed whilst preserving the illusion of the sovereign and rational individual that underpins the notion of liberal democracy.

This categorisation is central to the operation of Foucault's expanded notion of disciplinary power, which extended into notions of both bio-power and governmentality. These notions seek to determine the apparatus through which that power flows and acts. They focus on the surveillance and management of populations, oftentimes through apparently benign agencies, some intrinsic elements of the wider state and some that act as proxies of the state, such as professional groupings. (Foucault's primary focus in this respect was the way in which psychiatry, as a branch of medicine, developed itself and made itself significant in respect to governmentality by its defining approach to normalcy and hence otherness (Foucault, 1988b).) There are many adjuncts to this field, streams that have wriggled free of medical science in this context in order to assert themselves: psychoanalysis, through the ideas of Freud and Jung; clinical psychology, of course; and occupational psychology (and its analogue, organisational behaviour), which is where much OD practice draws its justification.

Techniques for sifting and sorting a population, categorising for the sake of the subtle and unfelt oversight and direction of a workforce, are rife in OD practice. Alongside MBTI and Belbin, there seems to be a boundless repertoire of instruments that seek to classify an individual and their behaviours in the workplace. Some are founded on self-assessment – the subject undertaking a review of themselves through their responses to key statements – and others rely on the assessments of both self and others.

WHAT DOES OD ACHIEVE?   119

Here, the self-assessment sits alongside the evaluation of responses from those above, alongside and below the subject in an organisation; the notionally panoramic nature of this perspective leads such instruments to be referred as 360 tools.

The popularity of anonymised responses to questionnaires in the context of a 360 assessment seems at face value justified: here is a situation wherein those with whom one works are offering supposedly honest assessments of you and your performance in the workplace. This is useful feedback, it would seem, which one can use to adjust behaviour in order to develop one's practice and overall effectiveness. However, it is worth noting two things here: first, oftentimes this work is undertaken against a construct of normalcy that no one engaged in that process has been actively involved in defining; and, second, if the workplace was an honest and human place in which people came together to address a common purpose, then everyone would feel able to offer candid real-time observations on presence and performance of themselves and others. It also represents an additional facet of the team as 'fierce manager,' about which I spoke earlier. These assessments often judge the individual against a schedule of expectations, and hence those with whom they work further embed the person into a regime of subjectification.

So, for example, in healthcare, a framework of managerial performance called the Healthcare Leadership Model (HLM) enjoys great currency (NHS Leadership Academy, 2013). It consists of nine domains, each encapsulating a standard area of practice in a corporate context: these include management with purpose, for results, and involving the engagement of others. People can commission a report for themselves wherein they invite those around them in the organisation (and oftentimes beyond) to rate them against key elements within each of those domains. Respondents are asked to assess practice in this way by judging against carefully crafted statements whether the person that they are rating across a five-point Likert scale is exemplary, insufficient or somewhere in between. The material collected is then rendered in report form, with the bulk of that document largely presenting quantitative data, where the individual being assessed is converted into numbers and patterns that inevitably feel to be distanced from the reality of human experience.

From a Foucauldian perspective, this has two effects: on the one hand, it is a surveillant instrument that serves to reinforce the panoptical nature of the modern workforce. It's not now merely the team in which one works that is undertaking the managerial work in the organisation; now, it is those for whom you work, with whom you work alongside, and who work for you. The scrutiny is caught in an instant – but it reinforces the idea that we are always being explicitly scrutinised by those with whom we share the working day and that this is in some way entirely legitimate. And so, on the other hand, this allows for the operation of disciplinary power with its subjectifying aspect: we achieve subjecthood through the ongoing assessments of those around us – and through the formal expression of those assessments against a model of organisational normalcy. Are we – in the eyes of others – an exemplary leader or are we largely insufficient in this regard? This subject is likely to seek the approbation of those around them, so will seek to change their behaviour in order to attain that. In this way, the surveillant scrutiny becomes embodied for us all. We no longer need to actually be watched in order to behave as if we are being watched.

OD is implicit in this practice, oftentimes guiding individuals and teams towards these sorts of instruments and activities. Invariably, this is done with notionally good intent, as if simply knowing more about oneself is an intrinsic good and that – on the basis of that feedback – one might develop oneself in order to be better. (As ever with such work, the underpinning notion is working with the people so that organisational effectiveness can be improved, regardless of the way in which this practice is seen to be drawing down and applying the notion of 'positive psychology' in the workplace (Lewis, 2011), which is the core underpinning to most of OD practice. It does so through such notions as encouraging people to develop a 'growth mindset' (Dweck, 2006).) Similarly, whilst a key facet of mainstream human resource management (HRM) practice, the activity around performance management and appraisal often fall under an OD remit. Certainly, where such frameworks use a ranking system, there is a clear sense of cut and slicing the workforce into good and bad categories, with the latter often requiring some remediation above and beyond the impact of being categorised as not being up to scratch in some arbitrarily designed schema. Oftentimes, responsibility for helping individuals or work groups to make the necessary adjustments falls to those who practise OD in the workplace. But the critique in this regard is even more profound: 'The appraisal does not so much discover 'the truth' about the appraised as construct it' (Grint, 2007, p. 61).

Overall, of course, it is possible that the presence of complex systems of performance appraisal in a great many organisations represents one of HRM's guilty secrets: if managers took time to speak to those who work for them on a regular and human basis, you would not need an elaborate and bureaucratised system of oversight in place to ensure that the worst of those managers at least spoke to their employees twice a year rather than hardly ever. Again, then, a common-sense structure in organisational practice is revealed as something that would not be in the least bit necessary if people related effectively and conversationally with one another whilst at work. These overbearing superstructures in organisational life is revealed to be compensatory regimes when one considers how much has been written about how ineffective they are in achieving the ends that they set for themselves (Coens & Jenkins, 2000).

Latterly, there have been numerous efforts to soften the edges of traditional appraisal. There are key aspects of this practice that many enlightened organisations struggle to encompass, not least the whole business of ranking staff, making linkages between that rating and reward (oftentimes in terms of pay progression or allocation of bonuses), and seeking to manage people through the objectives that are set for them each year. This management by objectives (MBO) approach is a decidedly mechanical and anti-humanistic means of thinking about the people who work in your business; it assumes that their only motivation for doing a good job would be the arbitrary target that has been pretty much plucked out of the air in the course of a formal conversation that is overburdened by the positional power of the workplace. Quite simply, the manager is entitled to review the member of staff – and to define what they will do in the workplace for the coming period. (Occasionally, this structure is overlaid by the notion that this is actually a dialogue in which the two parties jointly craft an outline of expected performance over the coming 12 months. This is merely a fiction, of course, regardless of how earnestly the manager believes that they are genuinely engaging with their direct report.)

Instead – taking the lead from psychological work on mindset mentioned above (Dweck, 2006) and with a nod towards neuroscience (Rock, 2008) – many employers have shunted the notion of appraisal from mainstream HR into OD, in light of the fact that new methods seek to emphasise the manager developing an ongoing coaching relationship with their employee rather than a managerially directive one. In one organisation in which I worked, we abandoned the traditional appraisal system, which is ordinarily constructed as a start of year conversation that reviews individual performance and sets expectations of performance in the coming year with a mid-year review scheduled to assess progress. Instead, the manager was prompted to hold quarterly progress conversations with their staff, founded on a 90-day purview instead of the standard 12 months.

Each of these conversations was expected to start with the manager inviting the staff member to reflect on their experience of the previous three months. The manager was then expected to articulate the challenges faced by their team in the coming three months (here, then, the fiction of the team, about which we spoke earlier in this chapter, reappears for the purposes of controlling the actions of individuals) in order to invite the employee to describe – their specific role notwithstanding – how they might work to enable the team to meet the expectations that existed on them. This practice was underpinned by managers feeling comforta-ble and confident to adopt a coaching approach to these conversations, drawing on the linked notions of the GROW model (Whitmore, 2017) and the idea of situational leadership, first outlined in 1969 (Hersey & Blanchard, 1969).

It might be argued that the reconfiguring of a quite transactional per-sonnel activity through two concepts that have common currency across OD as a practice indicates either a humanising of the activity – or a means of obfuscating the underlying dynamics of the relationship between the manager and the managed. Certainly, in a passing conversation one time, my interlocutor pointed out that, in truth, none of the amendments to ap-praisal that have been seen over recent years – of which this was just one small example – have seen the 'abandonment' of appraisal. Instead, it has merely been significantly revised, doubtless the better to improve an ex-perience where each staff member is pointedly yet obliquely reminded of their subaltern position.

This is not to say, of course, that this is a deliberate subterfuge on the part of those with power. This obfuscation is merely an element of the wider discourse around progress – the historical notion that things will inevitably get better – and the notion that things improve for everyone in light of these shifts. My point here, of course, is not to make a value judgement as to whether that is or is not the case: my intention instead is to underscore the fact that these cosmetic adjustments – profound though they might at first glance appear – do not fundamentally affect or alter the underlying power in the workplace and the outcomes of its action.

Colonising change

I have saved until last here the area of corporate life where OD perhaps makes its biggest claim – and which is a significant feature of working in organisations. As a practice, it has staked for itself a claim to support organisational effectiveness through working through people. In that regard, it puts a great stay in the notion of change, as something that is important to organisational refreshment. Its view of change is not simply that it is an inevitable feature the workplace, particularly in a context where people are regularly speaking of an environment that is – using the acronym VUCA, which business has borrowed from the military – apparently volatile, uncertain, complex and ambiguous (Mackey, 1992, p. 2). Instead, it takes the perspective that change is something that can be caused in an organisational context. It conceptually and actively inhabits and promotes a strong sense of linearity in regard to this, regularly mobilising the notion that the very idea of change is both plannable and deliverable through action and effect.

To a large extent, it founds this particular notion on the somewhat sterile work of John Kotter, who has made a career of rinsing through his one key idea again and again, thereby creating an illusion of refreshment and intellectual development that is patently absent on closer inspection of his schema. At root, Kotter promotes the illusion that change in organisational context is achievable through the application of a mechanistic eight-stage process (Kotter, 1995, p. 61). Although sometimes referred to as a model of emergent change and excused from that perspective from accusations of determinism (By, 2005), it sows in the mind of leaders and OD practitioners the illusion of being able to enact a meaningful sense of cause and effect in a complex adaptive system like an organisation.

The focused claim of OD as a practice in respect to supporting change in organisations is underpinned by two precepts: first, that any structural change, such as reviewing processes and procedures or reshaping how the organisation is configured, requires interventions to pull the people affected along and into place in light of this shift; and, second, related intimately to this sense of having coercively to pull human beings into fitting the shape of the organisation that is agreed as the 'right' one, is the idea that a key area of this work is around the ethereal notion of organisational culture. Hence, OD professionals are often seen trying to apply a humanistic sheen to technocratic redesign of the workplace. And that technocratic application is oftentimes in pursuit of the apparently common-sense notion of improved performance as filtered through the expectations of a capitalist economy. Increasingly, of course, that idea is questioned as we recognise that we can no longer keep seeing the planet as something that is there for us to ceaselessly exploit (Zizek, 2018, p. 34).

The problem with the alignment of OD with wider adjustments to workplace structure is that the popular fiction about organisational change promotes the notion that it is a simple matter of drafting a linear plan, dotting it with milestones, and setting people to work on it. This approach fails to acknowledge what people tend to know, namely, that plans very rarely come to fruition as they were originally envisioned – and that, even when reality does approximate the image that the people who drafted this picture of an idealised future picture, there is an ebb and flow in organisational life, where things reset to where they were. During the introduction of an approach to agile working I observed recently, which entailed converting a reduced number of work stations to hot desking, it took less than a fortnight for people to – quite legitimately, in my view – start adding personal effects to those desks (their coffee cups, an item of stationery such as a pen, a family photo): to my mind, they did this for two reasons: first, from a practical sense, it was a way to secure a desk close to the rest of their team rather than find themselves dispersed around the building; and, second, from a psychological sense, it added a homeliness to an otherwise stark and somewhat inhuman pen in which all people are expected to do is dispassionately deliver 'performance.'

This is an anecdotal observation of how change is invariably less 'sticky' than those promoting and seeking to deliver it imagine because of the way in which human subjects react to contextual circumstances. The person in the workplace is the object of a change in structure – but is equally a subject whose presence in this context reshapes that idea of change and the plan to achieve it. This is particularly the case where people resist collectively yet tacitly. Elsewhere, the literature around OD enjoys contesting the popularly espoused notion that 70% of change efforts are likely to fail: some authors comfortably call upon research to assert this notion (By, 2005), while others – through scrutiny of the provenance of this idea – refute it (Hughes, 2011).

My observations from practice are that any such initiative is unlikely to deliver in a traditional Lewinian sense, where we impose the linear and calibrated ideal of unfreezing, moving, and refreezing (Lewin, 1947), as the observation about agile working seems to confirm. There is an important conceptual caveat to add at this point: this three-step approach to organisational change does derive from Lewin, as indicated, but has been amplified (and, as a result, distorted) by the lifting of this simple schema from the theoretical context in which Lewin raised it and by its blithe application to a range of change settings (Cummings, et al., 2016). Models notwithstanding, it certainly seems to me that change efforts will engender change, by the very nature of the intervention, so declaring them unsuccessful is probably mere sophistry. Similarly, it seems unlikely to me – on the basis of experience – that the anticipated change will be realised to the letter. In light of this, all sides seem to be wrong – and all that we are sensibly left with is an active inquiry into change and how it is experienced in organisational contexts.

Of course, moving away from these somewhat quotidian representations of change to a more philosophical position is helpful in this context. Here, the work of Robert Chia, a writer who orients towards ideas drawn from a range of positions, including Bergsonian understandings of time, is helpful to disrupt the common-sense notions on change that prevail in and around the business. In essence, Chia persuasively argues that the faulty premise in our thinking about organisations is that they seek to default to stability, which means that change in this context is invariably privileged as something that has to be actively 'done' to the structures and the people. Instead, he posits the notion that organisations are stabilised patterns of relations that appear on the surface of ceaseless change, the way in which a crust might appear on top of a lava flow (Chia, 2014). This leads to the assertion that 'Organization aims at stemming change but, in the process of doing so, it is generated by it' (Tsoukas & Chia, 2002, p. 567).

This means that, while the traditional response is to endeavour to act upon the organisation through a transformation plan, we should instead aim to relax our presence in the organisational setting to allow change to take its organic course. To return momentarily to volcanology to illustrate the point around intrinsic change and the appearance of organisation,

Lava is molten rock generated by geothermal energy and expelled through fractures in planetary crust or in an eruption, usually at temperatures from

700 to 1,200°C (1,292 to 2,192°F). The structures resulting from subse-
quent solidification and cooling are also sometimes described as lava.
The molten rock is formed in the interior of some planets, including Earth,
and some of their satellites, though such material located below the crust
is referred to by other terms.

(Wikipedia, 2018)

We should encourage the change implicit in human organising to force its
way through the organisational crust; managing change therefore means
allowing it to happen, rather than seeking to impose a model of change
on the terrain. However, most OD practice today is deeply concerned with
being seen to accelerate and normalise plans for change, at the same time
creating the illusion of engagement in it as a process for all who are subject
to it – and working actively to incorporate those who do not immediately
become enchanted by its technocratic allure.

This seems to me to be especially the case in that most elusive realm in
terms of organisations eager to engender change, namely the question of
culture. The very term remains elusive, with a range of definitions in play,
even before you land on the sensitive issue in relation to the supposed differences between culture and climate in an organization (Denison, 1996).
Yet, despite this, senior leaders increasingly fetishise the notion that culture in a firm can be directly altered according to some master plan, supported by professional services firms who indulge the notion that a simple
checklist approach to this complex issue will deliver what you think that
you want. Fortunately, others working in the field are motivated to apply a
more attentive eye to this general assumption; they observe that culture is
intangible, oftentimes an artefact of other practices, and so not amenable to
being changed in any meaningful way (Ogbonna, 1992).

Those working from a more critical perspective accuse the very notion
of 'culture change' of being – through the lens of Orwell's '1984' – a totalitarian effort at control (Willmott, 1993). Specifically, it is argued that
these cultural efforts can be read in the following way: 'Far from lifting or
diluting management control, corporate culturism promotes its extension
through the design of value systems and the management of the symbolic
and emotional aspects of organizational membership' (Willmott, 1993,
p. 541). In essence, the organisational focus on the manipulation of culture is more to do with guaranteeing the incorporation of the workforce
through their deliberate 'enculturation.' In truth, most of us recognise

culture as the product of the relationships between individuals and the way in which the group legitimises and mediates those through a range of artefacts. An additional element that sits on top of this, of course, is its productive capacity to sustain itself and oftentimes to develop over time and regardless of change in the group personnel (Schein, 1997, pp. 3–15) but that judgement seems to desert us as OD practitioners when we are commissioned to do work on culture, particularly when we are asked to work on 'changing' it.

The suggestion that culture extends management as argued above holds great credence for me. One author periodises management orientations towards lifting productivity, from bureaucratic control (where reward is manipulated) through humanistic control (where satisfaction is key) to culture control, wherein myth and ritual is manipulated to generate love of the firm (Ray, 1986); this seems an honest appraisal of the impacts of the shifts in organisational practice that are discernible over time. And this is an area of activity, of course, which OD practitioners readily occupy, oftentimes without much critical thought as to what they are being asked to do. One author observes that,

> Organisational psychologists have always maintained a close relationship with practising managers and this interchange has grown even stronger as top management increasingly commission them to assist in corporate culture initiatives. Practitioners tend to perceive their efforts as benign and in accord with their espoused humanistic ideals. Few practitioners ever question the ethical-moral ramifications of their activities and typically view themselves as benignly applying knowledge derived from their training in the "legitimate field of scientific inquiry" that is organisational psychology.
>
> (Bagraim, 2001, p. 43)

At a recent event I organised where organisational culture was explored from an anthropological perspective, the conversation in the room took its time to slide below the surface of the day-to-day thinking and practice of those present – yet, when it did, a wealth of topics arose which are rarely perceived, let alone acknowledged, in this area of work. Chief amongst these was the issue of how much of this work reifies culture, in order to indulge the illusion that an agent outside of that structure can act upon it with the intention of changing it. This fiction of being able to exteriorise oneself from the culture that prevails in a given setting was necessary in order to be able to reconcile with what leaders in organisations often ask OD practitioners to do.

The flipside of this is that each and every individual in a given context will have within their gift – through their reflexive awareness and ability to act differently, both individually and collectively – the capacity to shape and reshape the culture in which they automatically find themselves. This, then, is how culture changes, not through grand programmes to reboot it but through the minute actions and interrelations that make up the organisation. Indeed, those grand top-down programmes are not merely benign yet ultimately unrealistic interventions; they end up serving an altogether different purpose of ideologising the workplace on the basis of what is tacitly perceived to be how people might best be controlled.

This cannot ever be unidirectional, as perhaps commentators from the Marxian perspective might assert. Indeed, as someone at the event took pains to underscore, there may be positive outcomes from such planned interventions. And, of course, those in the workplace should not be seen as mute recipients of this ideology: resistance, as noted above, remains a key element of the richness of life in the workplace – and resistance to efforts to change culture continue to undermine the idea that this type of intervention is meaningful and effective. Alongside all of this, the discussion encompassed a range of other ordinarily bracketed off notions in our conversations about culture. These included: the regularly disregarded place of power in the workplace; issues of individual ethics and the interplay with organisational constraint; and the vital place of emotion, again a concept that we tend to see as problematic in our day-to-day experiences of the workplace.

In many cases, projects designed to transform corporate culture tend to focus on two closely interlinked items: first, the idea of values, particularly values to be shared across an entire organisation, regardless of its reach or complexity; and, second, either implicit or explicit in relation to those values, a set of behaviours that are expected in a corporate context. I have already mentioned the biggest exercise of this sort in which I have been involved as a practitioner, which involved an organisation with a headcount of around 1200 people. It arose as a direct response to an intense period of corporate restructuring that, at one point, saw two-thirds of that workforce formally at risk. As levels of morale sank and a sense of profound disruption resonated around the organisation, the response of senior leadership was to embark on an initiative around culture.

This was articulated as an effort to put the firm back in contact with its values base, to recapture (in some fashion) all that had motivated people to work for the organisation in the first place. The work – stretched over a prolonged period and delivered in conjunction with external expertise – supposedly engaged 500 staff and clients in order to generate an owned set of six corporate values. A range of techniques – including appreciative inquiry focus groups – were used in order to spark what was seen as an organisation-wide conversation. Where senior leaders saw dialogue, others might reasonably have observed that two monologues were taking place: the organisation speaking soothingly to the workforce without being heard; and the staff robustly pushing back to the organisation, articulating their negative experiences of the restructuring, including loss of position, status, salary, and colleagues, to which the organisation largely paid lip service. In such cases, I am often reminded of the horrific scene in the film *Dangerous Liaisons* (Dangerous Liaisons, 1988), where the Vicomte de Valmont – in unwillingly giving up his lover, Madame de Tournel, as part of the wider machinations in the piece – endlessly repeats that it is beyond his control (YouTube, 1988).

The outputs from this work were two-fold: six commonplace values, to which now the whole workforce was expected to align; and a matrix of behaviours in traffic light coloured columns, with green those that 'we' would like to see more of and 'red' those that we would not expect to see. Insofar as the fiction was that people had been actively involved in the formulation of the values and had expressed opinions about behaviours that related to each of the six, it was discursively legitimate to use the term 'we' in the promotion of this work – but it seems reasonable to observe that this was not a sense of ownership felt at large. But the use of 'we' helpfully defines what would be acceptable in this context – who could think differently about these values and behaviours when 'we' have all worked to craft them? – and hence who would become the Other by not aligning with those values and behaving in a way that was not consonant with them.

As a postscript to this, the arrival of a new Chief Executive in the organisation led them to suggest that six values were too many. An exercise was undertaken to reduce them down to three. (In keeping with the wider sense of vagueness around corporate culture, there is no clear indication beyond personal preference why six is too many values and three is just right, other than that we obsess about Goldilocks options without much serious thought about what this means. I recall a conversation between senior leaders about reconfiguring the number of business units in an organisation: 'It feels like six is too many, yet four is too few,' opined one; 'Would it be five, then?' queried the other, helpfully.) Interestingly, the passage of time allowed the senior leadership to disregard the fiction of engagement that had underpinned the generation of the original set of values in order to feel confident to discard the supposed 'work' of the whole workforce in creating them. And, in truth, I doubt that anyone in the workforce seriously felt that their honest endeavour was being thoughtlessly cast aside, although shamefully – as the OD practitioner who had invested very heavily in the initial exercise – I ended up feeling a profound sense of betrayal and loss, given the commitment that I had given to it, and perhaps the psychic effort that had been required to bury away the clear conflict between the overall activity (its motivations, construction and delivery) and my own occupational values.

Conclusion

I have sought in this chapter to look afresh – and from a somewhat oblique angle – at the common-sense work that is undertaken under the rubric of OD. It has not been my intention to denigrate those who work diligently in the field, seeking to humanise the workplace whilst thereby supporting organisations to derive greater effectiveness through those human connections and interrelations in the workplace. I am one of that number – and hope, despite this critique, to continue working in the field.

That said, organisational life is not straightforward, particularly when one firmly locates it in its social, economic, and technical context: it is capitalism that defines our means of production and the relationships that derive from that, in terms of employers and employees, managers and shareholders, and so on. And so OD practices should not go without being properly scrutinised, particularly when so many working in the field cleave to the notion that this work is progressive, humanistic, and (at the most extreme) liberatory.

This chapter demonstrates, I hope, that not all is as it seems. The impact of OD in a capitalistic organisational context is manifold – and carries all manner of unintended consequences. At worst, OD is a means of veiling the worst excesses of modern work and the places where it takes place, fostering illusions of involvement and sometimes even empowerment. At best, it is seeking to ameliorate those excesses – but from firmly within the context in which that work can take place. It simply does not challenge the underlying organisational premises – and, by that omission, serves unwittingly to reinforce them.

But it was not my intention to offer a solely negative view of all that can be done under the general rubric of OD. The conclusion I reach from drawing from the experience across my years of practice is that there is much that could be said to be wrong with OD – but that there is potentially a more authentic and honest way to practice it, one that will resonate with the ideologies of empowerment and involvement that so many organisations promote but do not observe. Their notional commitment to these ideas opens up a space where OD practitioners can – if they so choose – work differently and in a way that represents a challenge to organisational life as it currently stands rather than simply reinforcing it. My ideas as to what that new approach to OD might look like follow in the next chapter of this book – and represent a call to action to all who think of OD as an activity that might offer a perturbation to the commonly accepted ways of being and doing in organisational life in the 21st century and beyond.

Bibliography

Anderson, P., 1979. *Considerations on Western Marxism*. London: Verso.

Bagraim, J. J., 2001. Organisational psychology and workplace control: The instrumentality of corporate culture. *South African Journal of Psychology*, 31(3), pp. 43–49.

Belbin, R. M., n.d. *Belbin home page*. [Online]. Available at: https://www.belbin.com/ [Accessed 14 August 2018].

Belbin, R. M., 2010. *Management teams: Why they succeed or fail*. 3rd ed. London: Routledge.

Benyon, H., 1975. *Working for Ford*. Wakefield: EP Publishing.

Bion, W. R., 2001. *Experiences in groups and other papers*. Hove: Brunner-Routledge.

Bjorkelo, B. & Madsen, O. J., 2013. Whistleblowing and neoliberalism: Political resistance in late capitalist society. *Psychology & Society*, 5(2), pp. 28–40.

Block, P., 2011. *Flawless consulting: A guide to getting your expertise used*. 3rd ed. s.l.: John Wiley & Sons.

Bourdieu, P., 1998. *The essence of neoliberalism*. [Online]. Available at: https://mondediplo.com/1998/12/08bourdieu [Accessed 1 August 2018].

Boyle, G. J., 1995. *Myers-Briggs Type Indicator: Some psychometric limitations.* [Online]. Available at: http://epublications.bond.edu.au/hss_pubs/26 [Accessed 2018 September 28].

Buller, P. F., 1986. The team building-task performance relation: Some conceptual and methodological refinements. *Group & Organization Studies,* 11(3), pp. 147–168.

Bushe, G. R. & Marshak, R. J. eds., 2015. *Dialogic organization development: The theory and practice of transformational change.* 1st ed. Oakland, CA: Berrett-Koehler.

By, R. T., 2005. Organisational change management: A critical review. *Journal of Change Management,* 5(4), pp. 369–380.

Cain, S., 2013. *Quiet: The power of introverts in world that can't stop talking.* London: Penguin.

Carey, A., 1967. The Hawthorne studies: A radical criticism. *American Sociological Review,* 32(3), pp. 403–416.

Carucci, R., 2018. *How to fix the most soul-crushing meetings.* [Online]. Available at: https://hbr.org/2018/02/how-to-fix-the-most-soul-crushing-meetings [Accessed 13 July 2018].

Case, P. & Phillipson, G., 2004. Astronomy, alchemy and retro-organization theory: An astro-genealogical critique of the Myers-Briggs Type Indicator. *Organization,* 11(4), pp. 473–495.

Chia, R., 2014. Reflections: In praise of silent transformation – Allowing change through 'letting happen'. *Journal of Change Management,* 14(1), pp. 8–27.

Coens, T. & Jenkins, M., 2000. *Abolishing performance appraisals: Why they backfire and what to do instead.* San Francisco, CA: Berrett-Koehler.

Cole, M., 2018. *On attentiveness.* [Online]. Available at: https://colefellows.wordpress.com/2018/06/06/on-attentiveness/ [Accessed 18 July 2018].

Cooperrider, D. L. & Srivastva, S., 1987. Appreciative inquiry in organizational life. *Research in Organizational Change and Development,* 1, pp. 129–169.

Criado Perez, C., 2019. *Invisible women: Exposing data bias in a world designed for men.* London: Chatto & Windus.

Cummings, S., Bridgman, T. & Brown, K. G., 2016. Unfreezing change as three steps: Rethinking Kurt Lewin's legacy for change management. *Human Relations,* 69(1), pp. 33–60.

Dangerous Liaisons, 1988. [Film] Directed by Stephen Frears. USA/UK: Lorimar Film Entertainment; NFH Productions; Warner Bros.

Denison, D. R., 1996. What is the difference between organizational culture and organizational climate? A native's point of view on a decade of paradigm wars. *The Academy of Management Review,* 21(3), pp. 619–654.

Devine, D. J. et al., 1999. Teams in Organizations: Prevalence, Characteristics, and Effectiveness. *Small Group Research,* 30(6), pp. 678–711.

Donzelot, J., 1991. Pleasure in work. In: G. Burchell, C. Gordon & P. Miller, eds. *The Foucault effect: Studies in governmentality.* Chicago: University of Chicago Press, pp. 251–280.

Doray, B., 1988. *From Taylorism to Fordism: A rational madness.* London: Free Association Books.

Dweck, C. S., 2006. *Mindset: The new psychology of success.* New York: Random House.

Emre, M., 2018. *What's your type? The strange history of Myers-Briggs and the birth of personality testing.* London: William Collins.

Fleming, P., 2005. Workers' playtime? Boundaries and cynicism in a 'Culture of Fun' programme. *The Journal of Applied Behavioral Science,* 41(3), pp. 285–303.

Fleming, P. & Sewell, G., 2002. Looking for the good soldier, Svejk: Alternative modalities of resistance in the contemporary workplace. *Sociology,* 36(4), pp. 857–873.

Fleming, P. & Spicer, A., 2003. Working at a cynical distance: Implications for power, subjectivity and resistance. *Organization,* 10(1), pp. 157–179.

Fleming, P. & Study, A., 2009. Bringing everyday life back into the workplace: Just be yourself! In: P. Hancock & M. Tyler, eds. *The management of everyday life.* Basingstoke: Palgrave Macmillan, pp. 199–216.

Foucault, M., 1983. *Discourse and truth: The Problematization of Parrhesia – 6 lectures given by Michel Foucault at the University of California at Berkeley, Oct–Nov. 1983.* [Online]. Available at: https://foucault.info/parrhesia/ [Accessed 1 August 2018].

Foucault, M., 1988a. Technologies of the self. In: L. H. Martin, H. Gutman & P. H. Hutton, eds. *Technologies of the self: A seminar with Michel Foucault.* Amherst: University of Massachusetts Press, pp. 16–49.

Foucault, M., 1988b. *Madness and civilization: A history of insanity in the age of reason.* New York: Vintage Books.

Foucault, M., 1991. *Discipline and punish: The birth of the prison.* London: Penguin.

Freeman, R. B. & Rogers, J., 2006. *What workers want.* Ithaca, NY: Cornell University Press.

French, J. R. P., 1964. Laboratory and field studies of power. In: R. L. Kahn & E. Boulding, eds. *Power and conflict in organisations.* London: Tavistock Publications, pp. 33–51.

Gabriel, Y., 1999. Beyond happy families: A critical reevaluation of the control-resistance-identity triangle. *Human Relations,* 52(2), pp. 179–203.

Garrod, B. & Ling, T., 2018. *System change through situated learning: Pre-evaluation of the Healthcare Innovation Network's Communities of Practice.* Cambridge: Rand Europe.

Greiner, L. E. & Schein, V. E., 1989. *Power and organization development: Mobilizing power to implement change.* Reading, MA: Addison-Wesley.

Grint, K., 2007. What's wrong with performance appraisals? A critique and a suggestion. *Human Resource Management Journal,* 3(3), pp. 61–77.

Han, B.-C., 2017. *Psychopolitics: Neoliberalism and new technologies of power.* London: Verso.

Hancock, P., 2009. Management and colonization of everyday life. In: P. Hancock & M. Tyler, eds. *The management of everyday life.* Basingstoke: Palgrave Macmillan, pp. 1–20.

Harrison, R. G., 1984. Reasserting the radical potential of OD: Notes towards the establishment of a new basis for OD practice. *Personnel Review,* 13(2), pp. 12–18.

Hassard, J. S., 2012. Rethinking the Hawthorne Studies: The Western Electric research in its social, political and historical context. *Human Relations,* 65(11), pp. 1431–1461.

Heimans, J. & Timms, H., 2014. Understanding 'new power.' *Harvard Business Review,* December, pp. 48–56.

Hersey, P. & Blanchard, K. H., 1969. Life cycle theory of leadership. *Training & Development Journal,* 23, pp. 26–34.

Hirschman, A. O., 1970. *Exit, voice and loyalty: Responses to decline in firms, organizations and states.* Cambridge, MA: Harvard University Press.

Hughes, M., 2011. Do 70 per cent of all organizational change initiatives really fail? *Journal of Change Management,* 11(4), pp. 451–464.

Institute for Organisational Development, 2019. *Membership.* [Online]. Available at: http://www.instituteforod.org.uk/membership/the-institute-for-organisational-development-why-join/ [Accessed 21 March 2019].

Jackson, N. & Carter, P., 1998. Labour as dressage. In: A. McKinlay & K. Starkey, eds. *Foucault, management and organization theory: From Panopticon to technologies of the self.* London: Sage Publications, pp. 49–64.

Kenny, K., 2018. Censored: Whistleblowers and impossible speech. *Human Relations,* 71(8), pp. 1025–1048.

Kleiner, A., 2008. *The age of heretics: A history of the radical thinkers who invented corporate management.* San Francisco, CA: Jossey-Bass.

Kline, N., 1999. *Time To think: Listening to ignite the human mind.* London: Ward Lock.

Kotter, J. P., 1995. Leading change: Why transformation efforts fail. *Harvard Business Review,* March–April, pp. 59–67.

Lave, J. & Wenger, E., 1991. *Situated learning: Legitimate peripheral participation.* Cambridge: Cambridge University Press.

Lawrence, T. B. & Robinson, S. L., 2007. Ain't misbehavin': Workplace deviance as organizational resistance. *Journal of Management,* 33(3), pp. 378–394.

Lazzarato, M., 2002. From biopower to biopolitics. *Pli,* 13, pp. 99–113.

Lewin, K., 1947. Frontiers in group dynamics: Concept, method and reality in social science; social equilibria and social change. *Human Relations,* 1(5), pp. 5–41.

Lewis, S., 2011. *Positive psychology at work: How positive leadership and appreciative inquiry create inspiring organizations.* Chichester: Wiley-Blackwell.

Lyubovnikova, J., West, M. A., Dawson, J. F. & Carter, M. R., 2015. 24-Karat or fool's gold? Consequences of real team and co-acting group membership in healthcare organizations. *European Journal of Work and Organizational Psychology*, 24(6), pp. 929–950.

Mackey, R. H., 1992. *Translating vision into reality: The role of the strategic leader*. Carlisle Barracks, PA: US Army War College.

Mayo, E., 1949. *The social problems of an industrial civilization (with an appendix on the political problem)*. Abingdon: Routledge.

McEwan, D. et al., 2017. The effectiveness of teamwork training on teamwork behaviors and team performance: A systematic review and meta-analysis of controlled interventions. *PLoS One*, 12(1), e0169604.

McKendall, M., 1993. The tyranny of change: Organisational development revisited. *Journal of Business Ethics*, 12, pp. 93–104.

McKinlay, A. & Taylor, P., 2018. *Foucault, governmentality, and organization: Inside the factory of the future*. Abingdon: Routledge.

McLean, A., 1981. Organisation development: A case of the Emperor's new clothes? *Personnel Review*, 10(1), pp. 3–14.

Menzies, I. E. P., 1960. A case-study in the functioning of social systems as a defence against anxiety: A report on a study of the nursing service of a general hospital. *Human Relations*, 13, pp. 95–121.

Metcalfe, B. & Linstead, A., 2003. Gendering teamwork: Re-writing the feminine. *Gender, Work and Organization*, 10(1), pp. 94–119.

Mir, A. & Mir, R., 2005. Producing the governable employee: The strategic deployment of workforce empowerment. *Cultural Dynamics*, 17(1), pp. 51–72.

Mumby, D. K., 2005. Theorizing resistance in organization studies: A dialectical approach. *Management Communication Quarterly*, 19(1), pp. 19–44.

NHS Leadership Academy, 2013. *Healthcare leadership model: The nine dimensions of leadership behaviour*. Leeds: NHS Leadership Academy.

Ogbonna, E., 1992. Managing organisational culture: Fantasy or reality? *Human Resource Management Journal*, 3(2), pp. 42–54.

Orr, J. E., 1996. *Talking about machines: An ethnography of a modern job*. New York: ILR Press/ Cornell University Press.

Oshry, B., 2016. *In the middle*. Boston: Power + Systems.

Oswick, C., 2009. Revisioning or re-versioning? A commentary on diagnostic and dialogic forms of organization development. *Journal of Applied Behavioral Science*, 45(3), pp. 369–374.

Perlow, L. A., Noonan Hadley, C. & Eun, E., 2017. Stop the meeting madness: How to free up time for meaningful work. *Harvard Business Review*, July–August.

Pittenger, D. J., 2005. Cautionary comments regarding the Myers-Briggs Type Indicator. *Consulting Psychology Journal: Practice and Research*, 57(3), pp. 210–221.

Pritchard, J. S. & Stanton, N. A., 1999. Testing Belbin's team role theory of effective groups. *Journal of Management Development*, 18(8), pp. 652–665.

Purser, R., 2000. The human relations myth unveiled: Deconstructing the history and origin of work teams. In: M. M. Beyerlein, ed. *Work teams: Past, present and future*. s.l.: Kluwer Academic Publishers, pp. 59–83.

Ray, C. A., 1986. Corporate culture: The last frontier of control? *Journal of Management Studies*, 23, pp. 287–297.

Reinecke, J., 2018. Social movements and prefigurative organizing: Confronting entrenched inequalities in Occupy London. *Organization Studies*, 39(9), pp. 1299–1321.

Reitz, M. & Higgins, J., 2017. *The problem with saying 'My door is always open.'* [Online]. Available at: https://hbr.org/2017/03/the-problem-with-saying-my-door-is-always-open [Accessed 18 July 2018].

Rock, D., 2008. SCARF: A brain-based model for collaborating with and influencing others. *NeuroLeadership Journal*, 1, pp. 1–9.

Rogelberg, S. G., Scott, C. & Kello, J., 2007. The science and fiction of meetings. *MIT Sloane Management Review*, 48(Winter), pp. 18–21.

Salas, E. et al., 2008. Does team training improve team performance? A meta-analysis. *Human Factors*, 50(6), pp. 903–933.

Salas, E., Sims, D. E. & Shawn Burke, C., 2005. Is there a 'big five' in teamwork? *Small Group Research*, 36(5), pp. 555–599.

Salmon, C., 2017. *Storytelling: Bewitching the modern mind*. London: Verso.

Saville Assessment, n.d. *Build talent with wave*. [Online]. Available at: https://www.savilleassessment.com/build-talent-with-wave/ [Accessed 4 October 2018].

Schein, E., 1997. *Organizational culture and leadership*. San Francisco: Jossey-Bass.

Schrage, M., 1995. *No more teams! Mastering the dynamics of creative collaboration*. New York: Currency Doubleday.

Sementelli, A. J., 2016. OD, change management, and the a priori: Introducing parrhesia. *Journal of Organisational Change Management*, 29(7), pp. 1083–1096.

Senge, P. M., 2006. *The fifth discipline: The art and practice of organizational learning*. New York: Currency/Doubleday.

Shepard, J. M., 1971. On Alex Carey's radical criticism of the Hawthorne studies. *Academy of Management Journal*, 14(1), pp. 23–32.

Stein, R. & Swan, A. B., 2019. Evaluating the validity of Myers-Briggs Type Indicator theory: A teaching tool and window into intuitive psychology. *Social and Personality Psychology Compass*, 13(2), e12434.

Sundstrom, E., De Meuse, K. P. & Futrell, D., 1990. Work teams: Applications and effectiveness. *American Psychologist*, 45(2), pp. 120–133.

Thompson, P. & Ackroyd, S., 1995. All quiet on the workforce front? A critique of recent trends in British industrial sociology. *Sociology*, 29(4), pp. 615–633.

Thompson, P. & van den Broek, D., 2010. Managerial control and workplace regimes: An introduction. *Work, Employment and Society,* 24(3), pp. 1–12.

Trades Union Congress, 2018. *I'll be watching you: A report on workplace monitoring.* London: TUC.

Tsoukas, H. & Chia, R., 2002. On organizational becoming: Rethinking organizational change. *Organization Science,* 13(5), pp. 567–582.

Valikangas, A. & Seeck, H., 2011. Exploring the Foucauldian interpretation of power and subject in organisations. *Journal of Management and Organization,* 17(6), pp. 812–827.

Wenger, E., 1998. *Communities of Practice: Learning, meaning, and identity.* Cambridge: Cambridge University Press.

West, M. A., 2012. *Effective teamwork: Practical lessons from organizational research.* 3rd ed. Chichester: BPS/John Wiley & Sons.

West, M. A. & Markiewicz, L., 2016. Effective team working in health care. In: E. Ferlie, K. Montgomery & A. R. Pedersen, eds. *The Oxford handbook of health care management.* Oxford: Oxford University Press, pp. 231–252.

Whitmore, J., 2017. *Coaching for performance: The principles and practice of coaching and leadership.* 5th ed. London: Nicholas Brealey Publishing.

Whyte, W. H., 1957. *The organization man.* London: Jonathan Cape.

Wikipedia, 2018. *Lava.* [Online]. Available at: https://en.wikipedia.org/wiki/Lava [Accessed 22 November 2018].

Willmott, H., 1993. Strength is ignorance; slavery is freedom: Managing culture in modern organizations. *Journal of Management Studies,* 30(4), pp. 515–552.

Woodhouse, D. & Pengelly, P., 1991. *Anxiety and the dynamics of collaboration.* Aberdeen: Aberdeen University Press.

YouTube, 1988. *It's beyond my control (Les Liaisons Dangereuses).* [Online]. Available at: https://www.youtube.com/watch?v=QlWsLStRAiw [Accessed 27 November 2018].

Zizek, S., 2018. *The courage of hopelessness: Chronicles of a year of acting dangerously.* London: Penguin Random House UK.

5

TOWARDS A TRULY RADICAL OD PRACTICE

On 25 September 2018, I posted a short paragraph on LinkedIn. I use the platform a good deal for professional purposes, sharing ideas and making observations in the hope that the network will engage in a virtual conversation on issues around organisation development (OD) practice. On this occasion, I made the following brief comment:

> Organisations would be better off spending money on meaningful consultation rather than on consultants. The lived experience and rich range of ideas for doing things differently reside in the workforce as opposed to expensive external "opinion".

Three days later, the post had attracted 3773 views, 21 likes, and 53 comments. This was the most activity I had ever solicited through posting something on LinkedIn. In truth, I had given little thought to the comments – they are implicit in my thinking, as this book will hopefully have shown – whereas on other occasions I have shared detailed material and fresh thinking from various quarters and stirred little interest out there in the ether. So, what was it about this posting that had caused such a reaction?

My view is that the sentiment underlying the post struck at the very heart of the justifications that OD practitioners assemble to rationalise their practice in the face of the confounding evidence that is instantly visible in organisational settings. As a general rule of thumb, the strongest push backs that I saw in terms of this post came from those who located their work in a tradition that suggests that OD work is in some way humanistic and progressive. Very often, these were expressed in terms of how the correspondent viewed their practice as significantly different in terms of engagement. This, of course, neglected the core quality of the original observation: that any intermediation by a practitioner has the potential to distort the voice of the workforce by passing it through that practitioner's filter.

This is not to say that many of these respondents are not endeavouring to do the best in a difficult arena. But their refutations showed a limited awareness of the distortions that their presence in a workplace – let alone the interventions that they fashioned and sought to deliver – might have in respect to that workforce. And, for me, it showed a worryingly resolute refusal to acknowledge the socio-economic context in which they sought to do this work.

One interesting element in this was that many of the comments that sought to self-justify practice in the face of this pithily delivered critique came from people who worked as freelance consultants. I could not help but reflect that the 'dull compulsion of the economic' – something to which the vast majority of us are obliged to show obeisance, in order to feed, clothe, and house ourselves and our families – was distorting the way in which these people were thinking about their practice: underpinnings and implications were disregarded, with the focus entirely on the superficial celebration of getting things done. The reverse of this was that very few who practised in organisations as a salaried member of staff took issue with the sentiment being expressed.

But, of course, it is not my intention merely to criticise, to carp from the sidelines about the work that people endeavour to do. My years of practice and the conceptual way in which I choose to engage with the world and make sense of it left me initially at an impasse in terms of my day-to-day work. But I retain an optimism about what OD can be and how it might have an impact on organisations and people who make them up. So, my earlier interrogation of current OD practice and my observations of what I perceive to be its impacts and implications is to be viewed alongside this chapter, which seeks to sketch out a fresh and different practice – a truly radical approach to OD – that I think could offer those of us who want what we do to be positive, authentically people focused, and freighted with rich meaning with an orientation by which to explore a different way of working.

In this chapter, then, I will explore seven aspects of that radical orientation, in order to offer practitioners access to ideas and potential practices that might positively refashion the work. Patently, many OD practitioners are content with what they do, how they do it, and what impact it has. I have applied a critique to that approach elsewhere in this book, but I recognise that the reaction of many to those views will be to seek to refute them and possibly dig in deeper to how they currently do their work. There may be others who are interested to come with me on a journey towards whatever that new approach to practice might be – and will throw themselves wholeheartedly into that project. I look forward to the collective inquiry that this will generate. And there will be those for whom the critique has resonated, to some greater or lesser extent, but who cannot commit to a root and branch overhaul of what they do and how they do it. They are very welcome also, for any positive impact is a good thing ... and offers insight into ways of doing things differently from a perspective other than the one I have sought to advance here. I have an earnest hope that this will open up a field-wide discussion amongst engaged practitioners as to how OD can be changed to better reflect the intentions of those who do this work – and those currently who are often the object of it.

The person and the power

The Foucauldian view of the way in which OD presents itself in the workplace context is one that largely seeks not to make a judgement about right and wrong, in terms of impact and outcome. The work that we do simply represents an expression of the discourse that prevails in the world of 'business' and, of course, also serves to reinforce that discourse. Critical writers from other traditions have taken a less kindly attitude to this issue: 'To put it bluntly, organizational psychology emerged to facilitate the bureaucratic processes of twentieth century corporate capitalism' is a declarative dismissal of an area of practice where many people feel that they are endeavouring to make a positive difference to others (Fischer, 1984, p. 172).

Unfortunately, this type of perspective tends to divide people into heroes and villains – and the synecdoche of 'organisational psychology' is a way of crudely implying agency to an entire field of practice.

It seems apparent, then, that OD practice is enmeshed in the production and action of power/knowledge in the workplace, which is both shaped by the prevailing discourse and, of course, serves to constitute it by those activities. Our work reinforces the notions that the organisation is an active collective, with all of its elements pursuing the same shared goal. Partly, this is a linguistic sleight of hand: we opt to use the term 'organisation' thereby usefully avoiding having to use the more obvious description of the company, the firm or, indeed, 'the business.' Interestingly, in my experience, the use of this latter term in the context of healthcare in the UK generates an extraordinary adverse reaction. Indeed, the attitude of clinical staff in the NHS towards notions of management – and their practical engagement in this –is largely negative, with one study reporting a significant number of those identified in the system as 'nurse managers' in a variety of roles at varying levels of seniority declaring that they actively disagreed with management values (Bolton, 2005).

And yet, in a capitalistic context, of course, the NHS is a 'business.' It doesn't dance to the tune of profit and loss, for sure, but it is constantly limited by the financial context in which it sits. There is money paid by commissioners for service – and providers of NHS services can be put into 'special measures' in respect to issues of either quality of care or financial management. For a private company, the market – in principle – flushes out issues of quality or cost. The travails of popular middle-class cake shop Patisserie Valerie underscore this, of course, with news that landlords for some of the properties occupied by the firm had to send in the bailiffs (Kinder & Ralph, 2018). For the NHS, the state acts as a proxy for the market. This does not alter the fact that the delivery of healthcare is conducted within a managed market and is not merely an altruistic provision.

So, for those of us practising in the public sector, our work might be said to veil the true nature of the relations of production as they play across the provision of such services. However, the work that we do is riven with the language of the market and business. We work to enhance organisational effectiveness by focusing our efforts on the people that make up the organisation. This, at its root, is the Janus-faced character of OD in context: we seek to deliver hard-nosed business effectiveness by acting upon the workforce in ways that appear humanistic. Importantly, the texture of our work weaves into the overall business discourse and serves to create the illusion that the modern workplace is in some way distanced from the crude functioning of a capitalist economy. Something has changed, we seem to say, and our work helps you to build the fiction that fundamentally your position in the workplace is in some way different – and, indeed, better.

There is a similar effect in the private sector: whilst the harsh realities of success and failure are writ large in businesses there, OD activity seeks to establish the fiction that the modern workplace is qualitatively different to that which prevailed when scientific management and Fordism was preeminent. Now, it would be foolhardy to suggest that they are not noticeable differences at a superficial level, certainly. But I would want to contest the underlying narrative – one that is woven tightly into the discourse of the world of work – that we have experienced a progressive move from a benighted state to an enlightened one. Initiatives around staff involvement, health, and well-being, culture management, flat management structures are, I contend, mere epiphenomena, activity conducted at such velocity and clothed in such noble language that they serve to obfuscate the workplace as a location where reluctance, resistance, and a general weariness about how things get done and how people are treated remain.

As one writer observes, many contemporary practices (and the technologies that we deploy in support of them) seem aimed at trying to manage the employee's soul: in this context, the modern employee should 'become self-initiating, take responsibility, and see for themselves what the organisation needs' (Villadsen, 2007, p. 1). In that sense, it goes beyond mere cosmetic shrouding, significant though that is in the workplace context: at a deeper level, this approach reinforces the notion that management is working to make work a positive experience, so to cavil about workplace issues would seem to be petty and ungrateful. It would appear that '...the employee should not be told what to do, but should be stimulated so as to "take initiatives by his (sic) own initiative"' (Villadsen, 2007, p. 2).

The flow of managerialism into the realms of the everyday seems apparent, as life outside of work is increasingly viewed through notions such as effectiveness, efficiency, entrepreneurialism, and measurement (Hancock, 2009, p. 7). This implicates my two friends I have mentioned who, at the beginning of each year, craft for themselves a set of 'family objectives.'

Work and home have folded into one another, in terms of the way in which managerial thinking and techniques have landed in their personal lives. However, as noted previously, other writers have critically discussed how everyday life is now being actively accommodated into the management of organisations, with the invitation being extended to the workforce to bring their identities, feelings, and lifestyles into the organisational space in order to foster 'fun' and ideas of diversity of voice (Fleming & Study, 2009).

From a Foucauldian perspective, of course, this discourse around working on the soul of the individual in the workplace represents the way in which power/knowledge has an amplified presence in the organisation. OD practitioners do not merely act in the spaces where people seek to work together; we also reinforce the relations that prevail in that context. As noted previously, one of the ways in which power/knowledge impacts is through its categorisation, with the implication that this activity defines normalcy – in this instance, what is seen to be acceptable or desired workplace practice by everyone in that workplace – and the Otherness that is generated in contradistinction to the prescribed normal attitude, behaviour, and interrelatedness with others. In OD, as soon as we are summonsed by a commissioner to undertake work to deal with a 'difficult' team, we are reinforcing the power in that context by subtly acquiescing to a model of normalcy to which the team in question does not comply. Despite what might be seen to be lack of positional power for the OD practitioner, it seems to be that our practice plays a key role in the way in which power/knowledge is created and experienced in the organisation.

Moreover, our work carries the imprimatur of the powerful in these organisations. I cannot think of an instance where an OD practitioner has been called in by the workforce, although some teams – demonstrating a high level of immersion in the prevailing discourse – may volunteer themselves through their manager for an intervention of this sort. OD is done at the behest of management in organisations – and so our agency in these spaces is given authority through that association and not, as we would like to perhaps hope, through a general acceptance of the efficaciousness of the work that we do and the benign experience of that activity by those with whom we work. So, as we appear in the workplace setting to work with people in the organisation, we are reinforcing two things: first, the prevailing discourse of the organisation, not least through what is seen as normal and hence what is seen as Other in this context; and, second, the hierarchy that exists in the organisation (or, in those organisations that maintain the fiction of having abolished management or having completely flat structures, the subsumed relations of authority that exist in lieu of formal structure).

Hence, many in the field begin to become bedazzled with the ways in which power might be used as a resource by which to advance the notionally progressive agenda of OD, thereby disregarding the ways in which OD is intrinsic to a more nuanced notion of power, particularly in the workplace. Some conflate the notion of power with that of organisational politics, offering sets of rules for conduct for OD in such a context, all of which leave the power at play in the space in which they are working unspoken and hence unchallenged (French & Bell, 1978, pp. 292–294). The passage of time has not diminished this notion: at a recent presentation at an OD event which expressly referenced the question of power, Mee Yan Cheung Judge was invited to offer the closing keynote and defaulted to an outline in respect to power that encompassed ideas such as using data to convince others and using organisational rules to advance our work (Cheung-Judge, 2019). Others become entranced by instrumentalist notions of positional power in the contexts in which they might find themselves working, as underscored here: 'To understand power in an organization, I must learn who the primary decision-makers are, where they are located in the managerial hierarchy, and how their decisions are typically made' (Burke, 1982, p. 137).

These things might reasonably be said to be structurally unavoidable in the context in which we find ourselves. But, as practitioners, we can either subsume ourselves to these effects – or we can seek to expose them in order that we might begin to subvert them. A starting point for us as practitioners might be to begin to rethink the goal of effectiveness. And there are critical traditions that might support us to 'unlearn' our practice to date – and to strike out as pioneers to define through our day-to-day activity a new way of doing what we do, one of which is anarchism. This may, at first glance, not seem to be the most productive body of thought and activity with which to engage when discussing organisation. But, in fact, as an anarchist author exploring this topic insists,

> You may think in describing anarchism as a theory of organisation I am propounding a deliberate paradox: "anarchy" you may consider to be, by definition, the opposite of organisation. In fact, however, "anarchy"

means the absence of government, the absence of authority. Can there be social organisation without authority, without government? The anarchists claim that there can be, and they also claim that it is desirable that there should be.

(Ward, 1966)

This helpfully lays the ground for us to investigate ways in which we might recast our work and reorient that practice so that the power implicit in conversations about effectiveness might be considered:

The anarchist conceptualization of organizational effectiveness requires additional considerations: *who set the goals and what are their social consequences?* And so an organisation would be defined as effective to *the degree to which all of its participants were involved in formulating its goals, to the degree to which its goals did not contribute to human discomfort, and to the degree to which it achieved those goals.* [Emphasis added]

(Ehrlich, 1996, p. 60)

If, as someone involved in OD, we opened any conversation with a commissioner of our services with this question – who set the goals and what are their social consequences – and explored the three implications that follow, it would make explicit the power in the context where we seek to practice. If we were then to carry this forward as the starting point for the work that we did with people in the workplace, it would not transcend the power at play but would surely draw attention to it and place it in a conversational space where it could be at least acknowledged and possibly challenged. The mere challenge, of course, does not necessarily kick over the statues. The world is rife with examples where challenge has expressed itself forcefully but the flow of a desire for a collective change ebbs as the system – and the power/knowledge formation – reasserts the status quo. The one that stands out most noticeably for me is the example of the Arab Spring as it manifested in Egypt, where the ebullient desire for change was absorbed into an institutional response. But it does at least allow people to think differently about their experiences and possibly imagine an authentic way in which a different and more positive sort of experience could be crafted.

The mistake would be to view a more radically oriented approach to OD as declaring a revolution, when instead it is presaging the liberation of thinking and the potential to inhabit the system the better to subvert it and unravel its myriad precepts. A Radical OD practice aims to allow people to explore the various ways in which they might deconstruct the discourse, thereby undermining its foundations in so-called normalcy and common sense. After all, too much revolution in human history has been about the voices of a dedicated few chiming noisily and pulling the vast majority of the others hither and thither, the best to serve that minority agenda.

This applies whether one is working with a group of staff delivering a front-line service directly to customers or to senior leaders in the Boardroom as they consider essential business decisions. In my experience, the latter oftentimes lapse into performative roles that sustain the illusion that power exists outside of the working relationships that they need to manage. One element of this performative presence is the deployment of a particular type of language, often referred to as management jargon. Back in 2014, it was reported that phrases such as 'ideas shower' and 'not enough bandwidth' (the latter meaning in truth that the organisation has overburdened me so significantly that I have no genuine opportunity to take on the additional activity with which it is now seeking to load me) were major causes of irritation in the workplace (Smith, 2014). Around the same, Professor Laurie Taylor presented an edition of his excellent Thinking Allowed programme that highlighted this type of language and asked, 'Why is meaningless speech in the workplace so ubiquitous?' (BBC Radio 4 – Thinking Allowed, 2017).

The map and the territory

This is not merely an irritating tic in organisational life: it recasts the conversations that are had in these spaces and supports a discourse where power does not have to be addressed. It allows individuals to inhabit a fiction where they do not have to speak out or indeed listen up to the truths that need to be heard by power. Another key strand of this fiction is, of course, the reliance by management on the presentation and representation of data. In the midst of conversations distinguished by the use of a very specific form of linguistic exchange, then, sits myriad images of reality that are so distanced from the practicalities of daily organisational life. The fetishisation of these artefacts – the GANTT charts, the spreadsheets, the risk registers, the strategic documents, and operational policies, all pointlessly overlaid – like a grotesque rococo ornamentation – with dazzling colours of red, amber or green – means that many organisations are engaging merely with a simulacrum of the reality that is actually experienced on a day-to-day basis by their employees. In respect to this notion of simulation, it is worth holding in mind that 'Simulation is characterized by a precession of the model, of all models around the merest fact – the models come first, and their orbital (like the bomb) circulation constitutes the genuine magnetic field of events' (Baudrillard, 2004, p. 372).

I highlighted earlier where a factory unquestioningly recorded a datum every day for 60 years and underlining the fictional quality of much data (Gray et al., 2015, p. 28). This illuminates for me the way in which organisations have – to an extent – substituted the map for the territory. The data hunger that exists in our organisations intermediates between people and their lived reality of day-to-day work in context. A fascinating practical example of this in recent times concerns the appointment of Alan Mulally as the CEO of the Ford Motor Company, where the observation is pointedly made that, 'Even when he tried to focus on the data, he found that different sources offered different numbers for different audiences' (Hoffman, 2012, p. 101). Beneath the positive noise of all of that data, it is suggested, Mulally found a company that had been going out of business for 30 years (Hoffman, 2012, p. 109).

This 'metric fixation,' as it has been described, has three components: the possibility and desirability of the replacement of judgement by numerical indicators; a fiction of accountability that is crafted from these metrics being made public; and the assumption that people in organisations are best motivated through carrots and sticks that relate directly to those metrics (Muller, 2018, p. 18). For me, this latter aspect is more nuanced than first appears, insofar as managing populations through statistical method is a key facet of what Foucault calls governmentality. The numerical webs that are spun in organisational contexts entrap through definition the subjects in that context. The individual succumbs to a view of the world (and those therein) that absorbs them into calibrations and categorisations. If the rating scale for your performance appraisal runs from 1 (meaning needs improvement) through to 5 (indicating the preferred level of performance of the ideal employee), it is the case that most caught unwittingly in this largely meaningless exercise would aspire to the higher rather than lower rating.

By this data effort, the member of staff no longer needs intense scrutiny and oversight: they are busy managing themselves, aware of this surveillant apparatus and accepting unquestioningly its premise. In the Foucauldian notion of governmentality, the management of populations is best attained – with a distinctive modern lightness of touch – by engirdling the object of that attention in a multidisciplinarity of measurement, which, in turn, effaces the person and discursively creates a reality to which we all then belong and interact.

OD as a practice is incorporated into the discourse that privileges this way of seeing the world – and hence how power/knowledge is experienced in the workplace. Indeed, OD pays obeisance to the scientism that inhabits organisational practice, as evidenced by its predominant model of activity which opens with what is invariably referred to as a 'diagnostic' phase (Block, 2011). One author envisages an initial effort in this regard as exploring needs and issues, identifying resistance and support, and looking at competence and commitment (Jamieson, 1995, p. 122). A grindingly dull yet wholly accurate definition of this aspect of OD practice suggests that it

> ...is aimed at providing a rigorous analysis of data on the structure, administration, interaction, procedures, interfaces, and other essential elements of the client system. The diagnosis, then, provides a basis for structural, behavioural, or technical interventions to improve organizational performance. Diagnosing a problem requires a systematic approach throughout the process. If organization change is to be effective, it must be based on a specific diagnosis of the problem.
>
> (Harvey & Brown, 1976, p. 123)

Unbidden to my mind springs the children's rhyme: 'Here's the church, here's the steeple, open the doors, but where's the people?'

So, the first significant act in the practice of Radical OD is to abandon the conceit of undertaking some objective exercise of diagnosis. Instead, the Radical OD practitioner should be seeking to immerse themselves in the lived reality of the context in which they are working rather than inhabiting the simulacrum of organisational life that is represented by the datasets so beloved of managers in this setting. Indeed, the task of the Radical OD practitioner should be to wean everybody away from the illusion that data offer insight into organisational life and to denature that familiar representation of reality through critique of its discursive impacts and overall determination. Large professional services companies will charm you with a partner and then let loose laptop-wielding recent graduates of MBA programmes to crawl all over your organisation, in order to craft for you a thick slide deck about their experience of slithering all over a superficial data version of your company. This is a tried but largely untested method that enjoys huge currency; where it has been tested – in this instance, in an NHS context – research suggests it offers little in the way of insight and improvement in efficiency, quite the contrary, in fact (Kirkpatrick et al., 2019). The fiction of management consultancy is exposed in this diligent review of its (lack of) impact, although we continue to allow it to hold sway over workplace thinking and practice.

I have worked in an organisational setting alongside one of these providers. My focus was on working to allow people to talk about their lived experience of their day-to-day work and the 'whys and wheres' of how it happened. Off the back of this conversation, I was eager to release the ideas for how things might be done better that these people were certain to have. Meanwhile, the professional services response was to produce a slide deck thick enough to stun an ox that notionally offered a meaningful picture of the company. Interestingly, a colleague of mine valiantly offered to get into the detail of this ridiculously thick document: in part, it was inconsistent – and, in some cases, downright contradictory, in her view. Yet the executive team in question was transfixed by this volume of data – like a rabbit hypnotised by a hungry snake – so the space did not truly open up for them to enjoy an authentic exchange with the people in the firm about the specific issue with which they were at that time consumed. As we withdrew from the work, our 'colleagues' from the professional services company apparently went from displaying an interest in our work and a desire to get alongside us in its delivery to open hostility to the idea and what it sought to achieve.

A Radical OD practitioner will work to shatter the illusion that the 'datasets in slide decks' are a true representation of reality – and instead encourage the agents in the organisation to connect meaningfully in order to engender a rich conversation. They will seek to move people beyond the 'metric fixation' in order to focus everybody in on the lived reality of one another in the work context.

But this is not an outcome in and of itself; it underscores the fact that the Radical OD practitioner is immediately and constantly aware of the power that inhabits the context in which they find themselves working. They also take a nuanced view of the way in which that power is generated and practically experienced. They will be aware that power is not ipso facto 'bad,' nor is it a resource for which we might scrabble in the workplace. A rich Foucauldian appreciation of power and its relationship to discourse opens a space for meaningful conversation about this. And – from that awareness – flows a responsibility to foreground the issue of power and how it is experienced in the workplace, rather than following the traditional view of bracketing off power in this setting and pretending that it has no presence in this work.

For a Radical OD practitioner, power **is** the work: exploring it, acknowledging it, amplifying it, and supporting others to critique it is the foundation of this new way of working. The abstraction associated with undertaking an 'organisational diagnostic' needs to be consigned to the dustbin of industrial history. Instead, the Radical OD practitioner needs to act as a meaningful conduit through which a rich and honest discussion of power can take place. And this applies as much to those organisations that ideologically shroud themselves in the ideas of post-bureaucratic or holacratic structure as to those more traditional corporations – such as NHS organisations – that rely very much (and still) on a command-and-control approach to management. In assuming this enlightened position, the Radical OD practitioner also recognises the way power exists between and through them and the people with whom they seek to connect in the workplace. OD reinforces the dominant discourse in organisational life and so acts as a particular type of facilitation of power. More than this, my presence as a practitioner carries with it a power in respect to my relations to the wider organisation, not least because of the way in which my work invites people to do things and they are inhibited from declining that invitation.

Parrhesia

Recognising and highlighting power in its context is surely an excellent starting point for an OD practice that transcends current expectations in corporate life. However, there is a wealth of discussion about the challenge of speaking truth to power in this regard, extending from the whole idea of whistleblowing through the extent to which an individual feels able to give voice to their reservations, concerns, and ideas about their lives in work. The observation of two people with whom I work closely in respect to this is deeply illustrative of the perils of failing to both speak up and to listen up to others:

> When dominant leaders begin to see themselves as unquestionably right, when those around them feel they can only say what is safe to say, then we have a perfect storm in which leaders who are disconnected from the day-to-day can persuade others through their own powerful rhetoric that their perspective of the world is reality. Alternative understandings and experiences are stifled with potentially disastrous consequences, as robust and informed decision-making becomes impossible. This is publicly visible in politics across the world right now and it is of equal relevance in the corporate world.
>
> (Reitz & Higgins, 2017, p. 5)

The leadership narrative discursively shapes notions of normalcy and hence of otherness.

We all of us in human interaction have an implicit responsibility to give voice to our opinions as to the shared reality that we collectively seek to construct. Where regimes of silence begin to crystallise in key areas of public discourse – where there are things that can and cannot be said and notwithstanding whether those proscriptions derive from a political perspective that might be described as conservative or progressive in terms of orientation – then our liberty as human agents and contributors to a wider exploration of human existence is unhelpfully inhibited. A civil exchange across the widest possible range of topics and ideas (something that seems to recede further and further into the distance as more and more people rely on social media in order to have those conversations) is essential to a vision of humanity enhancing its understanding and developing its presence in the world. This is a genuinely progressive way of engaging with thought and practice, whereas mainstream progressive politics that inhibits candid exchange actually runs counter to the idea of reason and enlightenment that notionally undergird that view of the world and how it should be.

As an undergraduate, I recall running across a greensward on the campus of the University of York, finding myself inadvertently at the head of a charge of protesters chasing after the philosopher Roger Scruton. He had just given an evening lecture and was being ushered to a waiting car as my 'side' indulged the grotesque notion of 'no platform' as a means of trying to prevent him from speaking at a seat of learning. Whilst I worked to maintain the illusion of speed, the bursar bellowing that anyone touching Scruton would be sent down led me to adjust my pace to allow him time to get into the car and drive away, prior to my heroic and breathless arrival. Depressingly, even at the time – in the very moment – I knew that this was wrong, both in practice and in theory. Yet, I was absorbed by the groupthink of the Left (and the associated desperate desire not to be excluded from its comforting confines) and so I sought to prevent someone speaking simply because I thought I did not like what he was likely to say.

The reverse of this coin, of course, is the responsibility that we share as individuals to be speakers of our truth as well as listeners to others. This isn't merely to engage in that old favourite on coaching courses of 'active listening.' It means a willingness to open up the space around you to allow myriad voices to chime in and to offer their interpretations of the reality that we share and to do so without negative reaction and resistance, or indeed retribution that we might, in turn, feel able to exercise. This is not a way of doing things – 'I actively listen when I am coaching someone but deny the voices of those around me at all other times' – but is instead a chosen way of being in each and every minute of the day.

So, any new approach to OD practice will need to have a foundation of working to hear (and to allow the expression of) all opinions and perspectives, regardless of how an individual might feel about the veracity or acceptability of those views. And a commitment to give voice to opinions and perspectives that, in a corporate context, might not sit comfortably. At the root of this is the Foucauldian mobilisation of the term 'parrhesia,' which is borrowed from Classical Greek thought and practice. Underpinning this is the sense that it means to say everything – but it is held in place by the honest relationship between the person and what they say: as Foucault notes, 'The one who uses *parrhesia*, the *parresiastes*, is someone who says everything that he has in mind: he does not hide anything, but opens his heart and mind completely to other people through his discourse' (Foucault, 2001, p. 12).

An additional core aspect of understanding this is through the acknowledgement that parrhesia carries with it a risk or danger in telling their truth – and this may be up to and including the chance of death as a result of that expression. For this reason, Foucault usefully notes that 'It is because the *parrhesiastes* must take a risk in speaking the truth that the king or tyrant generally cannot use *parrhesia*; for he risks nothing' (Foucault, 2001, p. 16).

Importantly, such speech acts are not merely about articulating a truth. They are instead a criticism, either of oneself (one might use *parrhesia* to confess to something that one had previously done) or of the person with whom one is in conversation, particularly where that person is possessed of a power that might impact on you.

Beyond merely calling attention to the power that exists in the workplace – and which is traditionally disregarded – the Radical OD practitioner needs to disrupt those two elements that underscore the inability to speak truth to power, namely conspiracies of silence in social settings (wherein an unspoken conversation may oftentimes reside) and active denial of some key notions in the discourse that surrounds us (Zerubavel, 2006). Furthermore, it is also the case that, while committing to this at a personal level, they should also encourage those around them to behave in the same way by creating a safe environment in which this can take place. To achieve this, of course, the Radical OD practitioner needs to be a *parrhesiastes*, giving frank voice to criticisms of their own position and those of their interlocutors despite the fact that this expression of their opinions might adversely impact on them, particularly in these circumstances their livelihood.

This goes to the heart of whether the Radical OD practitioner is engaging authentically with where they are working and the people that make it up – or whether they are simply serving to reinforce the discourse that exists across business in a capitalist society. Many current practitioners in our field are content to mislead themselves into thinking that they are serving a noble aim – through a personal commitment to ideas of progressivism and humanism in the workplace – when they are actually serving the interests of the way in which things have always been. Their activities, overwritten with the sterile practices mentioned earlier in regard to diagnosis in organisational settings, cannot be liberating for those in the workplace because they simply reproduce the status quo by overlaying it with the illusions of engagement and development.

There is no problem with practising in a way that serves to reinforce the way things are, of course. It is not how I would want to be seen to be working, but it is entirely consistent with the history of OD as a key element of supporting the management of enterprises to improve their effectiveness through working on the workforce in a capitalist context. But it is somewhat dishonest to practise in this way whilst deluding oneself and/or deluding others that this is a more sophisticated and involved way of doing this work. It is my assertion that there is a bifurcation in the history of OD at this juncture, whereby practitioners can choose to either recognise their practice as a business function that supports capitalism to get more from the workforce or to embrace the idea that their work in the workplace has political potential to be liberating – and which might offer a prefiguration of what human organising might look like if it were freed from the dead weight of organisation in all of its forms.

Like the blues singer Robert Johnson, we will all of us find ourselves at a crossroads such as this. In the Johnson myth, the Devil took his soul in exchange for the capacity to play the guitar exquisitely. The alternative option in this context, of course, was for Johnson to take the intrinsically human direction and commit to daily practice of the guitar in order to find a way of playing (doubtless not as perfect as the talent that the Devil might grant). As practitioners, we will be mindful of our own professional crossroads – and judge how best to orient ourselves when difficult decisions present themselves.

Organising not organisations

When I was around eight or nine years old, my family moved to Streatham, in southeast London. This area is blessed with a large common, which was an utter joy for children and, I suspect, remains so. The common was some way from where we lived, as we tended to live in flats above shops, insofar as my father worked as a window dresser for a large chain of shoe stores and this was a benefit of his employment. I started to attend Sunny Hill School there, where I was very content, made good educational progress, and developed a circle of friends. (Children are often surprisingly welcoming of incomers, fascinated by those who come from elsewhere and eager to hear of their experiences. At the age of 10, we moved again – this time into the first property that my family properly owned – and I had another positive experience with transferring into a new school.)

Out of nowhere, my friends and I decided that we should form a club that would centre around the building of a den on Streatham Common. This was an intensely exciting notion for our small group and we embraced the business of organising this with great gusto. Our expeditions identified a suitable place for a club headquarters and we began to stake our claim to it. At some point here, a gear shifted: we agreed that boundaries to the club needed to be set, which would involve each member being issued with a membership card. My mother, surprisingly sanguine on reflection about us all trooping off some way from her oversight, had started to express some concern about all of this – I think there was a news story in the South London Press at around this time about a man on the common speaking to children, a report that was unusual at that time but might be more commonplace in contemporary times – and I ensured that our membership cards included a number of rules about club conduct, including the stipulation that we should be aware of strangers.

My recollection – admittedly somewhat hazy nowadays – is that the issuing of these cards marked a turning point in the life of our association: our excitement at the initial notion and our endeavours to make it a reality saw a gradual attenuation of our commitment to it as formality introduced itself into this initiative. This could be seen as a very youthful life lesson in bureaucratisation: the virtue of this approach, of course, consists in the technocratic way in which it smooths off variance, commits a collective towards the attainment of expressed goals, and depersonalises those processes, the better to ensure equality in terms of administration of resource. This is balanced, of course, by the tendency for those arrangements to develop a dysfunctionality wherein one can perceive '...a transference of the sentiments from the aims of the organization onto the particular details of behaviour required by the rule' (Merton, 1994, p. 146).

This relationship between organising and organisation seems vital in terms of how we might find ways to work together effectively to common purpose (Weick, 1969). So, it has been interestingly argued that organisation has a tendency towards bureaucratisation, which can be thwarted by engendering circumstances through the encouragement of local autonomy and orientation towards a purpose defined at a sub-organisational level (Abrahammson, 1993). This, of course, sounds like a prefiguration of holacracy: the organisation as a flat structure without hierarchical design. Crucially, though, Abrahammson introduces the key concept of the 'mandator' into his analysis in order to clarify how power's presence can be discerned even as superficially things look to be different. His definition of this idea is simple: 'The mandator is the party who sets up the general tasks to be carried out by the administration' (Abrahammson, 1993, p. 14). In this schema, the mandator may be an individual – such as a CEO (think Tony Hsieh in Zappos, one of the first organisations to endeavour to be holacratic) – or a group, such as an executive team, shareholders, and so on.

I am minded here to underscore two simple facts: first, as people initially come together in the hope of delivering on a shared purpose, the role of mandator might be said to be genuinely shared across that group; second, an organisation begins to ossify as the fervour of that initial phase of organising cools, the role of mandator may formalise in a single person or group of individuals, despite what might first appear to be a free association. This is important in terms of OD practice, as oftentimes we take our instructions as a practitioner from the mandator in that context, which means we are invisibly supporting the 'deep organisation' that lurks below its public appearance. In respect to that latter, as organisations dabble in notions of engagement or supposedly post-bureaucratic arrangements, 'It is important, …, that one does not confuse *quantitative* changes, which increase work control, with reforms that lead to a *qualitative* change in the basic power relations in the enterprise, i.e., a change of mandator' (Abrahammson, 1993, p. 114). The Radical OD practitioner expressly gives the mandator its name in the course of their work … and seeks to move beyond cosmetic adjustments to structure, philosophy, and practice to call the mandator (and its agenda) into question.

One might wonder why organisations are seemingly so very content to feign employee involvement at this time. The Foucauldian view of this is simple: when our incorporation into wider social arrangements is premised on the idea of liberal democracy and all of its associated freedoms, it would be disruptive for the workplace not to be reinforcing this notion – or, indeed, through its practices and relationships, to be seen to run counter to it. This explains the extreme public reaction to the expose of working conditions at Sports Direct, where a piece for *The Guardian* newspaper by an undercover reporter was published under a headline that described their experience as a day at the Gulag (Goodley & Ashby, 2015) and an *Independent* article reported on testimony from workers in the company offered to a UK Parliamentary Select Committee (Rodionova, 2016). The latter cites one worker testifying to the Committee about their humiliation at work:

> Whilst I was there, your pick was timed to the second. If your pick was late you got a strike. But when the aisles are full of other pickers, this is impossible to meet. We still had to suffer humiliation over the Tannoy, with your name called out so that everybody knew.
>
> (Rodionova, 2016)

There is, however, notionally another pay-off to organisations of indulging the fiction of engagement. As far back as the late 1950s, the argument was being promoted – partly arising out of the experiences that gave rise to the Human Relations school of thought in organisational practice – that worker involvement in the organisation gave a significant pay-off in terms of company performance. One study, built on empirical material but with a strong focus on the workforce making its presence felt via unionisation and its associated collective action, made the case that various collaborative models of workplace organisation where the management and workforce cooperated in order to give employees a greater sense of involvement offered enhancements in productivity (Melman, 1958).

At one point, Melman notes from his findings that 'The workers' decision process had a considerable impact on the characteristics of management, demonstrating, for example, that managerial supervision of the traditional sort could be dispensed with while plant operations were carried out at high efficiency' (Melman, 1958, p. 197). But capitalism wants to have its cake and eat it: it wants the benefits of involving its workforce in the fiction of involvement in decision-making whilst leaving the mandator tucked behind the curtain, like the tiny little man who turns out to be the eponymous character in The Wizard of Oz. But this incorporation goes beyond productivity: it serves a deeper aim in respect to power, by allowing the formation of an illusion that the worker enjoys liberties in the workplace that are consistent with those that they supposedly have as citizens in a liberal democracy.

Interestingly, in this early exposition of staff engagement and its benefits in terms of organisational effectiveness, the notion of the supposedly sovereign individual in a work context is yet to take flight. It is a product of its time, in terms of industrial sociology, with an orientation towards corporatism and the effacement of the person in favour of a formal collective. And, of course, it would seem redundant at this point to note that trade union arrangements mirror the trajectory outlined at the start of this section, where a group moves from organising to become an organisation. There is a yawning gap of time between the Tolpuddle Martyrs congregating secretly under a tree and Unison's huge headquarters on London's Euston Road – but also a relatively short distance between people working together and the formalisation (and bureaucratisation) of that. In the specific examples cited in Melman's work, it is possible to suggest that the corporatist model represents a restructuring of the mandator in this industrial context.

The role of the Radical OD practitioner is to focus on organising – supporting people to sustain their enthusiasm, personal engagement, and sense of purpose in respect to coming together with others in order to get things done – and to hold at a critical distance the organisation that forms around this extremely positive activity. This needs to be done even though the formal organisation – through its managerial authority – may have commissioned us to do this work. Therein, of course, lies the power of *parrhesia* and the need for us to engage with it seriously. Where the organisation is predominant and overly determining of activity in this work context, the Radical OD practitioner needs to nudge people to see this reality and to have the courage to critique and undermine it off the back of their own experiences and expectations.

It is worth noting at this juncture that these tendencies – and our work to try to thwart them – are immanent in every possible setting where organising occurs, including those contexts that might be seen as expressly politically progressive. We have already noted the immersive study of the experiences at the Occupy London site that sprang up outside St Paul's Cathedral in 2011–2012 articulates an interesting tension arising out of the organising and formal organisation: the former had a strong ideological orientation, of course, while the latter tried to manage practicalities in respect to how to be exemplary of that new vision of politics that they were seeking to articulate. As the camp expanded its membership to involve rough sleepers, they struggled with reconciling the behaviours of some of those new arrivals – and debated the amount of resource that was increasingly committed to provide a service of welfare to them, in keeping with the compassionate politics that they sought to articulate (Reinecke, 2018).

Our challenge as Radical OD practitioners is to reverse this. Partly, this is about returning to some of the psychodynamic work that was done with groups, particularly in respect to their work on tasks. So, for example, Wilfred Bion's writing up of his experiences in groups – arising out of his post-World War II oversight of a large psychiatric hospital – discusses two coexisting situations that live within a human group: the work-group mentality directs the attentions of those therein towards the achievement of an aim or aims; meanwhile, the basic assumption mentality – which both precedes and succeeds the coming together of a group – refers to the human relationships and the emotions associated with same (anxiety, guilt, anger, etc.). In seeking to expand on this, it is observed that,

> The man [sic] who asks, "When does the group meet again?" is referring, insofar as he is talking about mental phenomena, to work group.

> The basic-assumption group does not disperse or meet, and references to time have no meaning in the basic-assumption group.
>
> (Bion, 1961, p. 172)

Patently, these two mentalities determine and overdetermine one another across the life of a group. And our practice needs to call attention to the ways in which these play out in an organisational context. At the most basic level, our appreciation, as facilitators in a space where there is a task focus or in which people are seeking groups for collaboration, is to draw attention to the focus of the work and the psychodynamics of the relationships that are seeking to deliver on that. Work that I undertook recently that sought to help a large group of disparate senior leaders from across a system to see how they were working together in regard to that ambition almost certainly ran aground because of the basic-assumption group in which uncertainty, existential anxiety, and all manner of other inter-relational issues were present. I failed in my practice at that time to speak out and give voice to what I genuinely felt lay at the very roots of their inability to make detailed and impactful progress.

A collaborator of Bion's was Harold Bridger, who – in his work – drew out this concept of a schismatic quality to group working to describe what he called the 'double task,' where we experience the pressure to do and complete a task to the exclusion of an awareness of how we are going about trying to do it as a group – and, indeed, the asking of the question as to whether what we are seeking to do is right and whether our means of going about this task are best suited to its achievement (Bayswater Institute, 2017). All work groups need time to disarticulate themselves from the primary task – the deadline, the expectation, the cluster of KPIs, and so on – in order to attend to a reflective exercise to explore that intensive experience in which they find themselves on a quotidian basis to determine whether it still makes sense, whether the way they have sought to get things done has been successful, and whether that purpose might need revising as well as whether there might be different ways of approaching the work.

It is not just this psychodynamic orientation that might help us as Radical OD practitioners to reverse the trajectory from organising to organisation. A second key aspect of that approach is about emphasising how formal organisation can unwittingly incubate within itself fresh thinking and new practices that fracture that carapace and allow something altogether different (although not necessarily new) to burst out and start making an impact. For instance, there is the excellent example of a church in the downtown of a large southwestern US city. Its dwindling congregation reflected changes in the socio-economic fabric of its locale, where it found itself amidst a large homeless population. Arising out of a number of small-scale conversations amongst its worshippers, the church made a number of small adjustments to its practice, beginning with offering breakfast to the rough sleepers with whom they shared this urban space, which begat even more significant shifts in their thinking and approach. Over time, these micro-shifts engendered further adjustments – the introduction of clinics for the rough sleepers, the growth (and shift in the nature of) the congregation as the homeless population joined the church, and so on – to the mutual benefit of all concerned (Plowman et al., 2007). The church changed and achieved growth; its neighbours gained practical resource from this adjustment. But this shift arose not through the formation of a grand plan for transformation but through localised conversation and connection between those who made up the church at that time.

The role of the Radical OD practitioner is to amplify this type of collective thinking and creativity, even when it might seem to run counter to the organisation. To that extent, we are not merely content to assemble 'tempered radicals' in the organisation, those who subscribe to its values but wish for it to be different from their perspective (Meyerson & Scully, 1995); we seek also to give space to discontent and resentment, the better that it might move from a negative focus – manifested in mere resistance – to a circumstance where that exasperated weariness of how things are in the organisation might be turned around into a vision of how things ought to be … and a commitment to work towards that end.

Hence, we work to unearth the 'guerrillas in the bureaucracy,' a term derived from a study that looked at how a traditional urban planning function in an American city experienced trying to function more locally and with genuine community involvement (Needleman & Needleman, 1974). In an interesting mirror of our earlier observations on organisational life in a liberal democracy, these authors observe that the very idea of a centralised planning function – a foundational notion to the activity and the occupational groups that seek to deliver it – runs counter to the underpinning ideas of a 'liberal' economy (where private development is often the motor in the system) and, indeed, to the liberal democratic notion of wanting to hear the populations voices when it comes to development of this sort (Needleman & Needleman, 1974, p. 165). They also discerned a tension between what might be seen to be traditionalists at the centre and the guerrillas on the periphery (Needleman & Needleman, 1974, pp. 185–219), so there is the need for a Radical OD practitioner to orient their work not towards consensus in this context, as is so often the brief that one receives from the manager commissioning the work, but instead to ascribe value to the difference that exists in that space and to allow real conversational exchange about that difference without trying to guide the meeting to an 'agreed solution,' which – in systemic terms – may simply not exist in reality.

An additional responsibility for us in this area of attending to organising rather than organisation is to hear the discourses at play. This means describing the dominant discourse – what it says and what effects arise from that articulation; drawing attention to the subaltern discourses that enjoy permission to sit alongside the dominant position but which are not allowed to supersede it; and foregrounding those discourses that are not even recognised as having currency whatsoever in that organisational space. Oftentimes, this latter position is perceived by indirect effect rather than direct attention to its precepts: it finds expression through defiance, dissent, and sedition in the context of the business. This needs to be heard, without doubt, but privileged only insofar as people will not have been mindful of its presence as a coherent pattern of thought about organisational challenge prior to this moment. People advocating these views might be described as 'disruptive' or 'difficult,' as someone who has not 'got with the programme,' and so on. These pathologising statements silence a diversity of voice, regardless of how difficult it might be in corporate life to hear these voices.

An example always springs to mind for me when considering this issue and how our practice needs to orient itself more authentically. In coal mining, there is a notion called 'pit sense,' the innate capacity of the collier to ensure their safety and those of others on the basis of situated understandings of the mine itself. It is founded on lived experience, is transmitted via apprenticeship, and often is expressed on the basis of intuition. A study demonstrates how commercial pressure to increase 'yardage' (as a measure of the amount of coal being mined) and external legal requirements in regard to health and safety led managers to overlay the practice of the miners with a bureaucratic superstructure which sought to eradicate pit sense, which was greatly valued by that workforce (Kamoche & Maguire, 2010).

Here, a legitimate practice is clumsily supplanted by a managerial initiative, which – despite its rational motivations around productivity and safety – merely dismisses the activity of those literally at the coal face in favour in an approach confected by the soft-handed souls in shirts and ties in their fluorescent-lit offices. Whether knowingly or not, it is expressed as a disdainful dismissal of the way in which miners have sought to guarantee safety for many years – and a safety that is of direct significance to them as people in the workplace. The Radical OD practitioner seeks instead to allow voices to be heard, regardless of how subaltern they might be felt to be – and despite the contextual shifts that might lead subaltern discourse from a place where it is tacitly tolerated to one where the action is taken to actively supplant or suppress it.

Reflexivity

Much OD practice is undergirded by the largely tacit notion that the contexts in which we work are in some way knowable. This is realised in practice through, for example, that model of OD consulting that envisages the work as a linear and logical sequence, from diagnostic phase through to some kind of evaluative activity. The former entails an engagement with that specific workplace, where the practitioner creates the illusion of getting to know the context by, for example, arranging interviews with key stakeholders or collecting a number of datasets in one place – material that purports to reflect performance, information about and from the workforce, other metrics that notionally offer insight. Interestingly, the latter phase of evaluative activity is often undertaken and expressed in the same numeric language, through notions such as return on investment; surveys undertaken before, during, and after the 'intervention,' and – at its most crude – the Net Promoter Score, which demands of people that they convert their experience of something into a number on a scale and thence into some formula that either offers reassurance through the expression of a percentage or might cause some concern as to how the work might have been undertaken more engagingly.

In reflecting on the history of OD, the following two elements are worthy of consideration in this regard:

> The basic assumptions of OD were influenced largely by a philosophy about people, work, organizations, and change that swept through many disciplines during the late 1950s and early 1960s... [while] the basic

techniques of OD stemmed from experiments conducted by applied social scientists in the early Twentieth Century.

(Rothwell et al., 1995, pp. 13–14)

For me as a practitioner in this field, these two foundational aspects seem
to generate a tension in terms of their relationship to one another, specifically insofar as the focus is declared to be on people – but this orientation
is realised through a reliance on scientism which haunts a wide range of
activities across society. By scientism, I mean the fetishisation of scientific
method and its associated notions of objectivity and experimental distance.
Immediately, then, the OD practitioner – even one notionally committed to
working in a dialogic way – is objectifying the people with whom they are
meant to work and reifying the organisation where they find themselves.

Whilst dialogic OD seeks to create some distance between itself and this
scientism, with key authors in the field making this claim and describing
some sort of entirely false binary opposition between traditional and dialogic
OD (Bushe & Marshak, 2009), at root it remains an activity that applies a notionally external focus to the lived experience of the people in a workplace –
and seeks to tease from them a view of their world to which all can subscribe.
It remains an epistemological exercise – albeit one that seeks to make people
aware of that which they already know – and not authentically one that is
ontological in orientation. Such an ontological approach would seek to create
space and time in which people in their work context and amidst their work
relationships might be allowed to be in a way that is unencumbered by the
intentions of facilitators to achieve an understanding or the sponsors of such
interventions, who might harbour a tacit vision of how those people might
work together better. Simply to be amongst those with whom you find yourself alongside in a work environment, to explore one's personhood in that
circumstance and to engage in free conversation, connection, and knowledge exchange (Cole, 2017), is a luxurious prospect. It also opens up an
opportunity to discuss openly the agenda – of the OD practitioner, of the
managers in the organisation, of the person who has asked for this work to be
undertaken – through the prism of power, as discussed earlier.

If the emphasis in our work is shifted towards being rather than knowing, then it seems sensible to suggest that we too – as practitioners – need
to rethink how we position ourselves in regard to the activities that we
undertake. The first position that a Radical OD practitioner would need to

assume in regard to this relates to the fiction of knowability; if we persevere with the erroneous notion that by assembling data, collating and codifying it, we can genuinely 'know' about the context whence that data has been drawn, then we are continuing to indulge the faulty notion that this material is in some way meaningfully connected with people's day-to-day experience of working reality. We end up displacing reality in favour of what we previously described as a simulacrum – and that becomes the object of our activity rather than finding ways to release the constraints on the subjects that exist in that context.

It is worth saying here that the focus on knowability is preeminent in traditional OD but equally undergirds dialogic OD, despite its efforts to set itself up as in some way as significantly different to standard diagnostic practice in the field. The dialogue remains for these practitioners a way to 'know' things in an all-encompassing way, something particularly noticeable in the key technique of the practice, namely appreciative inquiry (Cooperrider & Srivastva, 1987). Meanwhile, the power/knowledge at play in that context might be said to be buried twice over, which is to say that, if diagnostic OD is actually, despite its declared values, reinforcing the dominant discourse from a hidden position, then dialogic OD could be said to be doubling down on that, in light of the way that it seeks to present itself as a progression on the old model that is more honestly engaged. Its place in the context and its practice in that space might look to be different and more positive but it – like its diagnostic counterpart yet from a significantly cloaked position – is enmeshed in power, reproduces it, and reinforces the discourse at play in the workplace.

To return to the exploration of reality and knowability outlined above, this is not to find ourselves in a post-modern morass, where the very notion of reality is endlessly interrogated until we all float free from any notion of a material grounding. Instead, it is useful to engage with the precepts of critical realism (Bhaskar, 2008), which accepts the essential presence of a reality that we all, as human subjects, experience – but which recognises how each and every one of us will be engaged in an individual act of interpretation, which – where civility acts as a basis and conversation is encouraged – we are in a position to exchange with others in order to arrive at a meaningful understanding of that situation and the way in which others have experienced it. To an extent, this philosophy represents a negative reaction to the certainties of scientism and the vagaries generated *reductio ad absurdum* by some post-structuralist thought. Its application has been interestingly explored – as a way of both conceptualising and investigating – in relation to the study of organisational life (Fleetwood & Ackroyd, 2004), but the most I would want to draw from it is a relatively superficial acknowledgement of the need to focus in on the individual presence in a shared reality in relation to the supposed knowability of that reality.

I have explored thus far the importance for the Radical OD practitioner to support those with whom they come alongside in order to work to encourage a shift of emphasis away from epistemology (the pursuit of knowability in regard to a location, situation, or collection of individuals) in order to focus on ontology (amplifying the presence of individuals in organisational life, their lived experience of that, and encouragement of exploration of shared understanding and meaning). This requires the abandonment of all simulacra of organisational life, whether that be numerical data or qualitative exchange amongst those people that are captured for (re)presentation to others in the company. To an extent, we might argue that it also entails the abandonment of technique as well: a conscious decision by the Radical OD practitioner not to assume that the application of a particular activity will unlock the mystery that they are charged to unravel by the sponsor of their work. Partly, this reflects an acknowledgement of how work of this sort is nowadays seen to take place in a complex adaptive system rather than a self-contained and clearly bounded sovereign organisation. The ideas of linearity and causality that underpin traditional organisational thinking and practice can no longer be sustained in face of contemporary challenges. Equally, it reflects an increasing recognition amongst some OD practitioners that OD as an activity extends far beyond the simplistic notion of exploring a context and thence recommending the application of some technique drawn from the field's seemingly boundless repository.

Beyond how the practitioner might approach their work and the things that they might pursue in that regard lies the matter of how that person realises themselves in that context. The shift in the work from epistemology to ontology presupposes a considerably more developed awareness of the need for reflective consideration of lived experience. But, for the practitioner, in particular, that does not go far enough: instead, the Radical OD practitioner needs to abandon the notion of distance and objectivity to embrace fully a commitment to reflexivity. Importantly, this goes beyond the current OD fascination with the concept of 'self as instrument,' a notion that derives from the practice of qualitative research (Eisner, 1991/2017). Its application as a way of thinking about diagnostic work in an organisational setting was recognised (McCormick & White, 2000) and the notion has been eagerly seized upon by leading figures in the field of OD (Cheung-Judge, 2001).

While 'self as instrument' betrays elements of reflexivity, it also seems to presuppose a level of detachment from the terrain in which the work is being undertaken, wherein the individual acts in a knowingly instrumental fashion, the better to undertake their commissioned and defined task. To my mind, self-as-instrument resides in the act of practice, while reflexivity is an intrinsic attribute of the mindful practitioner. The former reinforces the power/knowledge at play in the context; the latter places an imperative on the individual to inquire into how they impact on that context – and, crucially, reinforce the dominant discourse and – to borrow a term from Althusser – engage in a notable act of interpellation, by which is meant, how the person is 'hailed' or, to use another phrase, subjectified by their situation located amidst a range of what are called ideological state apparatus, that encompass *inter alia* the family and formal education (Althusser, 1970/2008). As a methodological sidebar, it is worth noting that Althusser's work in this regard, particularly in respect to his idea of interpellation, prefigures Foucault's work around discourse and power. This is understandable, insofar as they were broadly contemporaries studying and then working in the same milieu, although Foucault felt intellectually liberated enough to shrug off the weight of Marxist theory thereby arguably fulfilling the theoretical journey on which Althusser had embarked (Kelly, 2014).

An awareness of our interpellation – that is, our subjectification through our relationships with a variety of authorities and other agencies – is a *sine qua non* for a truly radical practice. We are 'hailed' by managers who embody the culture of the organisation, and defined in that context in relation to the authority of its leaders and its economic imperatives. All of these interleaved factors shape our presence as an OD practitioner. Without the critical interrogation of these determinants, we are unable to recognise how our selfhood is designed and realised by the socio-economic context in which we reside – and so cannot release ourselves in order to begin a critique of that circumstance.

Self-as-instrument is a notion which partially acknowledges the presence in context but does so – to my mind – in a way that implies a scientific orientation towards an object with which the instrumental Self engages. In doing so, it generates two effects: a supposition of 'engaged detachment,' with the practitioner relating to the context but collecting data about it in a supposedly objective fashion; and an associated reification of a social context, which serves to concretise the work and thereby delimit its required infinite contingency. In contrast, the notion of reflexivity makes no distinction between the subject who studies and the object that is studied; they are as one, which is a vital perspective where one is seeking to orient one's practice in an authentically systemic direction. In this sense, 'Reflexivity is thus the constant awareness, assessment and reassessment by the researcher of the researcher's own contribution/influencing/shaping of intersubjective research and the consequent research findings' (Salzman, 2002, p. 806).

In respect to generating a greater appreciation of reflexivity, I will share with you a practice experience where I am fairly sure that I was reflective and active but not as reflexive as I might have been. Just recently, I was facilitating a large group of 140 clinicians to support them to enhance their understanding of leadership as a practice in the system of health and social care. It was apparent during the day that the participants tended to listen to the first part of any instruction prior to engagement with an activity but invariably filled the room with a conversation that overwhelmed the facilitator trying to put everyone on task in the course of the second part of the instruction. Broadly, the three other facilitators with whom I was working and I were pretty sanguine about this. However, as I sought to introduce an exercise, it happened again and I was mindful that the room had really only had partial instruction. I tried to call the room to order and, if anything, the conversations grew even louder.

In the moment, I felt two needs: the first was to assert myself in the space, which is something that was obviously bound up with the power that inhabited that terrain and how it implicated me. Linked to that was an anxiety about losing control of the room – although this is a moot concern, as I was working with a room of 140 adults, all of whom could quite reasonably make a judgement as to how their time together might best be used for them as a professional cohort. Instead, I felt an urgent requirement to impose my vision on the room and to ensure maximum engagement across the cohort with what it was that I wanted them to do, which goes to the very heart of what I have been discussing in terms of

OD as a supposedly people-oriented practice that actually merely serves the dominant discourse, in terms of the common-sense notions, practices, and expectations in a work context that shape how it is experienced (and accommodated to) by human subjects.

My second need might be said to be marginally more noble: I urgently felt a sense of curiosity as to what was going on in the space, what the interrelationships and attitudes might be that were governing this meeting of a large number of people, the majority of participants, and a small group of facilitators. This was amplified by the fact that, when I did eventually reassert control of the room, all 140 people fell into what felt like an extremely sheepish silence. This was no doubt partly because I had opted to call attention to what was happening in the room rather than simply speed past it: this manifested itself in my practice by explicitly calling attention to my need to know what was happening in the space, describing what I had seen (namely, that I had been speaking to the room and that, before I had finished, a large number in the room started speaking to one another and hence over me), and then drawing attention to the fact that the room was now utterly quiet in light of me describing this.

Clumsily, I realised at the time, I had intervened in the space on the basis of an unacknowledged irritation and with limited attention to how I might have surfaced the dynamics more supportively for this group. (This was compounded by the fact that my practice has limited development in respect to group dynamics, so I was personally ill-equipped to do the work I had started down the route of trying to do.) Patently, though, my intrinsic existence in this system shapes and defines the system: this was apparent in terms of the reaction in the room to my drawing attention to what I had experienced. I think in this I was aware of self-as-instrument – and, in so being, I was content to isolate myself from the human connectivity in the room.

My experience in this respect – and the thinking that I outlined prior to exploring this example – reinforces the idea for me that the Radical OD practitioner needs to eschew the notion of self-as-instrument in favour of reflexivity that acknowledges self-as-catalyst. It is not merely a reflective awareness of the context in which the practitioner finds themselves: it is an intense recognition of their subjectivity as an implicit and inseparable part of that context. The simple schema that largely underpins every model of reflective practice can be said to be this: What? So what? Now what? (Borton, 1970). Hence, reflection as a professional activity tends to see the experience as mere material to which one might apply a critical and pseu-doscientific eye. It carries with it a sense of abstraction, where the person who is embodied in the 'What' that appears at each of the three stages can exist outside of the experience in order to scrutinise it. Reflexivity does not "thingify" experience, but takes it as the starting point for an orientation in real time of the practice that we want to offer in our day-to-day lives.

Philosophically, much can be drawn from Heidegger's ontology in order to make some sense of this position. Commentators on the work of this notoriously difficult writer offer an intriguingly accessible summary of the key issue here when they suggest that

> ...the separation of subject and object denies the more fundamental unity of *being-in-the-world (Dasein)*. By drawing a distinction that I (the subject) am perceiving something else (the object), I have stepped back from the primacy of experience and understanding that operates without reflection.
>
> (Winograd & Flores, 1988, p. 31)

This idea of Dasein suggests an entanglement for us with the world and not any form of separation. This is important in respect to our thinking about how we practice. For example, to explain this, the example of a worker using a hammer is used:

> A workman reaches out for a hammer, instinctively weighs it in his hand, and begins to work. Each blow is hammered out with tiny, imperceptible adjustments of velocity and trajectory – adjustments that the workman (sic) does automatically and is barely aware of making...The movements in his hand are realized in movements in the hammer in such a way that the hammer serves as an extension of the workman's hand. In this way the hammer and the workman are together, entangled. The moment the workman begins to contemplate the hammer as a separate object or "thing", something gets in the way: something doesn't work properly, and the very Being of the hammer gets lost. To simply stare at the hammer, to think about it as a separate "thing", does not reveal anything of the *Being* of the hammer.
>
> (Royle, 2018, p. 7)

The implications of this particular understanding of existence are manifold, encompassing the fact that there can be no such thing as a neutral view-point; that practice should be privileged over theory; that representation clouds our understanding (e.g., familiarity with the use of a hammer is a greater value than knowledge of a hammer); and that meaning is socially formed, with the contentious observation being that 'A person is not an individual subject or ego, but a manifestation of Dasein within the space of possibilities, situated within a world and within a tradition' (Winograd & Flores, 1988, pp. 32–33). This, then, helps us to understand what reflexivity might mean to a Radical OD practitioner, as they do their work in space and time. The knowability of the world as an organising precept of our practice falls away under the weight of this world-view, to be replaced by a focus on our very being – and the ways in which that shapes all that goes on in the worldly circumstances where we offer our presence in respect to developing organisations.

An existential view of organisational life

This thinking, of course, falls within the general rubric of existentialism, traceable from writers such as Kierkegaard and Nietzsche through Heidegger to Sartre. Before moving on to a consideration of how Sartrean existentialist thought might play a part in helping the Radical OD practitioner to position themselves in regard to their work, I just want to pull through another concept from Heidegger, which is his idea of *thrownness*. Again, the best way, I think, to access this notion is through an example offered in Winograd and Flores (1988), which relates to imagining oneself chairing a meeting of 15 or so people. The meeting is made up of strong personalities with a variety of differing opinions about the purchase of a new computer system, which is the key item of business for the meeting. Hence, your chairing of this session is a delicate matter of engagement, balance, and direction, with the express purpose of supporting those in the room to reach a reasonable position.

A number of observations in respect to the idea of *thrownness* are then made in order to illustrate it. First, there is the existentialist certainty that you cannot avoid acting; even a choice not to act is an act in itself, so you are 'thrown' into action without choice. Second, there is no space in which to reflect in such a context, because the ontology of being the chair of the meeting is action in the very moment, so one is thrown upon one's instincts constantly. Third, the effects of actions cannot be predicted, because that ontology is infinitely contingent. Fourth, reflections after the event will generate representations but these are only apparent afterwards and certainly not in the moment; the hammer has its being in its use, not in one's knowledge of the hammer. Fifth, linked to this, every representation is an interpretation, so there will be myriad views of the same circumstance; and, lastly, language is action, so there is often a false dichotomy drawn between speaking and doing (Winograd & Flores, 1988, pp. 34–35).

To my mind, these observations seem to run counter to the way in which most of us experience organisational life. For example, most business practice is solidly based on the illusion of predictability, whether it relates to profit forecasts or undertaking large scale restructures or efforts around organisational change according to some delicately calibrated plan. We privilege the 'knowing' of things in this context when secretly most of us who consider such things harbour a very real anxiety that this is merely an illusion – and that our lives in the workplace are actually lived in a state of something akin to confusion. We excitedly embrace ideas of 'evidence-based practice' without celebrating what might arise from 'practice-based evidence,' which would take our ontology as the starting point of our experience in work rather than the idea that, by accreting layer upon layer of knowledge and data, we somehow come to understand the world as an object in relation to which we are entirely separate.

Similarly, in relation to this point, the illusion of knowability leads inexorably to the conclusion that there is a reality to which we all orient that is solid and agreed. This, of course, effaces the important recognition that the act of being – including having a presence in a work system – is not about a sovereign subject's orientation to a concrete reality: instead, the individual is engaged in constant acts of interpretation and so the reality of which they are an intrinsic and largely indistinguishable element is individually recognised, collectively explored, and socially constructed. Yet the average Board or committee meeting is invariably indulging the fiction of a single objective reality to which the 'organisation' needs to adjust or take actions to shape. Notwithstanding the moot point of agency in this respect – the metonymy of the word organisation tends to lend to the concept the idea that it is seamlessly collective and acts in the world as a single entity – it means that a great deal of attention in a company is devoted to matters that are merely epiphenomenal, when the nuts and bolts of organisation life and practice are left largely unattended.

I have often made the observation that an organisational chart will reflect the structure that people have attempted to apply to the circumstances they face, while underneath that there is a system of complex interrelation-ships, accepted ways of being, and connections that actually see the work of the firm being done. The idée fixe that supposed knowability equips an 'organisation' to craft the world in a way that it sees fit is a distraction that obscures how work actually gets done, which is ontologically, i.e. through being in an organisational context. This brings us back to that important distinction that exists between organising and organisation: many senior leaders attend to the latter and fail to recognise that the former is the motor of their enterprise and needs to be actively encouraged. The Radical OD practitioner, then, needs to constantly work to orient everyone in organisa-tional life towards lived experience rather than abstracted representations – and needs to explain (as best they can) that the traditional reassurances that senior leaders have created for themselves are illusory – and a focus on the collective lives across the company and the way in which they intersect and interrelate is where their attention should be and not on the colourful GANTT charts and spreadsheets.

Finally, in consideration to our example of chairing a meeting outlined above, there is a tension between language being seen as an act when the discourse of modern business is cluttered with expectations that people in organisations should move quickly to decision and that talk gets in the way of 'getting things done.' But speech is an act, of course, and conversation is the way in which organising is realised, in many ways. This is not to in-dulge the sophistry that attends dialogic OD, where it is often declared that the conversation is the change. Instead, the conversation offers insight into the doing of things differently to which the interlocutors must make an ontological orientation for it to manifest meaningfully. In light of this, the Radical OD practitioner should feel confident to foreground conversation as a means of working through the challenges of organising – and of being in an organisation – so that it is, in fact, the core element of their practice. That means engaging with negativity around 'talking shops' – and having the courage in these circumstances to defend conversation and what it gen-erates as a significant human and productive activity that stands in contrast to the fetishisation of action as something in contrast to speech.

Just to reinforce the above, it is worth highlighting the role of the Radical OD practitioner as a myth-buster, someone who, as a *parrhesiastes*, speaks out and calls out the constraints in which people have allowed themselves to become entangled, thereby enabling them to see this and to explore how to change these circumstances, both individually and collectively. In work I have recently been undertaking with my colleague John Higgins, we have explored the way in which some myths extend across social and organisational life and inhibit both. These include, first, the myth that everything is in some way fixable, from a human body enduring illness through to a supposedly 'dysfunctional' organisation; second, that perfection is the only standard that is worthy of pursuing; and, lastly, that there is always just one true way of doing things. In our view, this – by no means exhaustive – list of myths tends to paralyse meaningful creativity in the practice of leadership and management and endlessly reproduces that which has always been. The Radical OD practitioner needs to have the wherewithal and the willingness to call out these shibboleths and encourage those with whom they work to engage with them critically. Hence, to abandon those myths means that the practitioners contend instead that: all moves are tentative; the vast majority of issues that we face are complex in their composition; perfection is an illusion, and an unhelpful one at that.

But there is also an ontological facet to the way in which this practitioner engages in this practice. It's not merely about engaging with an existentialist perspective in an abstract way and in relation to one's engagement with – and encouragement of – others in a work context. As Sartre explains (and with apologies in advance for the gendered nature of the writing),

> When we say that man chooses his own self, we mean that every one of us does likewise; but we also mean that in making his choice he also chooses for all men. In fact, in creating the man that we want to be, there is not a single one of our acts which does not at the same time create an image of man as we think he ought to be.
>
> (Sartre, 1988, p. 37)

Importantly, he goes on to note that, 'If we have defined man's situation as a free choice, with no excuses and no recourse, every man who takes refuge behind the excuse of his passions, every man who sets up a determinism, is a dishonest man' (Sartre, 1988, p. 59).

This encapsulates a number of key elements of Sartre's existentialist thinking. First, it throws light on the notion of existence preceding essence, which is to say that there is no one true self to which we are working. Instead, we are defined by the myriad choices in the moment that we make in our existence – and that this, in turn, defines us as a person and – at the same time – defines all of humanity as a collective. And, second, any effort on our part to eschew that choice is an inauthentic way of being, and this is particularly the case where we seek to surrender our specific freedom to choose through some excuse; this is what Sartre refers to as living in 'bad faith.' Hence, the Radical OD practitioner recognises that their life is built through the chain of choices that existence compels us to make – and refusing that responsibility is to act inauthentically. From an existential perspective, there is no 'radical' essence that precedes an individual's practice; instead, their practice choices, in turn, define what radical might mean to them and to others.

Implicit in all of this is a Sartrean notion of freedom, a freedom that is wholly inescapable. To explore this further,

> A person can never surrender his freedom. He can never make himself an object causally determined by the physical world because the very project of surrender, the very attempt to render himself causally determined, must be a free choice of himself.
>
> (Cox, 2014, p. 48)

This means that the Radical OD practitioner needs to embrace the freedom that lies at the very heart of their practice and – through their free choices – shape themselves and the wider practice field (and beyond). But the exercise of that freedom needs to be reflexive and mindful so that our practitioner does not merely seek to surrender themselves to the context in which they find themselves working, which is – as we have seen above – a choice in and of itself.

Work exists that seeks to locate existentialism in the workplace and this offers a helpful signpost towards how a Radical OD practitioner might consider their work from this perspective. It is suggested, for example, that it is a philosophy that is helpful in the context because, first, it focuses on the primacy of the individual and their interactions with the workplace as formative of them and others; second, decision-making and ethics are intrinsic to existentialism and to organisational life; and, lastly, it offers a way of understanding the meaning of work (MacMillan et al., 2012, p. 39). In terms of developing meaning, productive linkages have been made between existentialism and Weick's work on sense-making, which has a strong presence in the field of OD (Blomme & Bornebroek-Te Lintelo, 2012). So, it is a notion that should, at least, be familiar to the mindful practitioner.

Meanwhile, another interesting route that has been explored is the relationship between existentialism and leadership, with an initial focus on the practice of leadership and its connections with topics such as freedom, responsibility, and meaninglessness in a workplace context (Lawler, 2005). Attention has, of course, also been paid to the idea of authenticity in leadership, which is a somewhat fuzzy-edged notion in a lot of scholarship but acquires a more grounded feel when viewed through the prism of existentialism (Lawler & Ashman, 2012). At root, the philosophy opens up a discussion around freedom and choice for the individual, something that is seen to have relevance in particular when we consider the modern vision of leadership. Indeed, this picture of the practice might reasonably be said to run counter to the familiar discourse around leadership, wherein – despite widespread notional allegiances to styles as wide-ranging as compassionate, inclusive and servant leadership – leadership still recurs in social and organisational life as a strongly individualised and heroic act, divided between those who deliver success (the leaders we love) and those who fail to achieve what is expected of them in respect to what we take to be their powerful position. Little exists between these two extreme polar opposites – and great relish is drawn from watching leaders leap into the positive or teeter and fall into the negative side of that very pronounced dichotomy.

Patently, the idea of giving an existentialist bent to one's professional practice links intimately to what I was saying earlier about *parrhesia*, which stands in the sharpest relief to the idea of living one's life in bad faith. This, of course, is not a suggestion of ideological veiling, where our choices are hidden by the beliefs that cloud our thinking and judgement. As Sartre explains, 'In bad faith there is no cynical lie nor knowing preparation of deceitful concepts. But the first act of bad faith is to flee what it can not flee, to flee what it is' (Sartre, 1988, p. 185). In fact, it might better be described as '...more like an ongoing project of self-distraction or self-evasion than self-deception' (Cox, 2014, p. 59).

The Radical OD practitioner, then, will deny the notion that there is some essential character to the idea of the person who does OD in favour of a vision that sees their professional self –and the broader idea of the practice in general – as realised by their existence as a practitioner. Similarly, the Radical OD practitioner will seek to place this sort of authenticity at the very heart of their day to day when seeking to get alongside a workforce to support them with how best to organise around a common purpose. Indeed, it would be an act of bad faith to focus on the organisation and not the existence of people seeking to organise together.

The organisation and its issues – its structures, functions, and inscribed processes – are epiphenomenal, despite assuming for itself the mantle of a key unit of analysis and practice for OD. It lends itself to OD activity, not least because the field has – to a large extent – built itself, in all of its manifestations to date – around the idea of the organisation as an essence that deserves our focus. But this is a distraction, for beneath this veneer – with its constant demands for attention, in terms of its dysfunctions and ineffectiveness – lies the key issue, which is organising and purpose. If mainstream OD practice tries to fix the organisation by working with (or, to put it more honestly, on) the people that inhabit that encrustation of previous organising, then Radical OD will seek to focus exclusively on the lived experience and thoughts and ideas of the people in order to fashion an authentic purpose and identify ways of coming together in order to attain that ambition. The idea of the 'organisation' needs to be entirely stripped from the equation; to do otherwise is to work with the workforce as if they were a mere instrument for organisational improvement, patently a practice that is intrinsic to the operation of power/knowledge in the workplace.

Herein lies a key aspect of Radical OD, namely the requirement to disturb the performativity that prevails in organisational life. This notion has two points of reference, one in respect to theatre practice and a more sophisticated and critically engaged origin in feminist theory. The former encompasses the way in which an actor might inhabit a role in order to meet the requirements of the overall narrative (Schechner, 2003). In the latter, located in thinking about feminism and the relationship between sex and gender, it is argued that,

> If gender is the cultural meanings that the sexed body assumes, then a gender cannot be said to follow from a sex in any one way. Taken to its logical limit, the sex/gender distinction suggests a radical discontinuity between sexed bodies and culturally constructed genders.
>
> (Butler, 2006, p. 9)

Using an existentialist prism and interrogating some key Foucauldian notions, Butler makes the case that

> If there is something right in Beauvoir's claim that one is not born, but rather becomes a woman, it follows that woman itself is a term in process, a becoming, a constructing that cannot rightfully be said to originate or to end.
>
> (Butler, 2006, p. 45)

This leads to the supposition that gender is something one does, as opposed to something that one is (Salih, 2007), hence gender can be said to be performative.

This can comfortably be extended into thinking about the role of 'employee,' 'manager,' or 'leader' in an organisational context. There is no fixity in respect to these terms other than through the dominant discourse that inhabits the social space wherein these roles are seen to prevail. From a Foucauldian perspective, these subjects and the relationship that we have with them are developed from the discourse that prevails, which is threaded through with practices, behaviours, and ideas that relate to power/knowledge. But the precepts of existentialism, alongside Foucault's notion of technologies of the self, where the subject is both created by the discourse and, at the same time, is able to act to define themselves in contradistinction to that discourse, support the Radical OD practitioner potentially to open up a space of inquiry wherein that performativity can be investigated and – potentially – shrugged off.

For example, a commission to work with a team 'in difficulty' or which gets described through the shorthand of being 'dysfunctional' – and we should hold in mind the fact that there is a whole realm of practice in the field which concerns itself with this elusive notion (Lencioni, 2002), so where the blithe and unthinking application of this definition serves to label a group of people at work in terms of their Otherness – then the Radical OD practitioner would actively seek to recast that perspective. Instead, they would extend an invitation to those involved to interrogate critically their discursive determination as 'dysfunctional' or 'difficult' in that specific context. After all, a wider organisational description of a team as 'dysfunctional' (herein, of course, the intimation of a biological metaphor, faintly tainted by a sense of medicalisation) might actually mean that this is a group of employees who are positive outliers in terms of the accepted culture and processes of the place where they work. Oppressive normalcy would seek to mobilise its capacities in order to silence subaltern discourses, of which this might be one.

A recent piece of research unwittingly underscores this, as the authors started to look into the whole issue of engagement and teams (Armstrong et al., 2018). I am minded to say here that the juxtaposition of these two ideas should be more than enough to set off alarms. To be flippant for a moment, the true test of how comfortable one might be in embracing the idea of a Radical OD practice is to see how visceral one's reaction might be to this concatenation of two fictional ideas in organisational life, as I have argued throughout. Here, then, is a piece of business school research that sanitises the context of its work by making no reference to the nature of the workplace, how paid employment is experienced by the vast majority in a capitalist society, the crude inequities that haunt that mode of production and the power that inhabits it. Indeed, the foundation of the work is the perceived problem of limited upticks in productivity despite the presence of a wide range of engagement initiatives, when the latter are widely held to support improvements in organisational performance.

The work contents itself with casting aside the traditional binary notion of people being either engaged or unengaged in the workplace in favour of a more calibrated model of four states. Only one of those states is viewed positively in this schema, namely what the authors describe as the 'Zone of Engagement,' which is where they normatively suggest teams should be (Armstrong et al., 2018, pp. 16–17). However, the other three zones that they purport to have identified – or confected – in light of the research demonise the teams there insofar as their behaviours are discursively unacceptable. Here we find a zone of contentment (where people coast towards retirement, eager to avoid challenge or stretch); a zone of disengagement (in which the autonomy and creativity of the human spirit is squeezed out by the sheer boredom and seeming pointlessness of the work that people are forced to do); and a zone of pseudo-engagement, where – to borrow a term from Scientific Management – the team members are 'soldiering' (Taylor, 1919, p. 30), by which was meant loafing, marking time, and playing the system. In other words, in the latter regard, they are engaging in acts of resistance to the dismal circumstances in which they find themselves.

This resuscitation of a central tenet of Taylorism and its application to the modern notion of teamwork seems particularly loaded to me. There is an ethical orientation to the mobilisation of the idea of pseudo-engagement, although its moral grounding is built upon the inequity of an unquestioned – indeed, wholly unexamined – wider social system. It chimes with a wider argument that scientific management has attained the widest possible range of its aims through its contemporary incorporation into wider organisational practices such as staff engagement initiatives and shifts in employment status, something that is helpfully referred to as Neo-Taylorism (Crowley et al., 2010). Ultimately, if these zones are meaningful – and that point remains moot, despite the supposed research underpinning it all – then the orientation needs to be inverted, so that the focus is drawn away from a pathologised workforce to a context in which work is patently deeply unsatisfying and so is the focus of thinking about organising and purpose.

So, the work here in respect to teams being problematised – if one were practising radically – would also be to explore the performative aspects at play in the workshop. How does the 'employee' appear in this discourse? How is the relationship between 'manager' and 'employee' discursively shaped and generally accepted? What would one's presence be like in this space if, first, there was no discursive shaping of 'employee' and, second, if – existentially – the person could turn up and express an unmediated version of their personhood? This is not easy work, as it goes to the very heart of our subjecthood, and traditional philosophy has seen that as something that we alone are enabled to shape, craft, and express. There will be a resistance to getting under the skin of all of this, yet it is intrinsic to an OD practice that seeks to privilege the person and critiques their relationship to what is then called the 'organisation.'

Deconstructing the layers

Thus far, the conversation about Radical OD has largely been concerned with reworking our personal and practice orientations. The imperative in this section is to now plant afresh on that uprooted ground where current thinking and activity resided in favour of taking the work off in a direction of more obvious activity and anticipated output and outcome. It is important to help people to scrutinise power as it presents itself in their working context – and vital to home in on the action of organising rather than privileging the organisation, which is a mere ossification of previous organising efforts. But ultimately the work that we undertake from the perspective of Radical OD has to be transformative, by which I mean that it supports people to think differently about the ideas, notions, and activities that they unwittingly undertake in the context of work – and offers them the chance to consider different ways of being, doing, and developing.

You will note that I am framing this in a way that places the responsibility for surfacing and exploring new ways of working firmly with those who do the work. This, of course, draws on the maxims developed in respect to living systems by Myron Rodgers on the basis of his long experience in this regard. In particular, he suggests that 'Those who do the work do the change' – and, more recently, he has begun to argue that 'The process you use to get to the future is the future you get' (Rodgers, n.d.). These seemingly simple observations – which for many of us in the field are truisms upon which we found our thinking and work – are radical, though, insofar as they run counter to much of what happens in organisations in a capitalist society. I see many instances where some obeisance is shown to such notions but where there is no obvious appetite to work to actualise these through an adjustment in leadership thinking or practice.

So, first, do those who do the work do the change ordinarily? No, that work is the preserve of managers (regardless of how well prepared they feel for such a responsibility – and the way in which this may adversely impact on their relationships with those that they manage); of project managers, who invariably create a fiction of what is happening through their production of brightly coloured charts and spreadsheets; and of 'change teams,' clusters of people from a variety of functions – including, inevitably, Human Resources. Then, second, is the fact that method is the midwife of outcome – indeed, might be said to be its parent, in that the DNA of the future will be derived from that of the approach taken to sire it – acknowledged by those involved in this type of activity? No, virtually every oxymoronic 'programme of transformation' that organisations trumpet and visit upon their workforces tend to use the methods and techniques (GANTT charts; SMART objectives; traditional hierarchical governance, replete with soul-destroying Task & Finish Groups; a linear focus that supports the illusions of causality, when organisational life can largely be seen as organic) that they have always used and which have never actually changed anything.

Behind much of this frenetic activity and providing cover for the hard-nosed realities that underpin such exercises, which invariably serve an organisational imperative which can be seen as at odds with the needs and expectations of the workforce, sits OD and its practitioners. In fact, the whole issue of managing change tends to sit at the core of OD as its chief concern. In offering practitioners, a selection of 'tools' in support of their work, one author groups these into five sections, thereby giving insight into what is popularly seen to fall within the remit of OD. These are: leadership development; employee development (with a focus on enhancing performance of individuals in the workplace); development of the ways in which the organisation functions (embracing improving meetings, communications, and work design); and, crucially, strategic planning and change management, with the focus on issues of diagnosis of problems and design of solutions, planning the delivery of change, and (inevitably) overcoming resistance (Silberman, 2003).

As a sidebar to this, it is always interesting to me that a field of practice that tends to work in a way that is largely intangible, in that it is strictly speaking about engaging and developing human relations in an organisational setting, indulges itself by using a range of terms that are drawn from the work of tradespeople. Thus, OD practitioners – as we see with Silberman's book title – often speak of using tools or having things in their toolbox. Similarly, the gatherings that they convene so often get spoken about as 'workshops,' which seems to conjure for me images of furnaces, hot iron and an anvil (and the production of material artefacts that are intrinsically useful, of course). It reminds me of a divisional director at an NHS organisation where I worked, who joked that, given my arrival at the meeting that he was leading, it was pretty certain that I would be pulling flipchart pens, blue tack and Post-Its out of my pocket very shortly. These are the tools of OD, although I sense they are far from worthy of that description. My father was a display artist and had a shed full of hammers, screwdrivers, saws, and industrial staple guns: I worked with him briefly and used tools to undertake my labour. Other than a fountain pen, I no longer actually engage with tools, in the proper sense, and to suggest otherwise is misleading.

To return to the discussion of change as a core element of OD, this applies as much in dialogic OD as it does in more traditional diagnostic OD. But, as intimated above, some people have tried to think differently about this aspect of the work, drawing the experience of the workforce to the centre of their practice. For example, my colleague John Higgins, heavily engaged at the time in the Ashridge Doctorate in Organisational Change, explains that,

> For a good while now,...., I have been moving away from universal models and grand theories – being drawn instead into an understanding of change as something more ordinary, more wrapped up in the day-to-day of people rubbing along together. This makes sense to me because it grounds my attention in the present and connects change to what is happening in the here and now, rather than in some idealised future or demonised past.
>
> (Higgins, 2014, p. xiii)

One reformist prefiguration of the ways in which one might properly take control of the idea of change as something that should derive from those people themselves, given their proximity to the work and their largely un-recognised ability to review what goes on and articulate different – and better ways – in which to do it appears in the notion of Communities of Practice. This derived from work undertaken around how people obtain competence in respect to their work. The starting point is an epistemology that underscores the idea that learning in this context is something that is situated and facilitated by what was called legitimate peripheral partic-ipation (Lave & Wenger, 1991). Notwithstanding that this can be seen to be a rather convoluted way of expressing the idea of apprenticeship (or, in the UK vernacular, 'Sitting next to Nellie'), it remains the case that this presentation of how workplace learning best takes place grounds it socially and underscores the idea that it is most effective when undertaken in and through practice, which makes it invaluable in terms of helping us to re-think learning in a work context.

One important aspect of this model is the idea of a Community of Prac-tice (CoP) as a place wherein apprenticeship occurs, rather than through the more traditional and individually focused relationship between a skilled person and their apprentice (Lave & Wenger, 1991, p. 94). This, in turn, became a focus for investigation in itself, leading to a more thorough ex-ploration of both practice and the communities that build around it. In the latter regard, practice needs to be seen as a site of complex and multi-layered understandings, activities, and mediated activities (Wenger, 1998, p. 47); regarding a community, it should be seen as in tight relation to that practice – and the means by which those involved make sense of what they do and how they do it (Wenger, 1998, p. 45).

All of which shapes the way in which we think about people in the workplace. We either view them at best as a 'human resource' to be mo-bilised or, at worst, as an asset to be sweated – or we see them as human agents, engaged in practice alongside a community of others and learning and developing through that. It leads to a stark distinction:

> [I]f we believe that productive people in organizations are diligent imple-mentors of organizational processes and that the key to organizational performance is therefore the definition of increasingly more efficient and detailed processes by which people's actions are prescribed [or, increas-ingly, proscribed, of course – MC], then it makes sense to engineer and

re-engineer these processes in abstract ways and then roll them out for implementation. But if we believe that people in organizations contribute to organizational goals by participating inventively in practices that can never be fully captured by institutionalized processes, then we will minimise prescription, suspecting that too much of it discourages the very inventiveness that makes practice effective.

(Wenger, 1998, p. 10)

A Community of Practice would appear from this type of exposition to be something that is organically implicit in positive organisational life. And where they are seen to flourish – and here it is worth recollecting the study of Xerox engineers and their informal, somewhat offline and positively deviant, CoP (Orr, 1996) as a means of thinking beyond the theoretical, useful though that definitional work might be – then there is clearly an expectation that we would want the organising that occurs through such communities to take precedence over bureaucratic attempts to add constraints to the lives of employees. As ever in such discussions, it is moot as to whether communities simply exist in certain organisational settings and do not appear in others – although Wenger went on to write the sort of 'How-to' book so beloved of busy senior leaders for whom the momentary tang of a new idea generates an excess of appetite for it (Wenger et al., 2002).

To that extent, as hinted at above, this type of activity could be seen as reformist, insofar as it suggests that it might be possible to negotiate with senior leaders to allow Communities of Practice to flourish when, in truth, the presence of such things in organisational life are implicit challenges to the arrangements of power that exist. I have wrestled with this paradox in practice for some time, trying to hold on to the potential of communities to disturb existing relations of power – but recognising that, in many instances, through containment and then abandonment, senior leadership react negatively to the existential challenge offered by these developments.

Holding to a pure vision of how Communities of Practice might affect the context in which they arise might reasonably be described as an impossibilist position, a term found in Marxian thought, which suggests that holding to a pure and unsullied version of one's vision of a better society means that the vision can never actually be realised (Wikipedia, 2019). And my experience to date is that participation in a Community of Practice can feel to be a liberating experience, one in which it is possible to suddenly feel valued in the workplace and which supports meaningful action from a grass-roots position (Garrod & Ling, 2018). It supports people to interrogate a key element of their day-to-day practice – although, to take a different view of this, it might also be seen that the way in which communities identify domains and specific areas of practice on which to focus fragments the overall flow of organisational life as experienced by the individual employee and those around them. Such fragmentation denies the opportunity to acquire a more holistic view of the workplace, whence one might make more critical explorations and craft even more incisive and holistic interventions to support a reworking of organisational life.

The Radical OD practitioner, then, sees the Community of Practice as a means of underscoring the social nature of the workplace and the making of meaning therein. They also see the CoP as a way of encouraging people to test the notions of empowerment and, through their reflexivity, to push at the boundaries of the discretion that is permitted, the better to see the potential if those boundaries were eased even further back – or removed altogether. But they can also serve to obfuscate, drawing a veil over the real question of agency and change in the workplace and reinforcing the power that exists in the workplace by making it seem 'natural' and wholly acceptable that those who work in organisations might only be granted a bounded discretion to do things differently.

The authentically radical take on this work is to mobilise key ideas from social movement theory and to apply them seamlessly into an organisational context. Whereas Communities of Practice have the potential to surface issues of power, the social movement approach proceeds from the centrality of power and builds organising out of that understanding. The CoP might tear down the curtain to reveal the old man behind it – as opposed to the all-powerful wizard of the imagination of the people of Oz – but it is not guaranteed so to do. It is not a *sine qua non* of the CoP that power is revealed; individuals may glimpse power in the course of their participation, perhaps in some instances they may collectively recognise the power at play in the realm in which they are working, but the Community of Practice is not necessarily a vehicle for meaningful change in attitude and activity amongst the workforce.

It would be unhelpful to think of Communities of Practice as being developments in the field of power that can comfortably be absorbed into the mainstream. Equally, it would be erroneous to suppose that they can be created by some higher authority in that field in order to soak up burgeoning resistance. Such perspectives play to the zero-sum view of power as resource held by one at the expense of another – and knowingly used in order to obtain key results in respect to offsetting the negativity that extant arrangements might engender. Without becoming too immersed in the somewhat obtuse philosophical corpus that has flowed from the jointly wielded pens of Deleuze and Guattari, it pays dividends to think of the ways in which CoPs might be thought of as lines of flight, pregnant with the possibility of creating change out of an assemblage of other lines that segment and create momentary stability in that setting. It is possible to suggest, in this regard, that a line of flight has the potential to engender significant change, to extend from the current assemblage in order to allow it to reconfigure (Deleuze & Guattari, 2004).

In so doing, however, it has the potential instead to merely undergird a marginally altered – but fundamentally unchanged – assemblage, not by the actions of individuals in authority but simply on the basis of its appearance and location. There are myriad practices that can be seen to have arisen from such circumstances, one example being 'urban exploration' as a recreational activity that is often seen to be transgressive (Garrett, 2013). Yet, some see this line of flight as susceptible to being systemically incorporated and hence deprived of its potential to create real change (Kindynis, 2015). Thus, brands begin to inhabit this activity as part of their efforts to market commodities, the whole thing becomes corporatised. Skateboarding moved from being something that sat outside of the mainstream and sought to surreptitiously colonise urban space to an activity where urban space was willingly offered to skateboarding by local authorities and the like. Now, of course, you are likely to find half-pipes in countless playgrounds up and down the country. To explicate how this concept differs from our more traditional understandings of social resistance, the following observation is astute and useful: 'Deleuze's idea of lines of flight can help us clear up a common misconception about the sixties counterculture. The counterculture was not fundamentally oriented *against* mainstream society. It was oriented away from it' (Rayner, 2013).

For the Radical OD practitioner, the emphasis is about generating a collective appetite for inquiry – and to support the development of the capacities to engage in the workplace with a critical frame, starting with an immediate foregrounding of the actions of power in that context. This would be a qualitatively different way of engaging a community, an holistic approach that, instead of homing in microscopically on a key facet of the things that people do in the workplace, encourages people to start with their presence in that space – and the forces and practices that exist there. That inquiry needs to lie at the core of an approach to active change, which can be helpfully derived from thinking about social movements. This is the frame within which genuinely radical inquiry can take place.

Understanding the idea of social movement requires us to codify to some extent those things that might reasonably be said to constitute them. These include a number of facets – numbering ten in one review of thinking in this area – which include: innovating (or supporting innovation); mobilisation of collectives for action; production of alternative knowledges (surfacing the subaltern discourses); redistributors of power, through challenge and reconfiguration of the power/knowledge in organisational spaces; and accelerators of change (del Castillo et al., 2016). As we have seen elsewhere, such social movements prefigure new organisational forms and exist as laboratories in which thinking and practice work together to generate new thinking in respect to the act of organising in contrast to organisation as a reified manifestation of human togetherness in pursuit of purpose (Reinecke, 2018).

In considering the fields in which social movements can appear, particularly in organisations in a capitalist society, the following is extremely relevant, especially for Radical OD practice:

> Some organizational fields are characterized by a distinct dominance order in which a few groups of actors operate at the apex while others survive on the bottom. In such instances, groups of influential actors have vested interests in preserving the social order. Consequently, structural innovations seldom emerge out of the center of a hierarchically-organized field, but instead, originate in the periphery, and may conflict with the interests of central players. Since actors at the periphery of a field – similar to those in the interstices between fields – possess little influence and lack resources, social movements are the vehicles of collective action by which new forms become established.
>
> (Rao et al., 2000, pp. 260–261)

In light of this, the Radical OD practitioner sees the periphery not as an outward boundary nor indeed a liminal space but as the location in which a great deal of the meaningful work in terms of OD will need to be undertaken.

Some might cavil at this, calling upon the importance of senior leadership in terms of performance and effectiveness in organisational contexts. This plays to a traditional narrative of leadership, which – regardless of espoused views of the practice – reinforces the idea of the 'leader' as a decisive person who works in a linear fashion with causality at the heart of this practice. This, as I've intimated in relation to the myths that John Higgins are currently exploring, inhibit thinking and what gets done under the general rubric of management and leadership in organisations, namely that everything is fixable; perfection is the only possible outcome and no other results can be countenanced, and that there is only one possible correct way to do something. Similarly, in work I did with Ljubica Pilja and Sherin Jacobs in respect to a presentation to the CIPD Student Conference in March 2019, the organisational context is overwritten with a number of paradoxes, including the relationship between how organisations publicly commit to support well-being in the workplace and create programmes of activity in this regard whilst sustaining a culture of 'busyness' where expectations of work are relentless.

A second paradox that we explored relates to the dominant discourse in regard to leadership – which encapsulates traditional notions of power, heroism and the use of charisma to attain one's outcomes – that can be seen to stand in contrast to the way in which a wide range of organisations publicly subscribe to the notion of showing compassion to their respective workforces. Hence, to challenge that discursive perspective, the social movement is a logical response, which allows groups of people to colonise the idea of compassionate leadership while, at the same time, challenging extant relations of power in the workplace. And that movement needs to burrow into and disrupt the cognitive dissonance at the heart of this, wherein our views of leadership simply do not tally – in fact, run counter to one another. What we say about leadership and espouse regarding what it ought to look like sits in contradictory relationship with what we see of leadership across society at large and in our organisations.

Finally, for those who maintain that an organisation's success resides in what a senior leader (oftentimes the Chief Executive Officer) or group of senior leaders might do, it is worth subjecting this taken-for-granted notion to critical scrutiny. In my field of healthcare, where – as previously noted – the CEO is simultaneously elevated to dizzying heights and, at the same time, aggressively penalised where things go wrong, a diligent and robust piece of research recently published seems to torpedo this idea, to my mind. The authors argue quite simply that, 'We find little evidence of CEOs being systematically able to change the performance of these organizations. We also do not find evidence that a change in CEO brings about an improvement (or even just a change) in performance' (Janke et al., 2018, p. 40). Yes, there are compounding factors in this specific context, which might leave one to query how this might translate across all industrial sectors and organisational forms: the fact that the NHS is determined and defined by government and political cycles and the sheer systemic complexity of NHS providers are noted in this regard (Janke et al., 2018, pp. 40–41).

But a Radical OD practice would seek to deflate the notion that heroic senior leaders are solely responsible for organisational outcomes; rather, it would put to the fore the idea that capacity for changing organisations for the better resides throughout – and at least one voice, that of employees, has either not been heard – or has been heard through a number of layers and constraints, through formal processes of 'engagement' (for which traditional OD is so often responsible). In this regard, I am less and less enamoured of the idea of writing things on flipchart paper, in light of the view that this action intermediates unnecessarily the flowing human process of organising, in favour of the creation of an artefact, which invariably disappears after the discussions. Commissioners of OD services favour the production of these artefacts, because they offer the illusion of measurability: they are erroneously taken to be tangible outputs from the event that was scheduled. Instead, they draw off the energy and (quite literally) inscribe the conversation into the discourse of power/knowledge that exists in that corporate context. The Radical OD practitioner will inevitably fall into the role of intermediary, from a structural perspective; their job, however, is to work towards disintermediation, allow the workforce to work directly on the organising issues at hand and not on the organisational exhibits that have to be produced to reassure those who curate the corporate museum.

Disturb the discourse, reveal the fictions

The Radical OD practitioner manifests a new way of working through an adjusted presence in the workplace – one which eschews the traditional approach where, having been commissioned by management, the practitioner carries the imprimatur of those who run the organisation, in favour of one where they present more authentically – and a different way of approaching their work, which requires them to actively adjust their focus. Overarching this is a responsibility to behave in an exemplary way, a means of acting in the space that requires them to efface themselves and to relinquish the sorts of control that resides in OD. The very production of an outline or a timed programme for an event presupposes that the group with which a practitioner will work can be led and directed through a process in order to achieve a specific outcome, either crafted solely by the practitioner or designed in conjunction with the senior leader who has asked for this activity to take place.

Similarly, as noted above, the 'capture' of the event, through whatever means – flipchart notes, graphic recorders, videotaping, and so on – actually reinforces the power at play in the context. Groups are 'directed' by the OD practitioner to constrain the free flow of their conversation in order to inscribe it (with at least one member of the group removing themselves from that flow in order to act as 'scribe'). This is not to enhance memory of the work but to give the organisation something measurable with which to hold the participants to account. All OD is doing is drawing the positivity out of human exchange and conversation in favour of implicating people in their own close supervision against targets. Hence, once more, the veneer of 'engagement' through the supposedly liberating 'away day' (dress casual, get out of the office, enjoy a nice lunch, play daft games, watch some big noises in corporate life spin out weak ideas into ten minute 'edutainments' via TED talks on video, get to josh around with colleagues, eat jelly beans from the bowl on the table, maybe start late and finish early on that day, etc.) is easily worn away to reveal all the old management imperatives and practices.

Passing some of this thinking through the prism of anarchist organisation, we land with two significant pre-requisites for change genuinely to take place and not simply that the past is endlessly reproduced: first, barriers to communication, thought and action must be aggressively destroyed; and, second, we need to foreground the simple axiom that 'You can't change the world if you expect to remain unchanged' (Amrod & Chernyi, 1996, p. 318). These precepts are antecedents of a rich radical practice in OD, both for the practitioner as an individual and in terms of the work that they seek to do in conjunction with others in the workplace. A new way of organising to meet common purpose requires those inhabiting this space to seek to tear down the barriers – what is ordinarily called the 'organisation' that has arisen around us or into which we have been accommodated – and also to recognise that transformation resides within each individual and in advance of the wider change that people might collectively seek.

This twofold way of being represents, in and of itself, an opening to the emergence of myriad small acts of resistance. Here, it is worth reorienting towards Foucault and his conception of power, which – whilst having more in common with anarchist thinking than Marxism – is more nuanced and less instrumentalist than either of those perspectives. Insofar as Foucault echoes Sartrean existentialism to decentre entirely the familiar notion that there is some human essence upon which power acts (and hence represses), it is vital to understand that he certainly does not disregard the oppressive character of power, in terms of the limitations that it sets upon individuals (Newman, 2007, p. 87). In fact, it is argued that 'Foucault sees resistance and power existing in a relationship of mutual antagonism and incitement – a relationship of *agonism*' (Newman, 2007, p. 87). Hence, our resistance is not an aberration, something rendering us maverick and somewhat *infra dig*. It cannot help but arise from power, in terms of both challenging and reinforcing it. To resist is wholly unavoidable – and it is a responsibility that the Radical OD practitioner will contentedly embrace, indulge, and amplify.

That resistance, of course, is not about lifting the cobbles and standing behind the barricades. Eventually, those cobbles become the bricks that are used to build the gulag where those who disagree are imprisoned – or the barricades end up as monuments of failed efforts at change. The work of resistance is personal and then thoughtfully collective. For example, calibrating power in terms of 'patterns of domination' allows for a deeper engagement with the way in which power exists in society – and this is work that can be done in the context of Radical OD practice. It is important that those patterns, which carry with them the air of common sense and hence enjoy a protected nature in human discussion, are interrogated and dismantled. Hence, one pattern can be said to be tolerance, which actually creates a circumstance where small doses of difference are allowed, whereas another, objectivity, offers a position undergirded by scientism that can be said to ignore the power-laden reality in which we find ourselves (Suarez, 2018, p. 19). Such common-sense notions naturally need to be cast into doubt by any Radical OD practice.

Hence, at root, Radical OD practice seeks to disturb the discourse and the apparatus that facilitates it, by which I mean the institutions, knowledges, practices, structures, concepts, and so on that represent the channels through which the discourse pulses and, at the same time, is formed. In so doing, our work begins to reveal the fictions that structure our lives. By fiction in this regard, I mean perspectives such as the progressivist idea that the workplace is in some way qualitatively different to that which prevailed in the late 19th century, in terms of power. But it also requires us to work at a subterranean level in terms of making sense of such fiction – and making connections with ideas and practices that would ordinarily appear to be entirely separate on the basis of a more ordinary epistemology.

So, for example, the pursuit of the idea of happiness at work shows – at a superficial level – what might be said to be an improvement in the experience of people in the workplace. But this is only possible if one views it through an historicism of 'then and now.' For we know that the motivations in this regard are not merely altruistic or solely focused on human betterment; it relates instead very closely to the idea of how best to maximise the exploitation of people at work without those subjects noticing it and hence pushing back against it, not least because it is imbued with the notion of progress … and who would want to be seen to contest that, particularly when those around you – through the fierce management of the 'team' – seem content with this. Many of us feel involved in our work these days through the processes of 'teamification' and practices around engagement – yet I would wager that many of us equally feel like outliers, discomforted by the workplace yet entangled in regimes of silence where we do not articulate those concerns in a workplace setting.

The elements that make up a radical practice

This chapter has sought to outline how a practitioner seeking to work differently in the field of OD might assume a fresh ontology, explore a new type of presence in the field of their work, and experiment with new sorts of practice, in terms of their relations in the workplace with both those from whom they take their commissions and those with whom they are expected to work. To recap, the seven orientations in a Radical OD practice are – to my mind – as follows:

(1) **Power**: The brackets that we tend to lock this into when we talk about the workplace need to be removed – and power needs to be not just openly acknowledged but actively foregrounded in the work that we call OD;

(2) **Parrhesia**: With power at the centre of these discussions, the Foucauldian idea of speaking out in the face of power regardless of how deleterious that might be to the speaker needs to be intrinsic to the work of OD, both through the practitioner and as a key aspect of the work that they endeavour to do with those with whom they find themselves alongside;

(3) **Organising not organisation**: The vitality of people coming together to organise for a common purpose is where energy and meaning come from interaction and not from the dry husk of organisation. The former precedes the latter – and the latter might be seen as the ossification of previous organising efforts, something that then bureaucratically hinders the lifeblood of organising on which human endeavour depends;

(4) **Reflexivity**: In light of the preceding three elements, there is a need to develop an astute understanding of how one's presence in the field impacts and shapes that field. And, equally, it is essential to recognise that the work that you do reinforces what is happening at that time. Much OD practice is a mere conduit for the reproduction of what is currently in existence. The practitioner in that space is contributing directly to that – unless they are keeping both their practice and – crucially – themselves under continuous review. This reflexivity offers the opportunity for their presence and practice to make a positive difference to the fields in which they work;

(5) **An existential orientation**: This advanced quality of reflexivity precedes an attitude towards one's practice – and the very issue of being in a work context – that is existential in outlook, that is to say, where personal responsibility, authenticity, candour, and an avoidance of the notion of essentialism shape the way in which the practitioner works – and encourages others to be in the organisational setting;

(6) **Deconstructing the layers**: The traditional understanding of the organisation in capitalist society preserves the idea that there are superiors and subordinates – and that those at the top are imbued with a competence that is required to 'lead' or 'manage' a firm, whereas those in subaltern positions are charged with operationalising the thinking from above. Even where companies are embracing the notional idea of self-managed teams, we see that this flattening of the firm is illusory and the new approach is still directed by someone at a senior level in the

organisation. Hence, to deconstruct those layers rather than to indulge the fantasy of having removed them, the workforce needs to be challenged to engage in deep inquiry – and to come together to do things in ways that actively address the question of power, which is where social movement theory can helpfully guide us; and

(7) **Disruption and revelation:** The discourse that dominates needs to be challenged constantly, not least so that other knowledges and power can be heard in the organisational context. And the fictions that shape our subjectivity in the workplace need to be teased apart and rebuilt in light of the stories of others.

Bibliography

Abrahammson, B., 1993. *The logic of organizations.* Newbury Park, CA: Sage.

Althusser, L., 1970/2008. Ideology and ideological state apparatuses (Notes towards an investigation). In: L. Althusser, ed. *On ideology.* London: Verso, pp. 1–60.

Amrod, J. & Chernyi, L., 1996. Beyond character and morality: Towards transparent communications and coherent organization. In: H. J. Ehrlich, ed. *Reinventing anarchy, again.* Edinburgh: AK Press, pp. 318–322.

Armstrong, A., Olivier, S. & Wilkinson, S., 2018. *Shades of grey: An exploratory study of engagement in work teams.* Berkhamsted: Hult Research.

Baudrillard, J., 2004. Simulacra and simulations. In: J. Rivkin & M. Ryan, eds. *Literary theory: An anthology.* Oxford: Blackwell Publishing Ltd., pp. 365–377.

Bayswater Institute, 2017. *The Double Task.* [Online]. Available at: https://www.bayswaterinst.org/2017/09/13/the-double-task/ [Accessed 21 January 2019].

BBC Radio 4 – Thinking allowed, 2017. *Management jargon: Why is meaningless speech in the workplace so ubiquitous?* s.l.: s.n.

Bentham, J., 1995. *The Panopticon writings.* London: Verso.

Bhaskar, R., 2008. *A realist theory of science.* Abingdon: Routledge.

Bidet, J., 2016. *Foucault with Marx.* London: Zed Books.

Bion, W. R., 1961. *Experiences in groups and other papers.* London: Tavistock.

Block, P., 2011. *Flawless consulting: A guide to getting your expertise used.* 3rd ed. San Francisco, CA: Jossey-Bass.

Blomme, R. J. & Bornebroek-Te Lintelo, K., 2012. Existentialism and organizational behaviour: How existentialism can contribute to complexity theory and sense-making. *Journal of Organizational Change Management,* 25(3), pp. 405–421.

Bolton, S. C., 2005. 'Making up' managers: The case of NHS nurses. *Work Employment Society,* 19(5), pp. 5–23.

Borton, T., 1970. *Reach, touch and teach*. New York: McGraw-Hill.

Bozovic, M., 1995. Introduction – 'An utterly dark spot.' In: J. Bentham, ed. *The Panopticon writings*. London: Verso, pp. 1–27.

Burke, W. W., 1982. *Organization development: Principles and practice*. Boston, MA: Little, Brown and Company.

Bushe, G. R. & Marshak, R. J., 2009. Revisioning organization development: Diagnostic and dialogic premises and patterns of practice. *The Journal of Applied Behavioral Science*, 45(3), pp. 348–368.

Butler, J., 2006. *Gender trouble: Feminism and the subversion of identity*. Abingdon: Routledge.

Cheung-Judge, M.-Y., 2001. The self as instrument: A cornerstone for the future of OD. *OD Practitioner*, 33(3), pp. 11–16.

Cheung-Judge, M.-Y., 2019. *The future of OD: Power, practice and possibilities*. London: s.n.

Cole, M., 2017. Rethinking the practice of workplace learning and development: Utilizing 'knowledge, connections and conversation' in organizations. *International Journal of HRD Practice, Policy and Research*, 2(1), pp. 7–19.

Cooperrider, D. L. & Srivastva, S., 1987. Appreciative inquiry in organizational life. *Research in Organizational Change and Development*, 1, pp. 129–169.

Corporate Rebels, 2018. *Bucket List*. [Online]. Available at: https://corporate-rebels.com/bucketlist/ [Accessed 14 February 2018].

Cox, G., 2014. *How to be an Existentialist, or how to get real, get a grip and stop making excuses*. London: Bloomsbury.

Crowley, M., Tope, D., Chamberlain, L. J. & Hodson, R., 2010. Neo-Taylorism at work: Occupational change in the Post-Fordist era. *Social Problems*, 57(3), pp. 421–447.

del Castillo, J., Khan, H., Nicholas, L. & Finnis, A., 2016. *Health as a social movement: The power of people in movements*. London: Nesta.

Deleuze, G. & Guattari, F., 2004. *A thousand plateaus*. London: Continuum.

Ehrlich, H. J., 1996. Anarchism and formal organizations. In: H. J. Ehrlich, ed. *Reinventing anarchy, again*. Edinburgh: AK Press, pp. 56–68.

Eisner, E. W., 1991/2017. *The enlightened eye: Qualitative inquiry and the enhancement of educational practice*. New York: Teachers College Press.

Fischer, F., 1984. Ideology and organization theory. In: F. Fischer & C. Sirianni, eds. *Critical studies in organization and bureaucracy*. Philadelphia, PA: Temple University Press, pp. 172–190.

Fleetwood, S. & Ackroyd, S. eds., 2004. *Critical realist applications in organisation and management studies*. London: Routledge.

Fleming, P. & Study, A., 2009. Bringing everyday life back into the workplace: Just be yourself!. In: P. Hancock & M. Tyler, eds. *The management of everyday life*. Basingstoke: Palgrave Macmillan, pp. 199–216.

Foucault, M., 1991. *Discipline and punish: The birth of the prison*. London: Penguin.

Foucault, M., 2001. *Fearless speech*. Los Angeles, CA: Semiotext(e).

French, W. L. & Bell, C. H., 1978. *Organization development: Behavioral science interventions for organization improvement*. 6th ed. Upper Saddle River, NJ: Prentice Hall.

Garcia, J. M. R., 2001. Scientia potestas est – Knowledge is power: Francis Bacon to Michel Foucault. *Neohelicon*, 28(1), pp. 109–121.

Garrett, B. L., 2013. *Explore everything: Place-hacking the city*. London: Verso.

Garrod, B. & Ling, T., 2018. *System change through situated learning: Pre-evaluation of the Health Innovation Network's Communities of Practice*. Cambridge: Rand Corporation.

Goodley, S. & Ashby, J., 2015. *A day at 'the gulag': What it's like to work at Sports Direct's warehouse*. [Online]. Available at: https://www.theguardian.com/business/2015/dec/09/sports-direct-warehouse-work-conditions [Accessed 21 January 2019].

Gray, D., Micheli, P. & Pavlov, A., 2015. *Measurement madness: Recognizing and avoiding the pitfalls of performance measurement*. Chichester: John Wiley & Sons Ltd.

Hancock, P., 2009. Management and colonization of everyday life. In: P. Hancock & M. Tyler, eds. *The management of everyday life*. Basingstoke: Palgrave Macmillan, pp. 1–20.

Harvey, D. & Brown, D. R., 1976. *An experiential approach to organization development*. 5th ed. Upper Saddle River, NJ: Prentice-Hall.

Higgins, J., 2014. Introducing the editors: John Higgins. In: K. King & J. Higgins, eds. *The change doctors: Re-imagining organisational practice*. Faringdon: Libri Publishing, p. xiii.

Hoffman, B. G., 2012. *American icon: Alan Mulally and the fight to save Ford Motor Company*. New York: Crown Business.

Jamieson, D. W., 1995. Chapter 4 – Start-up. In: W. J. Rothwell, R. Sullivan & G. N. McLean, eds. *Practicing organization development: A guide for consultants*. San Diego, CA: Pfeiffer & Company, pp. 105–137.

Janke, K., Propper, C. & Sadun, R., 2018. *The impact of CEOs in the public sector: Evidence from the English NHS –Working Paper No. 18-075*. Boston, MA: Harvard Business School.

Kamoche, K. & Maguire, K., 2010. Pit sense: Appropriation of practice-based knowledge in a UK coalmine. *Human Relations*, 64(5), pp. 725–744.

Kelly, M. G. E., 2014. Foucault against Marxism: Althusser beyond Althusser. In: H. J & W. J, eds. *(Mis)readings of Marx in continental philosophy*. London: Palgrave Macmillan, pp. 83–98.

Kinder, T. & Ralph, A., 2018. Patisserie Valerie landlords 'had to send in bailiffs'. *The Times*, 18 December.

Kindynis, T., 2015. *Urban exploration as deviant leisure*. [Online]. Available at: https://vanhoben.wordpress.com/2015/09/27/urban-exploration-as-deviant-leisure/ [Accessed 21 February 2019].

Kirkpatrick, I. et al., 2019. The impact of management consultants on public service efficiency. *Policy and Politics*, 47(1), pp. 77–96.

Lave, J. & Wenger, E., 1991. *Situated learning: Legitimate peripheral participation*. Cambridge: Cambridge University Press.

Lawler, J., 2005. The essence of leadership? Existentialism and leadership. *Leadership*, 1(2), pp. 215–231.

Lawler, J. & Ashman, I., 2012. Theorizing leadership authenticity: A Sartrean perspective. *Leadership*, 8(4), pp. 327–344.

Lencioni, R., 2002. *The five dysfunctions of a team: A leadership fable*. San Francisco, CA: Jossey-Bass.

MacMillan, S., Yue, A. R. & Mills, A. J., 2012. Both how and why: Considering existentialism as a philosophy of work and management. *Philosophy of Management*, 11(3), pp. 27–46.

McCormick, D. W. & White, J., 2000. Using oneself as an instrument for organizational diagnosis. *Organization Development Journal*, 18(3), pp. 49–62.

Melman, S., 1958. *Decision-making and productivity*. Oxford: Basil Blackwell.

Merton, R. K., 1994. Bureaucratic structure and personality. In: H. Clark, J. Chandler & J. Barry, eds. *Organisation and identities: Text and readings in organisational behaviour*. London: Thomson Press, pp. 144–149.

Meyerson, D. E. & Scully, M. A., 1995. Crossroads tempered radicalism and the politics of ambivalence and change. *Organization Science*, 6(5), pp. 585–600.

Muller, J. Z., 2018. *The tyranny of metrics*. Woodstock: Princeton University Press.

Needleman, M. L. & Needleman, C. E., 1974. *Guerillas in the bureaucracy: The community planning experiment in the United States*. New York: John Wiley & Sons.

Newman, S., 2007. *From Bakunin to Lacan: Anti-authoritarianism and the dislocation of power*. Plymouth: Lexington Books.

Orr, J. E., 1996. *Talking about machines: An ethnography of a modern job*. New York: ILR Press/ Cornell University Press.

Plowman, D. A. et al., 2007. Radical change accidentally: The emergence and amplification of small change. *Academy of Management Journal*, 50(3), pp. 515–543.

Rao, H., Morrill, C. & Zald, M. N., 2000. Power plays: How social movements and collective action create new organizational forms. *Research in Organizational Behaviour*, 22, pp. 237–281.

Rayner, T., 2013. *Lines of flight: Deleuze and nomadic creativity*. [Online]. Available at: https://philosophyforchange.wordpress.com/2013/06/18/lines-of-flight-deleuze-and-nomadic-creativity/ [Accessed 21 February 2019].

Reinecke, J., 2018. Social movements and prefigurative organizing: Confronting entrenched inequalities in Occupy London. *Organization Studies*, 39(9), pp. 1299–1321.

Reitz, M. & Higgins, J., 2017. *Being silenced and silencing others: Developing the capacity to speak truth to power*. Berkhamsted: Hult Research.

Rodgers, M., n.d. *Our Maxims*. [Online]. Available at: http://phillipskay.com/?page_id=126 [Accessed 14 February 2019].

Rodionova, Z., 2016. *The 7 most shocking testimonies from workers at Sports Direct.* [Online]. Available at: https://www.independent.co.uk/news/business/news/sports-direct-mike-ashley-worker-conditions-minimum-wage-ian-wright-investigation-a7149971.html [Accessed 21 January 2019].

Rothwell, W. J., Sullivan, R. & McLean, G. N., 1995. Introduction. In: W. J. Rothwell, R. Sullivan & G. N. McLean, eds. *Practicing organization development: A guide for consultants.* San Diego, CA: Pfeiffer & Co, pp. 3–45.

Royle, A., 2018. Heidegger's ways of being. *Philosophy Now,* April/May, Issue 125, pp. 6–10.

Salih, S., 2007. On Judith Butler and performativity. In: K. E. Lovaas & M. M. Jenkins, eds. *Sexualities and communication in everyday life: A reader.* Thousand Oaks, CA: Sage, pp. 55–68.

Salzman, P. C., 2002. On reflexivity. *American Anthropologist,* 104(3), pp. 805–813.

Sartre, J.-P., 1988. *Essays in existentialism.* New York: Citadel Press.

Schechner, R., 2003. *Performance theory.* New York: Routledge.

Silberman, M., ed., 2003. *The consultant's big book of organization development tools: 50 reproducible, customizable interventions to solve your clients' problems.* New York: McGraw-Hill.

Smith, C., 2014. *The 13 worst office jargon phrases staff love to hate.* [Online]. Available at: https://www.theguardian.com/careers/careers-blog/worst-office-jargon-phrases-staff-love-hate-management-speak [Accessed 20 December 2018].

Suarez, C., 2018. *The power manual: How to master complex power dynamics.* Gabriola Island: New Society Publishers.

Taylor, F. W., 1919. *Shop management.* New York: Harper & Brothers.

Villadsen, K., 2007. Managing the employee's soul: Foucault applied to modern management technologies. *Cadernos EBAPE.BR,* 5(1), pp. 1–10.

Ward, C., 1966. *Anarchism as a theory of organisation.* [Online]. Available at: http://theanarchistlibrary.org/library/colin-ward-anarchism-as-a-theory-of-organization.pdf [Accessed 26 January 2010].

Weick, K. E., 1969. *The social psychology of organizing.* Reading, MA: Addison-Wesley.

Wenger, E., 1998. *Communities of Practice: Learning, meaning, and identity.* Cambridge: Cambridge University Press.

Wenger, E., McDermott, R. & Snyder, W. M., 2002. *Cultivating communities of practice.* Boston, MA: Harvard Business School Press.

Wikipedia, 2019. *Impossibilism.* [Online]. Available at: https://en.wikipedia.org/wiki/Impossibilism [Accessed 14 February 2019].

Winograd, T. & Flores, F., 1988. *Understanding computers and cognition: A new foundation for design.* Reading, MA: Addison-Wesley.

Zerubavel, E., 2006. *The elephant in the room: Silence and denial in everyday life.* New York: Oxford University Press.

6

AND WE LAND, WHERE?

Some years ago, I acquired a book that – at that time, at least – I was interested to obtain. I did not consider it a serious piece of work; instead, it was a promotional item, advertising the services of a company, which sought to promote 'happiness' in the workplace. It made the case – off the back of research and practical experience in terms of case studies of particular companies – that it was the responsibility of businesses to ensure that their workforces were happy. This manifesto, as it declared itself to be, set the scene thus:

> Imagine a workforce where people are energised and motivated by being in control of the work they do. Imagine they are trusted and given freedom, within clear guidelines, to decide how to achieve their results. Imagine they are able to get the life balance they want. Imagine they are valued according to the work they do, rather than the number of hours they spend at their desk.
>
> (Stewart, 2012, p. 9)

Imagine, indeed. And, as an eager OD (organisation development) practitioner, I took these sentiments at face value. In doing so, I disregarded that carefully inserted caveat – 'within clear guidelines' – and the definition of the workplace as somewhere where people sit at desks. Instead, I was absorbed by some of the precepts promoted in this book: the idea at its core was to get out of the way of the workforce and afford them autonomy in their jobs, meaningful recognition of talent and ensuring a match between that and the work that people are asked to do, thereby focusing on making your workplace somewhere that people feel valued and sense that they are making an ethical contribution (Stewart, 2012, pp. 121–122).

Crucially, the main thing that I missed in my reading of this material was its orientation. It spoke of people at work but did so in a way that rendered that workforce as a mere object. In fact, the book speaks exclusively to the audience of managers; its message is how the work of management can be adjusted whilst leaving the fundamentals of management wholly untouched. The happy workplace is in the gift of managers – and it is created by their actions, in relation to a workforce that is a resource that can be acted upon and adjusted in this way. And so, on reflection, I am moved now to observe that my OD practice at that time was blind to these subtle issues where power is largely unaddressed in discussions about the workplace. The book seemed common sense to me: my job in OD was to work in the organisation, particularly with managers, to help them to manage in order to get the best out of the people that they supervise.

Interestingly, the book's message and this company's focus was part of a wider socio-economic trend. The New Labour administrations after 1997 had latterly enthusiastically embraced this notion of 'happiness' as something that needed to be actively promoted throughout society and into the workplace. In this regard, they were advised by a senior economist in this respect, called Richard Layard: as *The Guardian* newspaper noted in a profile of Layard, 'A Labour peer since 2000, he has been able to influence first Blair's administration and then Brown's into making his happiness agenda government policy' (Jeffries, 2008). His happiness agenda seemed to pivot around the notion that, despite our increased affluence, it was not necessarily making us happy (Layard, 2011). A partial response was psychological: it was argued that more psychiatric provision, particularly in respect to approaches such as cognitive behavioural therapy (CBT), should be offered and access to this service should be improved.

As is so often the case, this seems a response to the symptoms rather than a radical approach that tackles the cause. It's akin to saying to someone who is constantly being hit on the head with a hammer, 'Would you like to talk about being hit on the head with the hammer and how you might best accommodate to it?' This is not to say that Layard and his collaborators are not making a helpful observation about the vacuum that exists at the heart of capitalist economies. As they usefully state,

> While basic living standards are essential for happiness, after the base-line has been met happiness varies more with quality of human relation-ships than income. Other policy goals should include high employment and high-quality work; a strong community with high levels of trust and respect, which government can influence through inclusive participatory policies; improved physical and mental health; support of family life; and a decent education for all.
>
> (Helliwell et al., 2012, p. 9)

The context of Layard's doubtless well-intended intervention tends to undermine his argument, specifically, that those Labour administrations who had given him his 'tsar-ship' in this realm were, at the same time, aggressively promoting the notion of New Public Management. This notion and practice appeared in the late 1980s and arose out of the neo-liberal economics and conservative politics of the time. Its outline can be stated thus:

> NPM is a set of assumptions and value statements about how public sector organizations should be designed, organized, managed and how, in a quasi-business manner, they should function. The basic idea of NPM is to make public sector organizations – and the people working in them! – much more 'business-like' and 'market-oriented', that is, performance-, cost-, efficiency- and audit-oriented.
>
> (Diefenbach, 2009, p. 893)

In so doing, it embraced a strong managerial orientation, through ritualised processes such as the annual appraisal, and tight budgetary management, all of which serve to make the workplace a more uncomfortable environment for those who earn their livings there (Gruening, 2001, Table 1).

As I look back on my responses to the happiness agenda – and review this previously held position through the prism of the argument that I have tried to craft in this book – I am acutely aware of the ways in which OD, as a field of practice, supports this vision, regardless of how untouched in terms of meaningful structural and cultural reform, our workplaces actually are. For many of us as OD practitioners, the notion of supporting wellness and well-being in the workplace is an explicit aspect of our role. Even where that expectation is not expressly stated, the work that we do requires us to orient to the workforce in order to support the wider requirements around organisational effectiveness. At root, then, the question is whether we can effectively engender (the illusion of) happiness in a work context, in order that we make the people with – or, rather, on – whom we work more productive (Oswald et al., 2009).

This latest turn – the shift towards an engagement with the active promotion of happiness – is, of course, not without its critics, some of whom locate it firmly within the history of OD practice, outlining a seamless periodisation from Taylorism through the Human Relations school to our current fixation on the somewhat intangible notion of workplace well-being as a key strut of OD intent in the workplace context (Davies, 2015, pp. 105–137). This is significant if one takes a critical view of capitalism and its constant need to refresh itself. To that extent, paroxysms of rebellion can be seen to have been previously hugely helpful in terms of that reformation of this mode of production. Without express rebellion, however, it is suggested,

> What if the greatest threat to capitalism, at least in the liberal West, is simply lack of enthusiasm and activity? What if, rather than inciting violence or explicit refusal, contemporary capitalism is just met with a yawn? Yet it is no less of an obstacle for the longer-term viability of capitalism. Without a certain level of commitment on the part of employees, businesses run into some very tangible problems, which soon show up in their profits.
>
> (Davies, 2015, p. 105)

Step forward, then, OD to fill this void and sustain the oppressive nature of the workplace that – in and of itself – makes people unhappy.

The economics of this notwithstanding, it is argued that '[W]e now go to work not because we necessarily have to but because the workplace is where we might realize ourselves' (Cederstrom & Grassman, 2010, p. 101). The locus of control moves in this formulation, away from social engagement and collective efforts at societal change to an interior focus on individualised production of the self. Moreover, within at least one field of critical thought, the very notion of happiness and the ideas of how human subjects might relate to it is problematised, in terms of a three-fold theoretical appreciation of happiness, namely the imaginary, the symbolic, and the real. This layered understanding, which draws on the psychoanalytic ideas and practices of Lacan, patently throws the taken-for-granted assumption of the subject and their notional happiness into sharp relief, thereby through psychoanalytic notions breaking this assumed relationship between the person and the wider sense of 'happiness' (Cederstrom & Grassman, 2010). Such an oblique perspective simply allows us to evaluate afresh the common sense idea that the pursuit of happiness is simple and linear – and, of course, easily attainable, through paternalistic provision and individual self-actualisation.

In this specific field of thought, it has been argued that resistances in the workplace have been borne of a desire for recognition – and that these resistances have taken the form of making demands upon management, requesting of management something that they are assumed within this schema to possess and which would have value to the employee if they were able to obtain it. But this highly individual person in the workplace is merely subjectified in this context rather than liberated by the transfer of some psychodynamic resource. Some see this negatively, of course, with the subject yearning for some item that may not exist but which is seen to be in the possession of management. However, a contrary view of this, it can be suggested, means that this subject in terms of their individuality is thereby equipped to attain both voice and an autonomy, as they will be defining themselves (and being defined) by an organisational ideal of happiness which will be endlessly elusive and thereby be experienced thus as something unobtainable (Roberts, 2005).

For me, this exploration of 'happiness' in a workplace context is a useful and illustrative way for me to try to consolidate what I have sought to argue in this book. First, nothing is completely as it seems. The kindnesses of the contemporary workplace may feel qualitatively different but the power that courses underneath remains unchanged – and its effect in terms of ensuring the persistence of current circumstances is unaffected by the superficial arrangements. Certainly, there is a palpable difference in my experience as a worker between being overseen through close surveillance by a supervisor with a stopwatch and attended to by a modern manager who is attuned (or perhaps entrained) to support my well-being and to grant me levels of autonomy to do my work. But that which underlays both these means of managing the person in the workplace remains unaltered by these cosmetic adjustments. Ultimately, I am personally moved to observe that the harsh overseer is more honest about their intent than the duplicitous humanistic manager. The former's purpose in interrelating with me in that way is explicit and I am better able to stand in contradistinction to it, especially at those times when I wish to engage in some collective resistance to what is happening in the workplace. Who, after all, would want to be seen to be resisting or rejecting kindness?

Second, in accepting that nothing is as it seems, it is necessary to see that everything that is taken to be common sense in organisational life should be subjected to deep scrutiny. This is to make the point that our attention should be drawn not merely to that which appears expressly iniquitous – the precariousness of zero-hour contracts, the 'busyness' of modern corporate life and its seemingly constant call upon all of our time (Crary, 2014) – but also to that which seems enlightened, progressive and positive, in relation to the trajectory of human development. This requires an openness to new ways of seeing things – and old ways, as well, that perhaps we have not found amenable to our overall view of the world or which seemed inconsistent with our values in the world (and particularly in regard to the way in which we seek to work and what we think about that). Hence, I have called extensively throughout on the thought of Michel Foucault and the corpus of work that has developed in line with that thinking, particularly in respect to subjecting organisational life to critical scrutiny. Elsewhere, I have called upon anarchism as a means of thinking again about humans and their capacity for organising in order to attain a shared purpose. Both perspectives allow us to think anew about things that are familiar to us, which is an essential way to ensure that we live an examined life.

Third, scrutinising common sense means not simply critiquing the common sense of others but engaging with all that we use tacitly to undergird our thinking and practice in the world. I was secure in my career and certain as to its direction until such time as I began to think about it from a fresh perspective. To be candid, for me, this adjustment was inescapable: exposure to new ways of thinking meant that I could not disregard them or convince myself that I had not seen them. And my view of the world has regularly undergone revision in the course of my life. I was initially wholly and actively absorbed by trade unionism and working

204 AND WE LAND, WHERE?

class politics as a young man. My attachment to it lessened as I immersed myself in the quest to develop a better understanding of those politics. At this time, I called myself a Marxist, although that too was finally subject to deep critical review as I began to think about the constraints that such an ideology placed on human thought (and, in many practical circumstances, human existence). It was in teacher training that I allowed myself the luxury of shrugging off the ideological straightjacket that my younger brother quite rightly and regularly accused me of wearing and permitting my mind to roam wherever it fancied. In thinking about education, I found my way to Foucault, which – in turn – led me to surveillance studies and my doctoral work.

Fourth, interrogating my common sense in a work context has led me to the perspective that I have endeavoured to articulate herein. It was prompted by a clear sense of an increasingly apparent dissonance between the values to which I cleaved in my professional life and what I took to be the impact of that work, in terms of how others experienced what I did in this context and what purpose it might inadvertently be serving. This led to the critique of OD practice in this book, which is not intended to be hostile to the field or to those who seek to make a difference therein but merely to offer a different perspective to what we do, how we do it, and what its implications might be.

Alongside that, of course, I have offered what I take to be a series of precepts which I sense might allow me – and whomsoever shares the critical view that I offer and has a willingness to try and do this work differently – to start to explore a different way of doing it. In essence, I want to investigate the potential for doing this work in a way where the dissonance that I perceived in my day-to-day practice might be bridged. However, my view in this regard is that, in order to work in a way that is humanistic and democratic, I need to embrace the critique and recognise that the way in which OD accommodates to circumstances in the workplace is not a positive attribute but reflects the way in which its mainstream practice shrouds itself in those values yet delivers to an altogether different agenda. Hence, without critique and an active commitment to a Radical OD practice, the practitioner is condemned to ceaselessly reproduce the current situation in the workplace – its power relations, its capitalistic underpinnings, and so on – regardless of their espoused values. OD as practised in the current context cannot reform itself and the context in which it is undertaken: to make a difference to what we do and to the places where we do it requires us to embrace an authentically radical approach, one that gets to the root of the issues and offers a different way of envisaging the world.

To an extent, this will involve putting myself into uncomfortable positions. Where OD is ordinarily an intrinsic part of management practice in modern corporate settings, this will entail moving out of that zone and approaching the world in a significantly more oblique fashion. So, for example, as noted elsewhere in this book, the contemporary discourse around organisational life is beginning to adapt to a position where management as an activity is seriously in question. People have become hugely excitable about holacracy and teal organisations, as we noted above. And, at face value, what's not to like about this? However, our radical engagement with this notion would aim to explore both its surface and that which lies beneath that veneer, which is hopefully what the reader saw being undertaken in the book. But it is not merely to take that more involved perspective on such notions: it is also to engage with the underpinning ideas that make this so very appealing in an organisational context and to articulate a vision of the end of management that is ethically and politically meaningful.

To take such a view is not simply to be critical of management as it currently stands; in this, one can indulge the post-bureaucratic fictions that are peddled in various quarters and imagine a reformed practice, which I take to be untenable. Instead, one must articulate a position wherein one is *against* management, which means running counter to the view that is widely held that 'Even if we don't share the faith in today's management, we often seem to believe that the answer is 'better' management, and not something else altogether' (Parker, 2002, p. 3). It means, as well, rejecting the taken-for-granted foundational building blocks upon which the edifice of management is built, chief amongst which is the reassuring but wholly unsustainable notion that the natural and human worlds are in some sense controllable. This is not just naysaying for the sake of being contrary in a corporate setting: simply, '[T]he version of managerialism that has been constructed over the past century is deeply implicated in a wide variety of political and ethical problems, and ... it limits our capacity to imagine alternative forms of organizing' (Parker, 2002, p. 11). I take the view that it is not merely that current management practice is fundamentally wrong; it is not even that management has negative implications in a wider context.

Yes, it does both these things, but it also closes down the space where, as human beings, we might talk about different ways of doing and of being, both in the workplace and beyond.

So, the double-challenge for our practice of Radical OD is to apply our own critical eye to our work and the context in which it takes place, whilst at the same time helping those alongside whom we are asked to work to do exactly the same – and, in so doing, to open a supportive yet challenging space wherein people can connect meaningfully with one another to understand the current context through collective inquiry and, with that as a springboard, to take the leap into thinking differently about how an altogether different type of future might be crafted. I was starting on this journey of imagining a completely revised learning and OD focus when I found myself drawn to considering how this type of work in an organisational context might abandon the traditional approaches in favour of a practice of containment that facilitates people to converse, connect and exchange knowledge (Cole, 2017). I had not at that point followed the logic of that thinking to apply a more radical and intrinsically critical engagement with the very context in which such activity takes place, which is what I have sought to do here.

That critical engagement may take us – indeed, is very likely to take us – to unexpected places. Hence, to return momentarily to the discussion of the active promotion of 'happiness' in a corporate and a wider social context, one possible vector to explore in this regard (once you have discarded the constraining boundaries that inhibit all-encompassing and meaningful engagement with the topic) is that 'Wellbeing policy-makers like Lord Layard insisted governments should take citizens' feelings seriously and use them as a guide to policy. But what if the electorate's feelings lead them to xenophobic and self-destructive voting decisions?' (Evans, 2017) As we struggle with the eclipse of traditional political establishments in favour of expressions of populist sentiment, this perspective is one that it is worth following to its logical conclusion, alongside more traditional explanations. It is a discomforting view, for sure, but needs to be included as part of the discussion. The alternative is to marginalise this perspective; indeed, it is to subsume it to a dominant discourse that defines that which can and cannot be said.

*

Amidst the myriad joys of being dad to a five-year-old son is the way in which it focuses me to drive on towards an unscripted future whilst throwing me back into fond reminiscence, whence I am able to derive the widest range of resources. When Thomas was a babe in arms and I was trying to settle him at night, lullabies deserted me, whilst the old music hall tunes that my grandfather constantly crooned came flooding back: he fell asleep on many occasions to a whispered rendition of 'When father papered the parlour' (Weston & Barnes, 1909). This backward and forward motion seems to be important when we consider how we present in a range of contexts. I am currently planning some work with my colleague Steve Hearsum to help a community of OD practitioners to think about how practice gets refreshed. Two things are shaping our approach: first, the fact that novelty and newness are fetishised in our society. We are ceaselessly seeking – and pointedly guided towards – the next new thing: Apple stores are besieged by people at the launch of some new iteration of the iPhone; Sunday supplements offer weekly guidance of what the next big thing is likely to be in fashion, in beauty, in food, in technology, in motoring, and so on; and publishing is cluttered with books that declare that they are sharing with their readership the next big idea. (I am not unaware of the irony of making this observation in the context of this publication, of course.)

Second, linked to this observation, we are mindful of the fact that, by constantly looking towards something yet to emerge in the future, we lose perspective on that which sits in our past. From a practice perspective, a wealth of experience resides in our hinterland. In that memory will be rich thinking and applicable technique that, because it is not deemed to be 'new' or 'cutting edge,' is seen to have no currency to how we might wish to work in the present. In fact, this sort of mindset seems to misjudge fundamentally the very idea of innovating and starting afresh. Indeed, we cannot speak about innovation in our current business context without excitedly declaring that it needs to be 'disruptive,' although critique exists of this widely accepted notion (King & Baatartogtokh, 2015). Again, this relates to thinking that has great influence in the current context that, first, size matters (everything must be big in scope and intent) and, second, that the creative process is in some sense akin to magic, conjuring new ideas and products out of absolutely nothing other than the innovator's imagination.

In this regard, it is worth considering the iPhone. The technology of which it is built was developed by Nokia. Hence, the innovation that led to

Apple's emergence as a global leader in regard to smartphones is built not on a major leap forward in terms of hardware: instead, it relates to what might be reasonably be argued to be a slight adjustment in thinking, one that oriented the smartphone away from telephony and positioned it in relation to computing, particularly in respect to the internet (Linge, 2017). It is argued – off the back of a review of the innovations in Nintendo, Nokia, and Apple – that innovation has three issues to be addressed: first, cognitive, namely whether the firm is equipped to recognise the need for innovation; second, behavioural, wherein the firm recognises the need but simply fails to act on it; and, third, there is an institutional element, wherein

> Employees are full of ideas, and have high hopes of making an impact in the world through their work. Companies may even strive to [be] innovative, at least in their strategy, but in practice the processes, management, and incentives don't support it.
>
> (Pontiskoski & Asakawa, 2009, p. 372)

For Radical OD, this sense of grass-roots talents being structurally and culturally inhibited rather than set loose is crucial to our notion that the lived experience of those at work and their capacity to think differently about how work gets done is a resource that urgently needs to be released from the organisational confines within which it is actively constrained.

So, in this instance, there is a backward and forward movement of the sort that I described in terms of parenthood: scanning the past for that which is still current and finding ways to adapt it to be future focused. To return to my relationship with Thomas, I have begun to play with him that simple childhood game where you alternately stack your hands and whomsoever has their hand at the base then pulls it out and puts it on top. This restacking is undertaken at increasing pace until such time as the rhythm is broken and the game collapses. Two things intrigue me about this in regard to the suggestion that we need to reorient OD towards a more radical approach: first, that whatever hand is on top is very soon absorbed into the stack. The 'new' hand appears at the top but is very quickly replaced by another hand; latterly, as the game progresses, that original hand will, of course, come back again to the top.

This underscores for me that Radical OD is not something new, in terms of model or technique. Far from it. It is – to return to the innovation schema alluded to above – a cognitive adjustment, founded upon a sense that something different needs to happen; similarly, it will need a behavioural shift, so that recognition is brought firmly into the practice realm. But we should expect institutional factors to constrain our fresh thinking and adjusted perspective, because – at its most potent – it seeks to fracture those old certainties in favour of a purpose with a profound ambition at its heart, namely to change fundamentally the nature of the workplace and our experiences therein. So, despite articulating Radical OD in a previous chapter in terms of a number of touchstones, these concepts are not discrete but minutely interleaved into a fresh ontology for those who wish to practice OD in a different way. It is not about a new body of knowledge, a new set of precepts, or a grouping of new 'tools and techniques' (the latter being, in my experience, something that many in the field desperately crave); it is about how you *are* a practitioner in the field of work – how you present in that space, in light of the application of critical thought (particularly in respect to any gaps that might exist between the values which you hold and the work that you find yourself doing in reality) and a willingness to bring to the fore that which traditionally has been cast into the shadows of organisational life.

Centrally, a Radical OD practitioner is someone who has reviewed and adjusted their fundamental relationship to the deep question of power – and, in particular, how it manifests in organisations. The ideas that I brought forward in order to encourage thinking about how OD might acquire a genuinely radical and profound orientation and impact – namely, a concentration on power as experienced by people; the practice of *parrhesia*; focus on organising not organisation; engaging in true reflexivity; taking an existentialist approach to action; deconstruction of the layers; and disturbing the discourse and revealing the fictions – intimate a personal adjustment rather than the taking up on new methods of doing our work. And this changed ontology will, inevitably, nudge the individual towards an accommodation with bodies of thought that traditionally have not informed OD practice.

Foucault, of course, has quite a presence these days in the relatively niche corner of scholarship that is given the epithet of critical management studies (CMS). Whilst much therein might seem arcane, it offers a range of altered perspectives on the context in which we find ourselves in the course of our working lives. It deserves to be drawn out of the shadows and announced in the more public arena of the workplace. Hence, the Foucauldian notion of power/knowledge – power as a productive force that exists within the mesh of relationships in which we reside as human agents rather than as a private resource, possessed by one at the expense of another – brings a different perspective to organisational life – and encourages the active development of that perspective through the notion of genealogical method and practices such as *parrhesia*.

Equally, given the linkages that are presumed to exist between the sort of attitude provided by Foucault and the political ideas that are encapsulated in the catch-all notion of anarchism, I have very consciously pulled some of those vital notions into the debate herein. Of all the political positions, anarchism has perhaps the most productive relationship with the concept of power: Communists merely wish to seize it, Socialists want to inhabit and use it, Liberals wish to sanitise it, Conservatives want to sell us the pretence that it does not exist. Anarchists, however, want to genuinely understand it – and see it as the chief challenge that any project that aims at human liberation needs to consider and overcome. In that sense, it is a heritage that we neglect at our cost, given what it might say to us about organisation in particular.

Hence, Malatesta's observation from the end of the 19th century continues to hold true – but requires of us to reconnect with the sentiment at its heart rather than merely to subscribe to what is socially present:

> Organization which is, after all, only the practice of cooperation and solidarity, is a natural and necessary condition of social life; it is an inescapable fact which forces itself on everybody, as much on human society as on any group of people who are working towards a common objective.
>
> (Malatesta, 1897)

This prompts the recommendation, one that resonates strongly with the ideas that I have tried to lay out, that

> We cannot assume that we will ever know the "one best way" to organize (to borrow Frederick Taylor's term), and might instead encourage debate about ideas that are different to the way we do things now – whether old, new, marginal, hidden, possible or imaginary.
>
> (Parker et al., 2014, p. 629)

So, the clarion call here – such as it is – is not necessarily to do things differently, following a fresh model and associated repertoire of techniques, but to seek to be different in the context of our work. Being different in such a context means calling to the fore that which is ordinarily obscured in the gloom of the unexplored (and invariably unacknowledged) background. By being different, there is a potential to explore different modes of practice through constant experimentation and testing of the boundaries which ordinarily we might feel obliged to accept.

Elsewhere, it has been argued that OD needs to reclaim its supposed progressive position through a return to Lewinian rigour and relevance, alongside a very public willingness by the practice to address what are called the 'big questions' (Burnes & Cooke, 2012, pp. 1415–1416). In the face of such a weak manifesto, the world stifles a yawn and turns back to the business of business, which – of course – is left wholly unchallenged by such a supposed theoretical volte-face. This is a reformist prescription that will merely offer succour to the system and support it to endlessly reproduce itself. To break that apparently ceaseless cycle of reproduction requires practitioners to burrow deeply into the most basic underpinnings of the system that currently exists – and to deracinate it, the better to prepare the ground for a fresh and more positive planting. This is why this new way of being in OD needs to be seen to be radical: it needs to go directly to the root of the issues, rather than skate around on the surface. That is where OD will add true value in terms of human potential and authentically organising for the sake of working towards a common purpose.

Bibliography

Burnes, B. & Cooke, B., 2012. The past, present and future of organization development: Taking the long view. Human Relations, 65(11), pp. 1395–1429.

Cederstrom, C. & Grassman, R., 2010. The unbearable weight of happiness. In: C. Cederstrom & C. Hoedemaekers, eds. Lacan and organization. London: Mayfly Books, pp. 101–132.

Cole, M., 2017. Rethinking the practice of workplace learning and development: Utilizing 'knowledge, connections and conversation' in organizations. International Journal of HRD Practice, Policy and Research, 2(1), pp. 7–19.

Crary, J., 2014. 24/7: Late capitalism and the ends of sleep. London: Verso.

Davies, W., 2015. The happiness industry: How the government and big business sold us well-being. London: Verso.

Diefenbach, T., 2009. New Public Management in the public sector organizations: The dark sides of managerialistic 'enlightenment.' Public Administration, 87(4), pp. 892–909.

Evans, J., 2017. *The end of history and the invention of happiness – CWiPP Working Paper No. 11*. Sheffield: Centre for Wellbeing in Public Policy/University of Sheffield.

Gruening, G., 2001. Origin and theoretical basis of New Public Management. *International Public Management Journal*, 4, pp. 1–25.

Helliwell, J., Layard, R. & Sachs, J., 2012. *World happiness report*. New York: The Earth Institute/Columbia University.

Jeffries, S., 2008. Will this man make you happy?. *The Guardian*, 24 June.

King, A. A. & Baatartogtokh, B., 2015. How useful is the theory of disruptive innovation? *MIT Sloan Management Review*, 57(1), pp. 77–90.

Layard, R., 2011. *Happiness: Lessons from a new science*. London: Penguin.

Linge, N., 2017. *Nokia had the world's best smartphone – Then came the 'inferior' iPhone* [Online]. Available at: http://theconversation.com/nokia-had-the-worlds-best-smartphone-then-came-the-inferior-iphone-70958 [Accessed 7 March 2019].

Malatesta, E., 1897. *Anarchism and organization* [Online]. Available at: http://theanarchistlibrary.org/library/errico-malatesta-anarchism-and-organization [Accessed 3 March 2009].

Oswald, A. J., Proto, E. & Sgroi, D., 2009. *Happiness and productivity – IZA Discussion Paper No. 4645*. Bonn: Institute for the Study of Labour (IZA).

Parker, M., 2002. *Against management: Organization in the age of managerialism*. Cambridge: Polity.

Parker, M., Cheney, G., Fournier, V. & Land, C., 2014. The question of organization: A manifesto for alternatives. *Ephemera: Theory & Politics in Organization*, 14(4), pp. 623–638.

Pontiskoski, E. & Asakawa, K., 2009. Overcoming barriers to open innovation at Apple, Nintendo and Nokia. *International Journal of Social, Behavioral, Educational, Economic, Business and Industrial Engineering*, 3(5), pp. 370–375.

Roberts, J., 2005. The power of the 'Imaginary' in disciplinary processes. *Organization*, 12(5), pp. 619–642.

Stewart, H., 2012. *The happy manifesto: Make your organisation a great place to work – now!* London: Happy.

Weston, R. P. & Barnes, F. J., 1909. *When father papered the parlour* [Sound Recording].

EPILOGUE

In conversations with Amy Laurens, the editor at Routledge, since the submission of this manuscript, we explored the idea of appending a 'how to' chapter to the book. We concluded that it might interrupt the flow of the text. Moreover, there was a strong sense for me as the author that these notions about how we might do organisation development (OD) differently needed to be tested in practice by people who find themselves sympathetic to the idea of Radical OD on the basis of this book.

To this end, I am hoping to build a community of OD practitioners who feel a strong impetus to work differently and potentially in the ways that I have outlined here. To support that, there are some resources in place with which I would encourage people to engage, should they be interested in taking this work forward.

First, there is a website, where people can constellate in order to access fresh thinking on Radical OD practice. This can be found at www.radicalod. org. Second, there is a Slack channel – which can be found at www.radicalod. slack.com – and this is where we will be able to support a potentially global conversation about our experiences, our fresh thinking, and our revised ways of practising OD.

Lastly, I would invite people in the first instance to reach out and connect with me via email at radicalod@colefellows.co.uk: in this way, you can share your contact details and your thoughts about Radical OD, and at the same time become part of the community of practitioners that will help to develop a more authentic and liberatory practice in organisations.

Mark Cole
25 April 2019

INDEX

Ackroyd, S. 113
action plan 5, 6, 51
Althusser, L. 17, 47, 62, 166
anarchism 144, 210
anarchy 144–5
anti-humanist conception 20
apparatus concept 26–7
appreciation 23, 27, 92, 159; of
    Foucauldian concepts 36; of
    happiness 202; of reflexivity 167
archaeology 16, 35
Archduke Ferdinand 40–1
autonomy 155, 199

Bakhtinian carnival 10–1
behavioural expectations 89, 113
behavioural science 3
Belbin, R. M. 102–3, 116, 118
Belbin team tool 102
Bentham, J. 18, 109
Bion, W. R. 101, 159

biopolitics 90, 91
Bolshevik revolution 99
budgetary management 200
bureaucratic control 127
bureaucratisation 155

capitalism: corporate 140;
    paternalistic 59; welfare 81, 104
capitalist economies 44, 49, 75, 97,
    142, 200
Carey's analysis 99
change management 13, 181
Chia, R. 125
climate control systems 96–7
CMS see critical management
    studies (CMS)
cognitive behavioural therapy
    (CBT) 199
cognitive dissonance 85
collaboration change 4
collectivism 96

colonising change: bureaucratic control 127; corporate culture 128–30; culture change 126; enculturation 126; geothermal energy 125; humanistic control 127; Lewinian sense 125; Marxian perspective 128; organisational contexts 125; organisational effectiveness 123; organisational life 124, 130; organisation-wide conversation 129; organizational membership 126; reflexive awareness 128; structural change 123; technocratic application 124; transformation plan 125
commissioning process 10
communication: barriers to 189; change in 4; from the corporate centre 52; organisational 7
Communities of Practice (CoPs) 103–4, 182–4
corporate capitalism 140
corporate culture 128–30
Corporate Rebels 43, 65–7
critical engagement 206
critical management studies (CMS) 14, 61, 209
cult-like culture 59
cultural impact 8
cultural reform 201
Cultural Revolution 64–5
culture change 4, 126
culture management 142
cynicism 6, 79

Debray, Regis 13
'deep organisation' 156

Deleuze, G. 14, 185
demanagerialised workplaces 54, 55
Diagnostic and Statistical Manual of Mental Disorders (DSM) 23
dialectical materialism 40
disciplinary power 18, 25; genealogy 34, 41–2, 63–4; implications 27–8; power/knowledge 21–2, 24; workplace organisation 80, 91, 110, 114, 116, 118
disciplinary techniques 19
Discipline and Punish (Foucault) 17, 21, 31–2
dispositif 42
'distributing authority' 55–6
dominant discourse 70, 77, 150, 161, 168, 177, 187
double-coded practice 74–5
'dysfunctional' organisation 173, 177

employee development 180
enculturation 126
engagement: agenda 88; commitment 53; critical 206; as fallocracy 69–70; pseudo-engagement 178; staff 61, 157; workplace 44
engender 'efficiency' 54
Enlightenment 41–2, 83–4, 98
event 'capture' 189
'evidence-based practice' 171
existentialism 174–5, 190, 192

fallocracy engagement 69–70
false periodisation 81
fictional quality 147
financial context 141

flat management structures 142
Flores, F. 170
Fordism 49, 114, 142
formal authority 79
Foucauldian preamble 93;
    apparatus concept 26–7;
    archaeology 16; common-sense
    practices 36; 'discourse' 26–7;
    genealogy 16 (see also genealogy);
    governmentality 27–9; intellectual
    development 16; language 26;
    normalisation 26; parrhesia 30;
    power/knowledge 30, 36 (see also
    power/knowledge); reflective
    practice 16; self-awareness 30;
    self technologies 24–5, 30; social
    practices 26; surveillance 17–19
Foucauldian prism 12, 107
Foucault, Michel 7, 11, 14, 16–36,
    41–2, 47, 61–3, 90, 147, 152, 190,
    203–4, 209–10
French, John 4, 79
Freud, Sigmund 114, 118
front-line service 146
Fuchs, Ben 62

genealogy 16, 210; anti-humanist
    and anti-essentialist 31;
    assassination 40; capitalist
    economy 44; causality 41; cause
    and effect 32; CMS 61; Corporate
    Rebels 65–7; cult-like culture 59;
    Cultural Revolution 64–5;
    defensive response 52;
    definition 31; demanagerialised
    workplaces 55; deployment 41;
    descent and emergence 34;

desynchronization 35; dialectical
    materialism 40; disciplinary
    power 34, 41–2, 63–4; Discipline
    and Punish 31–2; discourses 35;
    dispositif 42; 'distributing
    authority' 55–6; emotional
    constellations 58; emotional
    reaction 59; engagement
    commitment 53; engender
    'efficiency' 54; Enlightenment
    41–2; fallocracy engagement
    69–70; global economy 54–5;
    governmentality 33; 'grey'
    literature 36; harassment policy 52;
    Hawthorne effect 44; health and
    social care 61; hegemony 62;
    hierarchy and bureaucracy 55;
    historicism 40; holacracy 55, 57, 59,
    60; homo economicus 54; human
    agency 31; human geography 59;
    Industrial Revolution 63;
    interconnectivity 63; internal
    logic fracture 62; interpersonal
    relationships 52; jigsaw
    element 30; large-scale social
    experiments 41; Lean practice
    56–7; legitimacy 58; legitimation
    crisis 51; liberal democratic
    discourse 42; linear approach 61;
    linearity 40; management
    culture 52; Marxian theory 62;
    Marxism 41; Marxist analysis 65;
    NHS 51–2, 56; NPM 54;
    organisational context 61;
    organisational effectiveness 61;
    organisational intervention 44;
    organisational life 44, 58, 68;

organisational response 51; organisational silence 57; organisational structures 54; organisational tree 60; paternalistic capitalism 59; peer-to-peer self-organization 60; periodisation 34, 42; piracy cost 69; policy documents 36; pot-pourri approach 67; power-knowledge formation 42, 64; progressive history moment 33; progressivism 42; psychiatry discipline 33; psychodynamic fashion 53; rebadging management 60; Rebel leadership 67; Renaissance 34; self-actualisation 68; self-improvement 67–8; self-management 54; self-organisation method 60; self-organising workplace 61; signal anxiety 58; social context 31; social relations 64; staff engagement 61 (see also staff engagement); staff survey results 51; Teal Organisations 54, 60; trusts 51; Unipart Expert Practices 56; Virginia Mason 56; work-life integration 59; Zappos 59–60
Gino, F. 67
Goffman, E. 21–2
governmentality 90–1, 117–118, 148
Gramsci, A. 62
Guattari, F. 185
Gurteen, David 89

hagiographic approach 75
harassment policy 52
hard-edged transactional activities 77

The Harwood Manufacturing Company 4
Hašek, Jaroslav 114
Hawthorne effect 44
Hawthorne studies 100
Healthcare Leadership Model (HLM) 119
Hearsum, Steve 207
Higgins, John 62, 173, 181
historicism 40, 42, 191
holacracy 55, 57, 59, 60, 205
homo economicus 54
HR function 6
Hsieh, Tony 59–60
humanistic control 127
humanistic ideals 8
human relations approach 99
'human relations myth' 104
human resource management (HRM) practice 120–1
Human Resources Development (HRD) approach 8–9

'Improving Worker Well-Being' 2
Industrial Revolution 63
informed decision-making 151
institutional element 208
intellectual development 16, 123
internal logic fracture 62

Johnson, Robert 154
Jung, Carl 114–115, 118

Kendall, G. 32
Kierkegaard, Søren 170
Kline, N. 87
Kotter, John 123

laissez-faire approach 6
Laloux, F. 54–5, 60
large-scale social experiments 41
Layard, R. 199–200, 206
layers deconstruction 192–3; change
    management 181; charts and
    spreadsheets 180; CoP 182–4;
    employee development 180;
    government and political cycles
    188; leadership development
    180, 187; legitimate peripheral
    participation 182; NHS 181;
    organisational contexts
    187; organisational life 183;
    organisation functions 180–1;
    organizational process 182;
    'programme of transformation'
    180; social movement approach
    184, 186; social resistance 185;
    strategic planning 181; 'urban
    exploration' 185; work context 179
lay-offs 4
leadership 6–8; development 180,
    187; function 110
Lean practice 56–7
Levi Strauss 1–3
Levi-Strauss, Claude 16
Lewin, K. 4–5, 75
liberal democracy 21–2, 118, 160;
    developments 99; discourse 42
'liberal' economy 160
Likert scale 44–5, 119
LinkedIn 43, 45, 52, 138

Malatesta, E. 210
management by objectives (MBO)
    approach 121

management culture 52
'managerialised' process 106
managerialism 54, 84, 106, 142, 205
Managerial Revolution 50
Marxism 75, 190
Marxist analysis 65
Marxist theory 62, 166
Marx, Karl 14, 40, 63
Mayo, E. 44, 98–9, 101, 104, 110
mechanical production 48
Melman, S. 157
metric fixation 147, 149
Mexican factory 2, 5
Mir, A. 81
Mir, R. 81
Mowles, Chris 112
Myers-Briggs Type Indicator (MBTI)
    102, 114–116, 118

National Health Service (NHS) 3,
    5, 46, 101, 141, 149; genealogy
    51–2, 56; layers deconstruction
    181; leadership culture 8;
    management culture 8; staff
    surveys 7
neoliberalism 96–7
neoliberal management reforms 8
neo-Marxist orientation 47
Neo-Stakhanovism 48
Net Promoter Score 162
New Labour administrations 199
New Public Management (NPM)
    54, 200
NHS see National Health
    Service (NHS)
Nietzsche, F. 34, 41, 170
normalisation 22–3, 25–7

Occupy London initiative 103
operational policies 146
organisational attitude 6
organisational awareness 77
organisational change management
    13, 79
organisational communication 7
organisational contexts 61, 125, 187,
    193; workplace organisation 76, 78,
    93, 95–6, 111
organisational culture 112, 124, 127
'organisational diagnostic' needs 150
organisational effectiveness 3, 10,
    61, 123, 141, 157, 201; workplace
    organisation 85, 97, 104, 120
organisational intervention 44
organisational life 7, 44, 58, 68,
    88, 92–3, 121, 124, 130, 146, 148,
    183, 203, 205; 'dysfunctional'
    organisation 173; 'evidence-based
    practice' 171; existentialism 174–5;
    false dichotomy 171; feminism
    176; improvement 176; issues 176;
    knowability 171–2; organisational
    chart 171; orientation needs 178–9;
    power/knowledge 177; pseudo-
    engagement 178; self-distraction
    175; self-evasion 175; Taylorism
    178; thrownness 170
organisational meetings 93
organisational normalcy 111, 120
organisational paradox 113
organisational politics 144
organisational redesign 76
organisational response 51
organisational structures 54
organisational tree 60

organisation discourse 102, 143
organisation functions 180–1
organisation needs 142
organizational control 81
organizational membership 126
organizational process 182
organizational psychology 140–1
organizational resource 107

Panopticon 17–19, 22
parrhesia 30, 158, 192, 209–10;
    'active listening' 152; business
    function 154; capitalist society 153;
    corporate context 152; corporate
    life 150; human agents 151;
    informed decision-making 151;
    progressive politics 151
participatory policies 200
peer-to-peer self-organization 60
periodisation 34, 42, 201; false 81
piecemeal process 48
'pit sense' 161
planned organisational change 76
policy documents 36
political development 28
positive psychology, in workpalce 120
post-anarchism 14
post-bureaucratic fictions 205
pot-pourri approach 67
Poulantzas, N. 62
power/knowledge 17, 42, 64, 141,
    143, 145, 191, 209; anti-humanist
    conception 20; definition 19;
    disciplinary power 21–2, 24; DSM
    23; 'humanness' 20–1; liberal
    democracy 21–2; normalisation
    22–3; organisational life 177;

Panopticon 22; psychiatric practice 23; reflexivity 166; Sartrean existentialism 20; society characteristics 21; 'zero-sum,' power 20
production line 2, 48, 50, 61, 102
productive process 48, 49
'programme of transformation' 180
progressive politics 75, 151
pseudo-engagement 178
psychodynamics 3, 159; resource 202
Purser, R. 98

qualitative changes 156
quantitative changes 156
quantitative reassurance 45

Rebel leadership 67
reflexivity 7, 16, 192; elements 162; health and social care 167; Heidegger's ontology 169; knowability 164; Marxist theory 166; Net Promoter Score 162; organisational life 165; power/ knowledge 166; scientism 163; self-as-catalyst 168; self-as-instrument 166–8; socio-economic context 166
regimes of silence 96, 151, 191
Renaissance 34
Robertson, B. J. 55, 59
Rodgers, M. 179

Salas, E. 101
Sartrean existentialism 20
Sartre, J. P. 170, 173–4
Saville Assessment 116
Schrage, M. 101

scientific management 42–51, 98, 142, 178
self-actualisation 68
self-as-catalyst 168
self-as-instrument 166–8
self-assessment 118–119
self-awareness 30
self-distraction 175
self-evasion 175
self-improvement 67–8
self-justificatory 9
self-justify practice 139
self-management approach 48, 54, 81
self-organisation method 60
self-organising workplace 61
self-surveillance 24
self technologies 24–5, 25–6, 30
Silberman, M. 181
Snowden, D. J. 45
social development 28
social justice 29
social movement approach 184, 186
socio-economic context 139, 199
staff engagement 61, 157; capitalist economy 49; Corporate Rebels 43; criticality level 43; discursive formations 45; *dispositif* 49; key performance indicators 45–6; liberal democracies 50; Likert scale 44–5; Managerial Revolution 50; mechanical production 48; NART 46; neo-Marxist orientation 47; Neo-Stakhanovism 48; NHS 46; periodisation 42; piecemeal process 48; productive process 48; quantitative reassurance

45; scientific management 43, 45, 48–9; self-management 48; sociopolitical context 50; Stakhanovism 48; UK economy 49; wage–labour forges 46; workplace engagement 44; workplace subjection 47; Zoom platform 43

Stakhanovism 48

structural change 123

structural reform 201

surveillance 24, 202, 204; 'automatic functioning of power' 19; disciplinary power 18; disciplinary techniques 19; Discipline and Punish 17, 21; docile subjects 19; modernity features 18; Panopticon 17–19; pre-modernity 18; Presidio Modelo prison 18; surveillance society 19

talent management system 82

Taylor, F. W. 9, 45, 48–9, 64

Taylor, Laurie 146

Taylorism 79, 98, 101, 114, 178, 201

Teal Organisations 54, 60, 205

teamification 191

'tempered radicals' 68, 160

Thompson, P. 113

trade unionism 203

trade union membership 80

transformation plan, organisation 125

'tsar-ship' 200

UK Parliamentary Select Committee 156

Unipart Expert Practices 56

Virginia Mason 56

wage–labour forges 46

wave questionnaire 117

welfare capitalism 81, 104

Wickham, G. 32

Willis Towers Watson 116

Winograd, T. 170

workforce participation 3

work-life integration 59

workplace engagement 44

workplace organisation: behavioural expectations 89, 113; Belbin team tool 102; biopolitics 90; Bolshevik revolution 99; capitalist economies 75, 97; Carey's analysis 99; climate control systems 96–7; cognitive dissonance 85; collectivism 96; colonising change see colonising change; CoPs 103–4; critical scrutiny 106; cultural adjustments 109; cynicism 79; data sources 84; diagnostic phase 76; disciplinary power 80, 91, 110, 114, 116, 118; dominant discourse 77; double-coded practice 74–5; economic life 80; emancipatory practice 102; 'engagement' agenda 88; Enlightenment 83–4, 98; false periodisation 81; fearless speech 95; Five Dollar Day 81; Fordism 98, 114; formal authority 79; Foucauldian perception 93; Foucauldian prism 107; workplace organisation: genealogical analysis 115; governmentality

90–1, 117–118; GROW model 122; hagiographic approach 75; hard-edged transactional activities 77; Hawthorne studies 100; health and social care 112; HLM 119; holacratic organisations 109; HRM practice 120–1; human agency 80; human relations approach 99; 'human relations myth' 104; human resistance 78; internalised discipline 108; large-scale research study 97; leadership function 110; legitimate response 78; liberal democracy 79, 99, 118; liberatory practice 85; Likert scale 119; 'managerialised' process 106; Marxism 75; MBO approach 121; MBTI 102, 114–116, 118; myriad micro-responses 110; neoliberalism 96–7; neuroticism 115; NHS 101; Occupy London initiative 103; organisational awareness 77; organisational change 79; organisational contexts 76, 78, 93, 95–6, 111; organisational culture 112; organisational discourse 102; organisational effectiveness 85, 97, 104, 120; organisational life 88, 92–3, 121; organisational meetings 93; organisational normalcy 111, 120; organisational paradox 113; organisational redesign 76; organizational control 81; organizational resource 107; Panopticon 108–9; parrhesia 95–6; personal resources 83; planned organisational change 76; power/knowledge 77; power modality 79; prelapsarian state 75; progressive politics 75; 'pseudo-teams' 98, 100; psychopolitical imperative 95; quality conversation 89–90; 'regimes of silence' 96; Saville Assessment 116; scientific management 81; scientific theory and practice 115; self-assessment 118–119; self-management approach 81; social contexts 86, 99; social regulation 81; 'Sociological Department' 81, 83; surveillance techniques 81, 88, 109; talent management system 82; Taylorism 79, 98, 101, 114; 'teamness' 105; Time To Think methodology 91, 94; trade union membership 80; wave questionnaire 117; welfare capitalism 81, 104; Western Electric 98; Willis Towers Watson 116; workplace activity 80; workplace practice 107; workplace surveillance methods 113

Zappos 59–60
Zoom platform 43

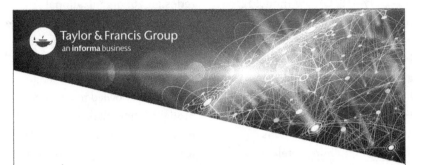